# HOME TRUTHS

## A Practical Guide to Buying, Selling and Investing in Property



**Bryan Pickup**
**and Wyn Derbyshire**

Published July 2010

ISBN 978 1907444 01 2



British Library Cataloguing-in-Publication Data.

A catalogue record for this book is available from the British Library.

Important disclaimer:
This book is only intended for guidance purposes and specific legal advice should always be taken before any course of action is pursued.

Typeset by Spiramus Press Ltd
Printed by Good News Digital Books, Ongar, Essex

Spiramus

102 Blandford Street, London, W1U 8AG.

For David and Ruth, who reminded me how important a first home can be.

*Bryan Pickup*

For David and Gwen Jones

*Wyn Derbyshire*

## Table of contents

CONTENTS

# INTRODUCTION

Property is a starting point for our sense of our own worth, both financially and socially. For most people, their home is their principal asset, representing 90% or more of their total wealth. So their property is their money, and their money is their property. To quote Ikea, 'Home is the most important place in the world'. Inevitably, this creates a tension between the emotional value of a home into which we invest whatever design flair and DIY skills we may have, and which shapes our and our children's memories, and its financial value for which we see the ads in the local paper, read the headlines and feel rich or poor according to whether the headlines suggest that prices are rising or falling. Whether we live at home or sleep on a friend's floor, rent or buy, our relationship with property defines the stage we have reached in our lives in the progression to adulthood, and whether we have yet 'made it' or not.

In successive generations since the First World War, we have moved from the wealthy minority owning their own houses and the rest renting (or living in the big house as domestic servants or on farms as agricultural labourers), to the situation today, where 70% of all homes in the UK are owner-occupied, 20% are 'social housing' and only 10% are privately rented. Putting it another way, whilst the population of the UK increased from 49 million in 1951 to 57 million in 2001, the number of private rented dwellings dropped from 7 million to 2.5 million and the total number of owner-occupied dwellings increased from 4 million to 17 million[1]. The Labour Government announced in July 2007 that its principal housing policy objective was to ensure that 3 million more homes are built by 2020[2], and most of these would be for owner-occupiers.

Margaret Thatcher's 'Right to Buy' was conceived in 1979 as a way of changing the electoral map by breaking up the tenants of council-owned estates (natural Labour supporters) into individual home owners (natural Conservative supporters). That policy has been hugely successful in shifting ownership patterns (and arguably the nature of the Labour Party – would there have been 'New Labour' without the Right to Buy?). Now almost every 25-year-old expects the 'Right to Buy' a home.

Residential property also represents a substantial proportion of the nation's wealth. In 2008, the value of all residential property in the UK was estimated at

---

[1] Source: Government Census - www.statistics.gov.uk

[2] Source: Green paper - Homes for the Future: (CM 7191) www.communities.gov.uk

£3,903 billion whilst the value of the British commercial property stock was estimated at £529 billion. Compare these figures with the estimated aggregate value of all UK companies listed on the London Stock Exchange (£1,288 billion[3]) and we can see that an understanding of how our property system works, with all its opportunities and potential pitfalls, is indeed important.

So, amongst the huge daily volume of information, commentary and advice about the property market, why this book?

It started with a conversation in a sunny back garden in SW19, with a young man settling into his career and a serious relationship, fed up with camping out with his parents or in short-term accommodation and feeling that if he didn't get a foot on the housing ladder now, he never would. But he didn't know where to start – should he move into or out of London? Should he move in with his partner? Should he mortgage himself to the maximum? And most of all, where could he get experienced and impartial advice? It continued with an anxious young couple, in a pub, trying to decide the figure to put in as a sealed bid for the house they had found, after a long search, which ticked all their boxes. So this book is for David and Ruth and all the other Davids and Ruths who know what they want, but don't know how to get it.

In one sense this book is a sequel to *Money and Work*[4] which provided a signpost to all those new to the world of work. *Home Truths* provides a signpost for all those who have entered the world of work and are now looking at the next stage of settling down by buying their first home. We start by considering renting, being a tenant, and then guide you through the process of getting your mortgage and buying, including financial and tax consequences. Looking ahead, we also explain the selling process.

However, we have broadened the scope of this book by including an overview of three areas which may appeal more to David or Ruth in 10 years' time, or to their parents now – opportunities allowing the average family in the last 10 years to invest its surplus wealth (often funded from the huge increase in value of the family home) in a variety of property-related ventures, such as buy-to-let, buying abroad and commercial property. As too many people have discovered since the onset of the Credit Crunch, these areas are full of uncertainty and risk as well as opportunity and profit, but risk and uncertainty can be minimised

---

[3] Source: Investment Property Forum research

[4] Spiramus Press, ISBN 978 1904905 48 6, published 2007

(though not eliminated) by developing an understanding of how these specialised areas of property investment operate. We seek to provide such an understanding in this book. And we also consider property issues that can arise in the later years of life such as property downsizing, equity release and inheritance tax planning.

This is not a 'do it yourself' guide in the sense of explaining how you can implement the mechanics of buying or selling property yourself without the help of professional advisers – you will save more money by shopping around for your furniture than you would by doing your own conveyancing – and it is not a ticket to becoming a property millionaire armed only with a television camera, paint and flowers. It is, however, intended to explain and give you control of the process of buying and owning a property of your own.

The economic melodramas of recent years have made everyone more anxious, more wary and more cynical about financial institutions. The lending institutions' reaction – lending only to the safest – has made the first step on the property ladder even more challenging. The housing and property investment markets have changed, but the fundamentals of human behaviour – the need to nest, the desire to invest – have not changed.

So the purpose of this book is to offer, in one place, enough information for you to assess your needs in the world of property thoughtfully, how to ask the right questions (and who to ask) and how to use the answers to achieve your dreams. We hope it will prove helpful to both first time buyers and more experienced property owners.

We have tried to cover a wide range of topics in enough, but not too much, detail to be interesting and useful. Please do not take this as definitive for every situation, and legal or other advice should be taken as needed for your circumstances. We have stated the law as at 30 June 2010 (i.e. post-General Election and emergency Budget) and we have flagged some changesfrom the previous Labour administration, notably the abolition of HIPs, but also changes in planning and social housing policies.

Bryan Pickup and Wyn Derbyshire
London
June 2010

# CHAPTER 1 THE PROPERTY SYSTEM IN ENGLAND AND WALES

## The big picture

We begin by explaining the property system in England and Wales from both a legal and a practical (procedural) perspective. In part this will be a history lesson, but in order to understand where we are, we need to understand where we have come from.

First an apology, for which we hope readers (and especially Welsh readers) will forgive us: in order to save repetition, we will refer to 'English' law and practice throughout this book – they are the same in Wales as in England[5]. This is not the case in respect of the legal and practical systems of property in Scotland and Northern Ireland; these systems differ in some important respects from that of England and Wales (particularly in some of the special terminology used) because the legal foundations were laid and have been built upon over centuries in different ways, although the broad principles of property buying remain largely the same.[6] Later in the book, we also cover the property systems in some other countries that have proven popular amongst British visitors seeking holiday homes in recent years.

## The legal framework

Because practice and procedure have developed from the legal framework, we will describe that first.

The first and most fundamental point to understand is the distinction between property meaning land and buildings and other kinds of property. Because land and buildings are valuable and (more or less) permanent compared to other kinds of assets such as personal property – livestock, cars, furniture, jewellery – or intellectual property (for example, the copyright in a book or film or design, or a trademark), special rules exist to define and protect ownership of them. To use a slightly old fashioned term to distinguish land and buildings from other types of property, they are 'real property', as opposed to 'chattels' or

---

[5] With a significant exception relating to planning – see Chapter 9.

[6] We give an overview of the key differences in Appendix 1.

other forms of 'personal property'. That provides the first clue to the history of land ownership in England: 'real' means 'royal'.

## Some history

For all meaningful purposes, the starting point of our present system of land ownership is 1066, when William the Conqueror assumed ownership of all the land and buildings in England having defeated the Saxon King Harold. This assumption of ownership by William was important, for he and his closest followers imposed a feudal system on conquered England (and his successors later extended it to Wales). A feudal system of sorts had existed in England before the Conquest, but the Norman version was far more rigorous and prescriptive than its Anglo-Saxon predecessor.[7]

Feudalism was born out of the anarchy and mayhem that arose in the wake of the collapse of the Roman Empire (at least in western Europe) in the fifth century. In those troubled times, kings and other noblemen (who often initially were little more than tribal leaders or leaders of warbands) maintained such law and order as there was (and maintained themselves in power) by armed force. To do this, they needed armed followers, but frequently lacked the financial resources to pay them, since coined money scarcely existed following the almost total collapse of the Roman economic system in the west. Moreover, the most powerful armed followers were knights – warriors on horseback - and they needed land and peasants to work that land in order to sustain their horses. And if they wished to remain in power, the kings and noblemen needed to retain the loyalty of their followers. The feudal system in Europe generally evolved to meet these needs by introducing a system of 'mutual obligations' between lords and vassals. The kings granted lands to their most powerful noblemen, which they held in exchange for their support in times of war. The noblemen in turn granted portions of their lands to lesser noblemen in exchange for oaths of loyalty and service from them, and so on, all the way

---

[7] In some places however (for example Kent, and those parts of the kingdom which had been subject to the rule of the Vikings), local land customs in force during the Anglo-Saxon era were to some extent recognised by the conquering Normans, thus complicating the English land ownership system in those areas in the centuries that were to follow. Some of these "local rules" continued to be recognised until well into the twentieth century, and were often of particular importance in relation to the inheritance of land.

down the ranks of society to the peasants (perhaps 90% of the population) tilling the fields, who held their lands (such as they were) in exchange for labour and food produce. Such was the system that William and his immediate followers imposed in England (and which is reflected in the survey that William commissioned of his kingdom 20 years after the Conquest, a survey which we today know as the Domesday Book). The English property system of today derives directly from the feudal system imposed by William – it thus derives from war and conquest.

Over the centuries, feudalism evolved to meet the challenges of changing societies in western Europe. One of the earliest changes was the introduction of lands and titles (for with awards of land frequently went awards of titles, many of them – such as Duces, from which we derive the word Duke – appropriated from the titles of Roman military commanders) that could be inherited. In its purest form – the exchange of land for services in war-time – the death of a vassal should have meant that the vassal's land (and the title associated with it) reverted to his overlord, since the widow and children of the deceased vassal could not fight and thus could not provide feudal services in exchange for land, and any adult sons might not prove as loyal as their father. In practice, however, kings were soon obliged to guarantee that sons (or at least the eldest sons) of fallen vassal lords could inherit their fathers' estates and titles, and the European system of nobility soon evolved. By the time William conquered England, the concept of inheritable land and titles within the feudal system was well established.

Another way in which the feudal system evolved over time was the extension of the ways (or tenures) that land could be held in exchange for various types of services (known as 'incidents'). Thus, holding land in exchange for services of a military nature (including the provision of armed horsemen for use in battle) became known as knight's service; services to the king of an honourable nature (such as performing the duties of chamberlain, or carrying the royal standard in battle) became known as grand sergeanty. Grand sergeanty and knight's services were together known as *tenure in chivalry*. Monasteries and other types of ecclesiastical lands were held in what was known as *spiritual tenure*. And there were other examples. Knowing the type of tenure attaching to a piece of land allowed one to determine the terms on which the land was held.

A common form of tenure was *tenure in socage*, whereby land was held in exchange for a wide variety of possible services (typically involving the provision of agricultural services). Over the years, tenants who held their lands by way of socage gradually escaped being subject to the obligation to provide socage services in exchange for lump sum payments to their overlords of money, known as 'quit rents'. A socage tenant owner who paid quit rent was thereafter no longer obliged to provide feudal services. Socage was important, since land was generally regarded as being held in 'common socage' unless it could be shown that it was held by some other form of tenure.

The forms of tenure just described - and others like them - were known as 'free tenure', since they were enjoyed by 'free men' or 'free tenants'. In fact, the majority of the population did not enjoy any form of free tenure, but rather unfree tenure. The essential difference between free tenure and unfree tenure was that free tenants, whilst they might have to provide some form of service, could not at law simply be ejected from their land without cause; unfree tenants – commonly known as villeins – enjoyed no such protection. Moreover, many were often legally obliged to provide such services and for such time as their feudal overlords might decree, and were in fact no more than common labourers. In many cases, the life of a villein was little (if at all) better than a slave and the feudal system effectively bound them to their overlords' lands and villages, and condemned them to a life of agricultural toil. The system was often harshly enforced, and villeins who tried to escape frequently found little support elsewhere as feudal lords (for all that they often fought between themselves) generally prided themselves on solidarity when faced with rebellion from their inferiors and went to great lengths to return absconding villeins to their feudal lords and the resulting feudal punishment (which was frequently of a grisly nature). As a social system, feudalism probably reached its peak of complexity and importance during the twelfth and thirteenth centuries; thereafter, as society slowly evolved, it began to disintegrate, its demise considerably hastened by the effects of the Black Death in 1348, which killed perhaps a third of the population, so devastating rural communities that it became much harder for feudal overlords to exact the services owed to them from the surviving peasantry, many of whom took advantage of the prevailing chaos to abscond and establish themselves afresh elsewhere. As a legal system of land ownership, and notwithstanding the Black Death, the complexities of feudalism took some time to disappear, but by the end of the seventeenth century, many of the more unusual forms of land tenure had been abolished.

It was not until 1925 that property law was put onto a modern, rather than mediaeval, footing. As a result, today there is only one form of feudal tenure left – socage – now generally referred to as freehold. Strictly speaking, if you 'own' freehold land in England and Wales today, you do so under the tenure of socage – albeit without generally being obliged to provide services to a feudal overlord. As a consequence (strictly speaking again) in fact no one 'owns' land in England and Wales apart from the Crown – a fact that has for generations astonished law students attending their first land law lectures. In practice, of course, it makes no difference; today a freehold 'estate' in land is tantamount to absolute ownership of that land. But it is an interesting historical distinction.

A few ancient or feudal peculiarities survived the 1925 changes, including the concept of 'the lordship of the manor' which can still be bought and sold along with various archaic privileges such as 'advowson', that is the right to appoint the vicar of a particular church, the concept of 'common land'; and the obligation known as 'chancel repair'. We explain the latter in more detail later in this chapter.

The feudal estates originally granted by William and his successors have now largely been broken into much smaller pieces but in theory it is still possible to trace the freehold of 35 Acacia Avenue back to an ancient royal gift.

One important form of property ownership we have not mentioned so far is that of leasehold property; that is, where a tenant rents property from a landlord. This is because the law relating to leaseholds arose independently of the feudal system, initially evolving out of the law of personal contracts rather than feudal land law. Over time, however, the laws relating to leaseholds came to be regarded as being subject to principles of tenure, which had arisen under the feudal system, and various aspects of the old laws relating to feudal forms of tenure continue to apply to the landlord and tenant relationship, albeit that relationship itself was not a feudal tenure. We discuss the distinction between freeholds and leaseholds below.

## The Crown Estate

There remains one other important form of land holding that we should mention, namely the land held directly by the Crown. This is, effectively, land that William and his successors did not bestow upon others, such as most of the seabed around the UK, and land below the high watermark, and such land now forms The Crown Estate. That logic is not just historical but continues: land that does not belong to anyone else, such as land owned by a company that is dissolved, also belongs to The Crown Estate and is known as *bona vacantia*. When the UK's territorial limit was extended from three nautical miles to 12 under the Territorial Sea Act 1987, and then again from 12 to 200 nautical miles by the Energy Act 2004, the extra miles of seabed naturally became part of The Crown Estate which is therefore intimately involved in off-shore developments such as wind farms, oil and gas pipelines and under-sea gas storage – in other words, The Crown Estate is an institution of the future as well as the past.

## Freehold and leasehold

In the modern world, it is important to understand the distinction between freehold and leasehold interests in land. Many Victorian and Edwardian houses were originally built by landlord property developers for the purpose of renting them to tenants. Such tenants therefore had leasehold interests in their houses rather than owning the freeholds themselves. As many property developers divested themselves of residential leases or were wound up, and with pressure from legal changes, most are now freehold; leases remain the building block for the commercial property investment world, but in the residential world are now found mostly in blocks of flats or other arrangements where the structure and facilities are shared between owners and need to be maintained collectively. Having said that, it is still possible to encounter houses and bungalows whose 'owners' have leasehold interests rather than freehold interests and pay 'ground rent'; this is not uncommon, for instance, in parts of Lancashire.

As previously noted, leases originated outside the feudal system as a way of allowing one person to use another's land in return for paying a rent. Rental income forms the basis of all property investment.

A lease is essentially a written contract between a landlord (or lessor) often but (not necessarily) the freeholder and a tenant (or lessee), by which the landlord allows the tenant to use the property as his own. A lease will typically have the following characteristics:

- it will exist for a fixed period of time;

- the tenant will be obliged to pay a rent (which can be nominal);
- the lease will be subject to positive conditions: for example, the tenant agreeing to repair and to insure;
- the lease is also likely to be subject to negative conditions: for example, not to use the leasehold property except as a home, nor to sell it without permission; and
- the landlord is likely to have a right to terminate the lease if the tenant is in breach of his or her obligations or, if the lease so provides, becomes insolvent.

In contrast, a freehold will typically:

- be permanent: that is, have no time limit after which it expires or otherwise ceases to exist;
- has no body 'superior' to it: in other words (apart from the Crown, and that only theoretically, no one has a 'superior' or overriding interest in the land); and
- can be used for any purpose, subject to any restrictive covenants, mortgage restrictions, adverse rights and planning laws.

## Why leasehold rather than freehold?

An essential difference between a freehold interest in a property and a leasehold interest is that the former is effectively absolute ownership of the property whilst the latter, ultimately, is not (although in the case of very long leaseholds, for example, the leasehold of a flat for 999 years, the leaseholder - the tenant – may be forgiven if he or she feels that they do in fact own the property). This being the case, it is interesting to consider why leaseholds – at least long leaseholds capable of existing for many years – have become so popular.

First, there is the economic motivation which can lead to the creation of leases – the lease is a mechanism for one person to use something belonging to somebody else for a period of time for regular payments, and then give it back at the end of the agreed period, so one person gets the use of the property and the other gets money (and the asset back to use themselves or let again). That logic still applies to short term arrangements – in fact, it is the basis of buy-to-let. To attempt to achieve this objective using freehold would effectively involve one party agreeing first to sell the property to the other, and then to repurchase it at a later date. Not only would this have potentially costly stamp duty consequences, it is not feasible from a legal perspective because the law does not recognise a right to buy back many years in the future or indefinitely; such consequences can be avoided by use of the leasehold mechanism.

Second, there is the legal technicality that it is impossible, or at least complicated, to impose obligations on a freehold owner which bind subsequent owners. By contrast, obligations in a lease bind all subsequent owners of that lease so that the landlord can enforce the obligations against successive persons owning the lease at any relevant time (technically this is known as 'privity of estate'). This may sound like academic theory, but if you consider the example of a block of flats where each flat owner is responsible for repairing their own flat but the landlord is responsible for the structure of the building – foundations, walls, roof – and its shared facilities (boilers, lifts, hallways and staircases) – to which the flat owner contributes through a service charge, it is crucial for the landlord to be able to enforce each flat owner's obligations to pay, and it is in the interests of the other flat owners that it does so, regardless of whether an individual flat owner may have decided to sell his or her flat to another person.

It follows that virtually all flats are leasehold. (As we mention below, commonhold was introduced in 2002 in an attempt to improve on the leasehold flat system but is still unusual in practice.)

It is for this second reason that 'flying freeholds' are to be avoided. Sometimes deliberately and sometimes by accident or lack of thought, situations have been created where a freehold includes land above or below another property. For example, in a row of houses, there may be an extension that juts out over the top of the garage of the adjoining property. In that situation, the owner of the extension above would not have any right to force the owner of the property below to maintain it, so that the supporting walls or structure may fail, risking the property above. Likewise, the person below will have no direct obligation from the owner of the upper part to repair the roof or keep his property watertight so it does not damage the property below. Even if, when these arrangements are first created, there are obligations of these kinds put in place, they are not enforceable after any change of ownership (since we are dealing with freehold property here). So, taking a long term view, the use of freeholds in this manner is not an appropriate way of dealing with such matters. By contrast, if the owner of the lower building granted a lease of the space occupied by the building above to the owner of the building above, then the obligations in that lease would be enforceable throughout the term of the lease against whoever owned it and at the end of the lease whoever owned it then would be obliged to remove the upper part.

So, as at 2010, the vast majority of residential properties are owned either as freehold, that is mostly houses, or leasehold, that is mostly flats.

Rather confusingly, there is no legal difference in principle between a long term lease, which represents a substantial and almost permanent capital asset paid for as a lump sum with usually a small annual rent often payable (called a 'ground rent'), and a short term lease or tenancy agreement, which is by its nature temporary and paid for in (usually monthly) instalments by way of rent. Both involve a contract by which a landlord grants to a tenant the right to use a defined space for a defined period of time for a sum of money. However, the financial and practical consequences are very different. A long lease will normally have a value and be capable of being sold or mortgaged: a tenancy will normally not be valuable or capable of being sold or mortgaged. For the purposes of this book, we will call the long term contracts leases, collectively leasehold, and the short term ones tenancy agreements or tenancies. We cover tenancy agreements in Chapter 2.

To confuse you further, we also need to draw a distinction between 'tenancies' and 'licences'. A licence is a personal contract allowing the licensee to use something usually for a fixed period in return for money – the licence fee. Examples are the permissions you buy to park in a car park, stay overnight in a hotel, moor a boat or pitch a tent or caravan. A licence does not amount to a legal interest in the land or building itself, whereas a lease or tenancy does. In the days when residential tenancies were heavily protected by the Rent Acts, it was common practice for 'landlords' to grant licences instead of tenancy agreements in order to avoid occupiers getting the protection the Rent Act automatically gave to residential tenants so as to limit the rents they paid, and to give them rights to stay (for life!) after their initial tenancy period expired. Following the leading case of *Street v Mountford* in 1977, the courts have looked at the reality of arrangements rather than the words used. Now that it is standard to grant non-protected tenancies as Assured Shorthold Tenancies, there is no need to pretend that a tenancy is a licence. Some out of date 'landlords' still think they should, particularly where they are letting to sharers.

## Typical lease terms

What are the typical terms of a lease

Unfortunately, leases are not standard documents and need to be read carefully to ensure they fit the circumstances of the particular building and flat, impose reasonable obligations on the landlord and nothing too restrictive on the tenant, and will qualify for a mortgage.

The standard provisions are:

- **Length of lease.** Most residential leases start with a period of at least 99 years, and often 125, 150 or 999 years. Leases with fewer than 80 years left to run need to be considered carefully, as they may not be acceptable as security for a conventional mortgage. Generally, leases with fewer than 55 years to run (that is, the mortgage term of 25 years, plus 30 years) are definitely not acceptable as security. Leases with 70 or fewer years to run may be unacceptable to some lenders.
- **Rent** – usually a fixed amount of anything from £1 to £500 per annum.
  - Sometimes with fixed increases, say doubling every 25 or 33 years.
  - Sometimes a peppercorn - legalese for 'nothing'.
- The **'demise'** – that is, what is included in the lease. This needs careful checking because mistakes are not uncommon and inevitably lead to problems.

You should check the lease plan carefully: does it include all the rooms, loft space, parking, storage areas, balconies that you expect?

Remember that the description of the demise (both words and plan – and usually the words override the plan) define what you have to maintain and repair as well as what you use, so external walls and roof should not be included if responsibility for these will be shared.

*Rights granted to you.*

You will need a right to use the common areas (unless you have your own front door), including shared entrances, halls, hallways, lifts, stairs, parking, gardens, refuse storage areas, communal areas. You may also need a right to access other flats in order to repair or decorate yours.

You will also need a right for services – water, sewage, gas, electricity, telecoms, cable TV to pass through the common areas of the block to your flat.

*Rights reserved to the landlord*

The landlord may need a right of access to your flat to repair or decorate the building, or shared facilities or services.

*Service charge*

The landlord should have an obligation to provide a comprehensive list of services – which will usually include repair and maintenance of the building, common areas, facilities and services, including decoration of the outside of the building and the internal hallways etc.

You must expect to pay a fair proportion of these costs, including a reasonable fee for the landlord to employ a managing agent.

*Insurance*

Unlike a house, where the owner will insure both the structure of the building and the contents, in a block of flats, usually the landlord will insure the structure of the building and the major plant and machinery – boilers and lifts and recharge the insurance costs back to the tenants, leaving the individual flat owners to insure their own contents.

*Use*

The lease will usually limit use of the flat to residential purposes. This will not prevent you from doing some work from home, but if you cause other residents a problem (for example, by having a succession of customers coming to visit you) you can expect complaints and possibly some legal action.

*Selling or sub-letting or sharing*

Depending on the terms of the lease, you may need the landlord's permission to sell your lease (and if you are buying, your seller may need permission to sell to you). If so, the request for this consent needs to be made to the landlord early, and as buyer you may have to provide references and other financial details to satisfy the landlord that you will be an acceptable tenant. Sub-letting may also need the landlord's previous permission. Sharing (that is, bringing in a lodger) usually would not, but this should be checked. If you have this in mind you will also need to check the user clause, which will often limit use to 'a single family'.

*'Good Neighbour'*

The lease will contain a long and repetitive list of restrictions on the way you have to behave as an occupier – no pets, don't throw waste down the drains, put carpet on the floors, don't play any instruments or music systems late at night, don't hang washing out of the windows and so on. These may seem petty (and in practice landlords are unlikely to try very hard to enforce them) but you should bear in mind how irritated you would be with your neighbours if they did not show you the courtesy of observing these rules.

## Leasehold issues

As we have said, as a generalisation houses are freehold and flats are leasehold. The number of leasehold houses has reduced over time due to some of the legislative controls we mention later.

By the nature of flats, whether within a house converted into two or more flats, or a large purpose-built block, some responsibilities must be shared. Someone has to be responsible for maintaining, decorating and repairing the structure and outside of the building, any internal areas in shared use such as hallways and staircases, outside spaces such as gardens and parking areas, shared facilities such as lifts and heating and entry phone systems, and employing any necessary staff such as a porter or gardener, or security staff. The landlord is usually responsible for those shared responsibilities, and entitled to recharge the costs through a service charge which is charged to the flat owners (leaseholders) according to the amount spent, in addition to the pre-set 'ground rent'. The landlord usually also insures the building and shared facilities, with the leaseholders being responsible for insuring only the interior of their own flats.

Usually, the landlord appoints a firm of estate agents to manage the block (managing agents) for a fee which is added to the costs and charged back to the leaseholders. The split of costs between leaseholders is usually set at the beginning of the leases on a mathematical basis – a simple 50% for a house converted to two flats of equal size, or a more complex calculation based on floor area if the flats are not of equal size – or as a 'fair and proper proportion' to be determined by the managing agents each year, and according to what is spent. Sometimes proportions are according to usage - for example electricity or water may be split according to sub-meters recording how much each flat uses.

As you can imagine, there is plenty of scope for argument about the cost and quality of the services landlords and managing agents provide. A distant landlord is never going to care about property as much as somebody who lives there. In the 1960s some landlords reputedly made a profitable business out of running the service charge and insurance arrangements for blocks of flats. Conversely, the typical property developer – both the small local 'converter' and the major house building company – have come to realise that the 'hassle factor' of dealing with blocked drains or replacing communal heating systems that inevitably come with blocks of flats as they age, is more trouble than it is worth. So, the legislators have stepped in and have given some protection for leaseholders, by imposing controls on landlords and managing agents.

So, partly as a matter of economic common sense and partly as a result of the legislation, the freeholds of many flats, and therefore responsibility for maintenance and insurance, have migrated to the leaseholders who own a 'share of the freehold' either directly in their own names or through a residents' company set up for that purpose. The owner or residents' company will then manage the shared facilities, again usually through a managing agent. The owner or residents' company is still subject to the controls imposed by the legislation, but is motivated by caring for the building in the long term interests of the residents, rather than money. In relation to new developments, the developer now usually pre-arranges that once all the flats are sold the freehold will be transferred for a nominal amount to a company owned by the leaseholders, who each receive a share in that company when buying their lease. In relation to older buildings, the migration of freeholds to residents is imposed by law.

The legislative controls imposed on leasehold landlords are highly complex and technical.[8]

Parliament's view over the last 40 years has clearly been that leaseholders should control their own freehold, for all the reasons we have explained.[9] Over

---

[8] Frankly, despite this legislation being intended to protect consumers, it is a minefield of complexity for leaseholders, freeholders, lawyers and valuers and we can therefore only give the briefest of summaries which, in line with the spirit of this book, should enable you to understand what you are told if you stray into any of these areas, rather than giving you the full set of tools.

that time, the power given to leaseholders to achieve that has increased significantly.

There are two separate strands to the legislation: one to address ownership by encouraging freeholders to sell to residents, and the other to ensure that freeholders deal fairly with maintenance and service charges.

*Leasehold houses*

Under the Leasehold Reform Act 1967, leasehold houses within certain criteria were given the right to force their freeholder to sell the freehold to them (known as 'enfranchisement'), or to grant a lease extension. The criteria originally included a residence qualification (that is, that the leaseholder had lived in the house for three years before seeking to buy – instead, since 2002, the qualification has been ownership of the lease for two years), and a maximum value limit, protecting many properties within the highest value central London landed estates such as Grosvenor and Portman (this was removed in 1993) and a low rent test, (that is, that the rent was less than 2/3 of rateable value – this was removed in 1996 except for houses in some rural areas) and a long lease test, that is, that the lease was for more than 21 years. This last test is still applicable. So, initially, the right to enfranchise was only for long term individual residents with long leases of houses with low rents, and not for the most valuable houses. Following the various changes, the leaseholder of any house where the lease was originally for 21 years or more can enfranchise regardless of rent or value and whether or not he/she actually lives there, as long as he/she has owned it for two years. This includes, perhaps surprisingly, companies and non-UK residents, and in some circumstances includes properties originally designed as a house but later used for business purposes (as is common in Mayfair, for example). There are exceptions where the freeholder has a special status, such as a local authority or housing association, The Crown Estate (unless they have agreed to recognise the Act in relation to that property) or the National Trust.

The price payable is a matter for expert valuers, but broadly is the value of the land (as opposed to the building on it) plus 'marriage value', in other words the

[9] It is of course co-incidental that a significant number of MPs live in 1930s mansion blocks where these problems were most prevalent.

extra value created by combining the freehold with the existing lease, which are usually worth more when combined than they would be as two separate interests. Clearly, the shorter the period left on the lease, the higher the 'marriage value'. If the freeholder and leaseholder cannot agree the price, it will be determined by the Leasehold Valuation Tribunal.

As an alternative to enfranchising by buying the freehold, the leaseholder can claim a 50 year lease extension instead, although some of the qualification criteria (low rent and upper value limit) which no longer apply to freehold enfranchisement do apply to lease extensions.

For the curious, it is worth mentioning that if a long lease of the type that could give rise to enfranchisement simply expires, the leaseholder can usually still stay in occupation, but must pay a proper market rent instead of the previous 'ground rent'.

Health warning – do not attempt to enfranchise or do a lease extension, or buy a property with a view to doing so, without specialist legal and valuation advice. If you want more detail before seeking professional advice we recommend LEASE, the Leasehold Advisory Service, a Government funded free advice service (www.lease-advice.org) which has a range of useful advice notes, and answers to frequently asked questions. For advice on what the Leasehold Valuation Tribunals can do, and how they work, see www.rpts.gov.uk.

*Leasehold flats*

If you thought the law on enfranchisement of houses was complicated, you ain't seen nothin' yet. We will try to keep it simple, but if you own, or are looking to buy, a flat in an older block or conversion which does not come with a 'share of the freehold', at some time you may have to deal with the issues we raise.

The underlying principle of the legislation is that landlords cannot be trusted to behave and leaseholders should be allowed either to buy the freeholder out altogether or if not, to take control of management of the block. Complexities arise because, in order to make this work, leaseholders need to act collectively.

This is a highly technical and specialist area and legal and valuation advice is essential before you take any action. The Leasehold Advisory Service (www.lease-advice.org) is a useful source of more detailed information than we can include here.

So, subject to various qualification conditions, leaseholders have a (collective) right to force the freeholder to sell its interest to them, under the Leasehold Reform, Housing and Urban Development Act 1993 as amended. This is known as 'collective enfranchisement'. The leaseholders must serve notice on the freeholder, typically through a company they set up for this purpose, to buy the freehold at a price which reflects both the value of the freeholder's interest and a half share of the 'marriage value'. As with enfranchisement of houses, the valuation is complex, and if a price cannot be agreed between the freeholder and the leaseholder, the Leasehold Valuation Tribunal can determine it. Additional complications for valuing blocks of flats rather than houses arise where (for example) the freeholder owns and rents out a few flats within the block, or garages, or there are unsold flats, or a caretaker's flat, or outside areas or a roof space with development potential.

This right for the leaseholders, collectively, to buy the freehold largely supersedes the right of first refusal given to them by the Landlord and Tenant Act 1987 – the effect of which was that if the freeholder decided to sell its freehold, it had to serve notice on the leaseholders and give them the opportunity to buy the freehold before putting the property on the open market. This legal requirement does still exist and the freeholder must comply with it or face criminal penalties. In some cases, a decision by the freeholder to sell the freehold will force the leaseholders to make their decision on whether to buy collectively, where perhaps only some leaseholders have previously been sufficiently motivated to trigger the 1993 Act procedure and force collective enfranchisement.

Particular difficulties arise where there is a mixed-use building, typically flats above shops or restaurants, or where the occupiers are a mixture of long leaseholders and short term tenants, or where the leaseholders differ in their financial circumstances so some are keen to buy the freehold but others are not interested, or cannot afford to. To qualify for collective enfranchisement, the decision to buy (and pay their share of the price) must be made by a majority of long leaseholders, at least two-thirds of the flats in the building must be occupied as long residential leases, and if there is a non-residential part it must not be more than 25% of the floor area of the whole building.

Alternatively, as with houses, individual flat owners can extend their leases, subject to various qualification criteria. This may be a suitable solution for some, where it is not practical to achieve a sufficient majority of leaseholders to enfranchise the freehold collectively, or the proportion of non-residential use is high enough to mean that the leaseholders do not qualify for collective enfranchisement.

The lease extension is by way of a new lease for 90 years plus the period left on the existing lease, at nil rent (in contrast, the lease extension period for a house is 50 years and there will be a ground rent payable).

This right is subject to a two year ownership condition, but not to a residence condition, so it is available to companies and non-residents.

The price payable is based on the amount by which the value of the landlord's interest in the flat is reduced by the lease extension – the longer the period remaining under the existing lease, the less this will be – plus half of the 'marriage value' (that is, the amount by which the value of the freeholder's interest in the flat is reduced by the grant of the lease extension). If the existing lease has 80 years or less to run, there is an allowance for the reduction in value of other property owned by the freeholder (for example, the remainder of the block).

The advantage of extending the lease is that the flat will be more marketable and therefore more valuable with a longer lease than a shorter one. In particular, leases with fewer than 70 years to run are less attractive for mortgage lenders, and conventional mortgage finance becomes difficult once the period left on the lease is below roughly 60 years. Since quite a lot of 99 year leases were created in the 1960s this will be an issue for an increasing number of leaseholders. Extending the lease, however, only benefits the individual leaseholder and does not resolve any of the common issues for flat owners relating to the quality and cost of maintaining the block as a whole.

The controls on management are, in ascending order of usefulness:

1. Freeholders can only charge costs which are within the scope of those provided for in the relevant lease clauses. So, for example, interest costs or

the notional rental value of a caretaker's flat have been disputed and disallowed where the lease wording was not sufficient to cover them. It is difficult to resolve such disputes without litigation.

2. There is a general requirement for freeholders to act 'fairly and reasonably' in spending what is, in effect, the leaseholders' money (the key case is *Finchbourne v Rodrigues*). This sounds great in principle, but is extremely difficult to enforce in practice.

3. The Landlord and Tenant Act 1985 imposes a very formal regime on freeholders and managing agents to justify significant expenditure, both on one-off items such as roof repairs and boiler replacements, and on on-going contracts such as lift maintenance or the appointment of a managing agent. It forces them to demonstrate value for money. This procedure is set out in Section 20 of the 1985 Act and various sets of regulations, and helpfully summarised by LEASE in their leaflet 'Section 20 Consultation' available at www.lease-advice.org. Briefly, the freeholder or managing agents must consult the leaseholders, and the tenants' or residents' association if there is one, if they intend to carry out works above a certain value, or enter into a long term service agreement.

In relation to works, the freeholder or managing agent must consult if any leaseholder would have to pay more than £250; in relation to service agreements the figure is £100 in any year. The freeholder must obtain and provide details of at least two estimates, one of which must be from someone independent from the freeholder. The leaseholders and the residents' association then have the right to comment and the freeholder must 'have regard' to those comments.

If the freeholder or managing agent fails to follow this procedure, the freeholder has to pay the excess over £250/£100 per leaseholder itself. In practice, this process takes three to four months to go through, which can be a problem if works are required urgently.[10]

Leaseholders who have experienced the joys of battling with managing agents over service charges and Section 20 will enjoy reading three cases where

---

[10] These rules apply in England; an earlier version not including service agreements applies in Wales, for the time being.

freeholders spent considerable sums on repairs which they could not then recover because they had failed to follow carefully enough the procedures for obtaining estimates and notifying tenants (in *London Borough of Islington v Abdel Malek* the leaseholder avoided a bill of over £10,000 where notice was given but it was inadequate because the works had already started); in *London Borough of Camden v Leaseholders of 37 flats at Grafton Way* 37 leaseholders avoided a bill for £13,600 each because the detail given was inadequate and in *Daejan Investments v Benson* five leaseholders avoided a bill of £54,000 each where the freeholder did not allow enough time for consultation on the estimates.[11] However, these cases are the exception rather than usual practice. Control of when and how to carry out repairs still remains with the freeholder. Properly advised freeholders can still incur and recover costs if they follow the right procedures.

The 1987 Act allowed leaseholders (collectively) to apply for the appointment of a manager to take over the management of their block from the freeholder where they could show mis-management by the freeholder. In extreme cases the leaseholders could force the freeholder to sell the freehold to them. As this inevitably caused disputes and legal costs, a wider 'Right to Manage' was introduced by the Commonhold and Leasehold Reform Act 2002 by which the leaseholders (collectively) can insist on the right to manage their building. There is now no need to prove that there has been mismanagement by the landlord or its agents, or to obtain the freeholder's approval. All the leaseholders have to do is create a 'Right to Manage' company, for which a standard template exists. For details of how to set up such a company, how to run it and how to take over control from the freeholder, again the Leasehold Advisory Service has more detailed advice available at www.lease-advice.org, including a leaflet called 'The Right to Manage'.

Using the 'Right to Manage' procedure rather than the collective enfranchisement procedure has advantages in some cases, for example where it is difficult to get a sufficient majority of leaseholders to enfranchise, or the non-residential proportion of the building is too high, and it avoids the need to pay for the freehold.

---

[11] The first two cases also illustrate an unforeseen problem with flats bought from local authorities under the 'right to buy' legislation – often they come with very substantial repair bills due to lack of maintenance.

Practicalities – it should not be overlooked that taking ownership of the freehold or control of management away from the freeholder does not solve every problem that can arise in blocks of flats. When the roof needs repairing, the outside needs painting or the lifts or boilers need replacing, those decisions need to be made, the works carried out and the costs paid. Inevitably, residents' associations, freehold owning residents' companies and Right to Manage companies are dominated by those with the inclination and time to take on those responsibilities and (as one of the authors knows from personal experience) being a director of such a company is mostly a thankless task, and not always a way to popularity with your neighbours. The complicated requirements for prior consultation and estimates for works or service agreements under Section 20 of the Landlord & Tenant Act 1985 apply just as much to freehold owning residents' companies and Right to Manage companies as they do to developer or investor landlords, but the residents' company will not have cash reserves to pay bills if you get the procedure wrong. Directors also need to comply with company law and auditing requirements, including a duty to act in the interests of the shareholders – that is, the leaseholders. Company law is not designed as a way of settling disputes between neighbouring flat owners, for example if some residents want to sell part of the gardens for development and others don't. Memories of the incompetence of the previous freeholder fade quite quickly (in one of the few reported cases on the appointment of a manager under the 1987 Act, *Taylor v Blaquiere,* a leaseholder disputed the expenditure proposed by the new manager). Some might say that the British have not yet adapted to the limited form of communal living, and of democracy, which is inherent in living in a flat.

## Other forms of ownership

Though the vast majority of residential properties are owned either as freehold, or leasehold, it is worth mentioning a couple of exceptions, if only so that if you find them you will know they are not 'normal' and you need specialist advice. Two are old, one is new.

*Copyhold*

This was a historic form of ownership, between freehold and leasehold (that is, a free interest but subject to the 'superior' interest of the lord of the manor). Copyhold was abolished as part of the major overhaul of the UK's property law in 1925. A few properties that have not changed hands since before 1925 still exist as copyhold. In 30 years of legal practice, we have encountered only two examples: a farm worker's cottage that had been passed down through the same family since before 1925, and the headquarters of a building society, which had been in their ownership since the 1880s. A copyhold title can be upgraded to freehold but specialist advice is needed.

*Rent-charges*

These were used in late Victorian times, particularly in Manchester, to create an ongoing 'rental' income for the developer of a housing estate. A (usually fixed) 'rent' is payable by the owner of the freehold to the rent-charge holder. Rent-charges are still sometimes used for commercial properties: for example, estates of small freehold factory or warehouse units, as a means of charging and enforcing payment of a service charge for the maintenance of the estate. Historically, they could be used in other ways too, but are now rare and (apart from the 'estate' rent-charge) can no longer be created and the historic ones will cease by 2037. Estate rent-charges will continue.

*Commonhold*

This is a new form of ownership, introduced by the Commonhold and Leasehold Reform Act 2002 to cater for the same maintenance/shared obligation issue which we have previously mentioned. Commonhold is based on an Australian concept, and is not very different from the 'collective' concept in parts of the US or the 'shared ownership' system in most of Continental Europe.

In a typical commonhold scheme for a block of flats, rather than a freeholder landlord (whether an investor or a residents' company) granting leases, receiving rents, insuring and maintaining the building, providing services and charging each tenant their share, the commonholder 'tenants' themselves own the common parts on a permanent and freehold basis communally, as well as their own flat, and so their 'ownership' of their flat is not time-limited. Moreover, they do not pay a rent and collectively control insurance and maintenance costs. By buying a flat in the block, they commit themselves to a commonhold scheme in the form of a 'Commonhold Community Statement' which regulates the responsibilities of each owner, collective responsibility for decision making about insurance and maintenance of the building and common parts, the collection of each owner's contributions to insurance and maintenance and so on.

In theory, commonhold is a sensible system but it is not well understood by developers, solicitors or lenders. A few schemes have now been established but they are rare and on current form are likely to remain so. It is not practical to convert an existing leasehold block to commonhold, so commonhold will only come into use as new developments adopt this legal structure.

One possible use of commonhold is as a mixed use scheme – where, in addition to residential properties, there are commercial buildings for shopping or leisure purposes, such as a cinema or health club, which share facilities and therefore the cost of maintaining them. Commonhold would also be an effective way of replicating a rent charge for an estate of small commercial properties, but again this is not an option that has been pursued to date except by a few brave pioneer developers.

## Land Registration

Historically, conveyancing was entirely based on paper title, in the form of title deeds. This meant that on each purchase of land the purchaser's solicitors would investigate title by reviewing copies of the title deeds, and then by checking them against the originals the vendor held. It was for the purchaser to satisfy himself that the seller owned the property and had good title to it, and to what extent the property was affected by third party interests such as rights, covenants or tenancies. This process would be repeated each time the property changed hands. Only experienced practitioners were able to understand the arcane way in which the conveyancing documents were (hand)written. Such a system was an art rather than a science, and weakness in title would be hard to discover, leading to disputes later. Disputes about ownership could only be resolved in the courts. The work involved was repetitive, inefficient and expensive.

To quote the Real Property Commissioners in 1830: 'The great difficulties which occur in selling estates and obtaining money on real security, the time which usually lapses before the completion of such transactions, and the harassing expenses and disappointments which attend them, are evils universally acknowledged'.

After a couple of failed or partial attempts, the Land Registry was established in 1925 with the task of creating a definitive register of all land (rather than buildings), owners and other interests in lands such as mortgages and rights to which land may be subject: a modern, comprehensive and accurate Domesday Book.

The land registration system has the great advantage of simplifying land transfer by establishing a register of information covering all matters relating to each registered title, including the name of the owner and the rights to which they are subject; providing an easier and standardised method of transferring ownership; and introducing a state indemnity scheme under which compensation is paid to a registered proprietor deprived of his/her title.

So, on a transfer of registered land it is unnecessary for the purchaser to delve into the past history of the land in order to ensure that the seller has a good title. A once-and-for-all investigation of title is conducted by the Land Registry at the time of first registration. All the purchaser must do is satisfy himself that the seller is the registered proprietor, subject only to those third party interests disclosed. This he can do simply by inspecting a copy of the entries in the register, which the seller can easily supply. The land registration system also means that procedures and standards are set nationally, to remove the local peculiarities that developed under the unregistered system.

The huge task of creating the nationwide register started slowly, with limited areas (mostly in London) subject to compulsory land registration only when a change of ownership took place. So, for many years, the land registration system existed alongside the traditional unregistered land conveyancing system described above. Gradually the areas of compulsory registration expanded to include other urban and then rural areas throughout England and Wales so that by 1990 registration was compulsory throughout England and Wales. By 2008 the Land Registry estimated that 22 million land ownerships in England and Wales were registered (although because rural land ownerships are inevitably larger in area, they estimated that this represented only 68% of the nation's land surface). Until 2003 the requirement to register land at the Land Registry arose only on a change of ownership (and not on a transfer by gift: for example, under a will) so land which had stayed in the same ownership since before 1925, or only passed from one owner to another by way of inheritance – for example, The Crown Estate, other landed estates, much government property and some long established company sites - was still not registered. In 2003 the Land Registry took the final step and imposed a requirement that all land, even The Crown Estate, is now subject to compulsory land registration so that owners of all land in England and Wales must apply to the Land Registry for registration by 2012. The Land Registry, in doing so, has an eye on both its own profitability (now that it is a semi-independent agency) and on the introduction of 'E-Conveyancing' – a move towards making the system for recording land transfers entirely electronic. This process has started, enabling some mortgage-related documents to be recorded electronically, but has some way to go. A system allowing for some electronic transfers of land ownership may be implemented by the Land Registry during 2011.

The Land Registry was identified by the Government in November 2009 as one of the assets it will sell to the private sector. It may not be coincidence that two weeks later the Land Registry announced 1,500 redundancies and the closure of seven regional offices, after announcing a loss of £130 million for 2008/9.

As a consequence of the obligation to register all land, the remaining unregistered land will slowly disappear, along with the archaic legal skills necessary to convey it. Once a property is registered, the title deeds will usually be retained by the Land Registry and in some cases sent to the Public Records Office. Some people have them framed or turned into lampshades.

The information held by the Land Registry is public and is now available online. The definitive version is that held by the Land Registry on its system and the paper versions (known as Land or Charge Certificates) are obsolete. Before 1992, the registered title was only available with the landowner's permission. In 2001, the Land Registry started to record 'price paid' information on the register (it had previously done so up to 1976 but then stopped). In consequence, the Land Registry and numerous other websites which have access to their data can provide information about local house prices, and the prices of previous transactions back to 2001 (and up to 1976). This has proven extremely popular amongst those who are keen to know what their neighbours paid for their houses, but less popular if you object to your neighbours knowing how much you paid.[12]

*Registration of leases*

The land registration system applies to leasehold property as much as it does to freehold land. Again, the application of compulsory registration of leases started slowly, so that from 1925 to 1986 only leases for longer than 40 years granted for a capital sum were registrable (unless the freehold was already registered). This was widened in 1986 to include all leases for 21 years or more and again in 2003 to include all leases for more than seven years.

Registration of a lease means, in addition, that it is also recorded on the freehold title, if that is registered.

Since most long-term residential leases fall into the registrable category even if granted before 1986, it is still important to check, if buying one, whether it is registered at the Land Registry and, if not, whether it should have been at the time: that is, whether the property was in an area of compulsory registration at the time the lease was granted. If it should have been registered and was not, the lease is invalid and cannot be effectively sold or mortgaged.

Again, over time, as the Land Registry captures information on all properties, all leases for seven years or longer will become registered, but seven year leases granted before 2003 will not.

*The form of a Land Registry title*

A typical Land Registry title consists of text in three sections: the property register, the proprietorship register and the charges register, plus a 'filed' plan showing the property edged with a red line, and is always produced as at a specified date. Sometimes pre-existing documents may be filed with the registered title – the lease if the property is leasehold, and other relevant documents such as those granting rights of way or imposing covenants over the property, if they cannot be easily summarised.

[12] The price paid has always been public knowledge in most other countries, including Scotland.

The Land Registry is an efficient and stable organisation (originally a government organisation, now an independent agency) and the accuracy of its information is guaranteed by a compensation scheme.

There are limitations to what it does. It records only the legal ownership of property, not who has the financial interest if different – so if two people own a property jointly, the Land Registry does not record what proportions they own (although it does record whether they are joint tenants or tenants in common – an important distinction for inheritance and tax purposes).

*Land Registry plans*

The plans used by the Land Registry for their filed plans are derived from Ordnance Survey data, which in turn is derived largely from aerial photographs. Inevitably, details of roads and buildings are sometimes out of date, particularly in relation to new developments. The scale of the plans (usually 1:1,250 in urban areas, or 1:2,500 in rural areas) means that the boundaries are not shown with pinpoint precision and disputes about boundaries can arise due to, or be encouraged by, the thickness of the red line on a Land Registry plan. Because of the scale of the plans and the thickness of the line, these plans are accurate to within only a few feet.

*Rights*

It is important to recognise that, useful as the land registration system is, not every right affecting land is recorded at the Land Registry; certain kinds of right are not covered (usually those affecting rural land). Rights can and do arise by long use rather than by the parties entering into an agreement, particularly rights of way for services and rights of light, and such rights may not be reflected in the Land Registry's records. In particular, the Land Registry does not always record rights of which the land has the *benefit*: for example, a right of way or a right for drains to pass across the land next door. Proof of these may be crucial to the continuing use of the property, and obtaining such proof may require a detailed review of pre-registration title deeds for the property benefiting, or the property subject to the right, or obtaining a statutory declaration from someone who has known the property for many years, to prove that the right exists.

Finally, the Land Registry will not record important information affecting the use of the property, such as planning permissions or restrictions, public footpaths or other rights of way, current or past mining activity, common land, chancel repair liability, flooding history or building defects and past or present disputes about ownership are not recorded there. This is why, if you are considering buying a property, your solicitor will need to carry out local and other specialised searches of the relevant authorities, and raise questions of the seller's solicitor (known as preliminary or pre-contract enquiries or 'CPSEs') and get satisfactory answers before you commit yourself to buy by exchanging contracts. We discuss this process in greater detail in Chapter 3.

## Freehold title issues

Generally, freehold is the safest type of ownership and the least likely to be affected by title issues. However, there are some potential problems for owners which may come up when you buy (or sell) and which are worth mentioning because they can have practical consequences or an effect on the value (and mortgageability) of a property, or lead to disputes.

Those which affect legal ownership or rights should be apparent from the Land Registry entries. The most common are:

*Restrictive covenants*

These are promises by a previous landowner not to do something, which are legally-binding on subsequent owners of the property. For example, in the housebuilding boom of the late 19th century when many houses were built on land sold off by landed estates, it was common that covenants were imposed that no house built should have a rental value of less than say £50 per annum. In the 1920s and 1930s suburban building boom, covenants to prevent more than one house being built per plot were common. In the 1990s, much more wide-ranging covenants against building an extension, or limiting the size of sheds or fences, were common. Covenants against 'nuisance' or 'interference' are usual where part of a garden is sold off for development. If buying a house which is new, or recently built, or which has been altered, it is important to check the detail of such covenants to make sure they have not already been breached and that if you plan, for example, to build a garage or extension those plans would not be frustrated by a covenant. With older covenants, such as the 19th century ones, specific indemnity insurance cover can be obtained. Some are more difficult to deal with – the authors know of a house subject to a covenant not to use it other than for 'people of the working classes'. Covenants against the sale of alcohol are common on land originally owned by the Church of England or some landed estates. The existence and relevance of covenants is one of the points to cover with your solicitor when you buy.

*Easements*[13]

These may affect the property, and can be a problem – for example a right of way for a neighbour to drive over your driveway, or a right for a gas main or a drain to go through your garden. Again, these should be apparent from Land Registry information. Easements usually cannot be changed or terminated without the agreement of the person who has the right so if you want to build a garage or an extension to your house over the top of a gas main (which is not allowed for safety reasons), for example, you would have to persuade the gas board to divert it first, at your expense.

Conversely, the property may require the benefit of easements - particularly rights of way, and rights for services – and if it does not, the owner of the land over which the right is required may be entitled to prevent that use (depending on how long it has continued). There have been a series of cases involving houses separated from a public road by a grass verge belonging to a landowner who seeks to charge a fee for the houseowners to gain access to their own properties. Again, this is for your lawyers to check.

Freehold or leasehold property can also be affected by the action or inaction of various local or other authorities – a new road proposal, previous planning applications, smoke control orders, various kinds of enforcement action (or by the actions or intentions of neighbours) past disputes, or proposals for building work. These are also matters to be checked through your lawyers at the time of purchase, and we go into more detail on how to achieve this, and how to interpret the results, in Chapter 3.

This is not an exhaustive list of potential problems. By way of illustration of a little known relic of mediaeval land law, which unexpectedly caused a major problem for one family, we will explain 'chancel repair'.

---

[13] Lawyer jargon for 'rights'

*Chancel repair liability*

Chancel repair liability originated from the tithe system that was used to finance church repairs. A chancel is the part of a church near the altar, usually reserved for the clergy and choir. In other words, it does not include the part used by the congregation. It still exists, and was brought to media attention by the widely reported case of *Parochial Church Council of the Parish of Aston Cantlow and Wilmcote with Billesley, Warwickshire v Wallbank,* which went as far as the House of Lords, the highest court in the UK. Mr and Mrs Wallbank who had (it transpired) acquired a property subject to chancel repair liability ended up with a bill of £200,000 to repair the chancel of their parish church, plus a legal bill of a similar amount. The Human Rights Act did not help them.

The principle, dating back to mediaeval times, is that the rector of a church is responsible for the repair of his church, and in return is entitled to tithes from the properties within his parish. This responsibility and benefit passed to the Anglican Church at the Reformation and is now with Parochial Church Councils.

It applies only to pre-Reformation parish churches with a chancel, so not to the Victorian parish churches in most cities, or to those of Catholic or other denominations. It is therefore primarily a problem in villages, although you cannot rely on that generalisation. Each property within a 'chancel repair' parish is liable, whether it is old or new, and whatever its value. The land owners are jointly and severally liable, so that each is responsible for the whole cost of the repairs, whatever their own property is worth.

There is no conclusive record either of parishes affected or of properties liable, although there is a 'Record of Ascertainments' maintained by the National Archives at Kew. It is possible to obtain a search of this Record, but it can be difficult to correlate that with modern place and property names, and up-to-date Ordnance Survey maps.

The Law Commission recommended the abolition of chancel repair liability in 1985 and The Church of England has accepted that it should be phased out.

This has not been implemented, but in response to the *Aston Cantlow* case there is now a requirement that all such liabilities must be registered against the relevant land at the Land Registry by 13 October 2013, so each parish should now be in the process of establishing what liabilities exist, which properties are affected and applying for registration of the liability at the Land Registry. If not registered by 13 October 2013, new owners will not be liable, although existing owners will.

It is possible to get insurance, which may be cheap for low-risk properties, but expensive or unavailable for high-risk properties.

Searches of the National Archives should still be carried out for properties where there is any risk though the results may be imperfect.

# CHAPTER 2 BEING A TENANT

## The big picture

In Chapter 7 we will look at the letting system from the 'buy-to-let' landlord/investor's perspective. Let's reverse the polarity and look at renting from the tenant/occupier's perspective in this chapter. Residential tenants do not get much coverage in the property pages of newspapers, or much help from estate agents or lawyers, so most tenants sign their tenancy agreements without taking advice, but without tenants the letting system, and the buy-to-let investment market, simply would not exist.

This section focuses on private sector tenants[14] and attempts to guide you through the maze. The private rental sector contained some 2.5 million homes as at 2006, an increase from around 2 million in 2000; those statistics probably understate the position significantly because many arrangements are 'unofficial'. Many of us, even those who follow the traditional middle class housing trajectory of parents' home to student accommodation, back to parents' home to sharing with friends to buying, will have been a tenant and may be again, perhaps as a result of a hiatus between house moves, or of a change of job location.

Unfortunately, despite its importance to the overall mix of housing available in the UK, the private rental sector has a poor reputation for quality and honesty - the shadow of the notorious 1950s slum landlord Peter Rachman still hangs over it, along with the image of Rigsby in the 1970s TV series 'Rising Damp'. As recently as 2006, the Law Commission in its report 'Renting Homes, The Final Report' found significant evidence of serious problems in the private rental sector regarding the physical condition of many privately rented properties and the way tenancies are created and managed, mostly (inevitably) at the cheaper end of the market. In fact, there are many reputable landlords and successful tenancies, and this poor reputation is unfair on many landlords who are trying

[14] There is another book to be written on the topic of public sector tenancies, that is, what used to be called council housing, and housing associations or 'registered social landlords'.

to run professional businesses, or in the case of many smaller landlords, trying to do the best they can.

The Government has announced that they intend to introduce a licensing system for landlords, although the details and date of this remain uncertain.

Nevertheless, there are still rogues around (despite a number of well-meaning government and local authority initiatives) and we hope this section of this book can help you to avoid them and other potential renting pitfalls, and to know your rights as a tenant in case you cannot.

## The legal background

Until 20 years ago, the private rented housing market was subject to a considerable degree of regulation, to control the amount of rent tenants paid, and to give them and their families 'security of tenure', that is the right to stay after the initial tenancy period expired. It was evident that these regulations were discouraging the renting of properties to private sector tenants, thus limiting the supply of available housing in the country and, from a public policy point of view, the ability of workers to move from one part of the country to another to find employment. To combat this, the Conservative Governments in the 1980s passed a number of Acts to de-regulate the private rental sector. In particular, the rent control and 'security of tenure' residential tenants had through the Rent Acts were removed for new tenancies so that since 1988, most new private sector tenancies have been created as 'assured shorthold tenancies', known in the trade as ASTs. Under an AST, the amount of the rent is freely negotiated between landlord and tenant, is not subject to any external system of rent control, and the tenancy does not carry with it any rights to extend or renew when the period of the tenancy expires, unless specifically negotiated.

It is outside the scope of this section to consider other types of tenancy agreements to which special rules apply, apart from 'assured tenancies' and sharing arrangements, which we will mention briefly. In particular, we will not cover regulated tenancies, that is those still subject to the Rent Acts (most such tenants are now elderly, and paying low rents) or other short-term rental agreements created before 1989 (which even though confusingly called assured tenancies or protected shorthold tenancies were significantly different in legal effect to today's ASTs), not least because by now, most will have now expired.

In addition, we do not consider tenancies of special types of properties such as farms or farmhouses or farmworkers' cottages, or where the landlord lives in the same property, or tenancies offered as part of employment, such as accommodation for a pub or hotel manager, or tenancies of commercial property – a shop or an office, or of mixed use, including, for example, the flat above a shop which the tenant will occupy. Special considerations apply for each of these (and in most cases the tenant under such arrangements will have more rights rather than fewer compared to an AST); because there are so many variables, you will need to take specialist advice if you are considering entering into a tenancy of any of these types. We are also not covering holiday lets from the occupier's point of view. Legally these are still tenancies even if they only last for a week, but in practice they are neither as significant nor as likely to give rise to problems as tenancies of a home.

'Assured tenancies' are those offered by public sector or quasi-public sector landlords such as councils or housing associations. The tenants have greater rights to stay than under an AST, and the tenancy period is usually longer, but these tenancies are usually subject to 'need' and waiting lists.

### Assured Shorthold Tenancies

So exactly what is an AST? Let's start by saying what it is not. A tenancy to a company, or at a rent over £25,000 per annum, or at a rent of less than either £250 per annum outside London or £1,000 per annum in London cannot be an AST. (The upper limit will increase to £100,000 per annum from 1 October 2010). Nor can ASTs be used by local authorities or housing associations.

ASTs are, however, the kind of letting you will normally be offered if you go to a letting agent (directly or via the internet) or respond to an advertisement seeking to rent a flat or other type of property to live in. The property you are seeking to rent may be offered furnished or unfurnished. Nevertheless, you are likely to rent by means of an AST and the principles will be the same either way. As we discuss in greater detail below, the rental period must be for a minimum of six months, but may be for longer.

## Finding a tenancy

For students, word of mouth, your students' union and accommodation officers can tell you where to look and what to expect, better than we can. In some cities, specialist student housing providers such as Unite (www.unite-students.com) provide an upmarket version of student living, in new or newly converted buildings, often with concierge services, at higher cost. These may be particularly attractive to overseas students. Strictly speaking, accommodation provided for students by educational establishments will not be as an AST and will be on a standard student contract. Private sector accommodation for students will be on an AST.

For young professionals looking for their first step out of the parents' home or after university, the easiest and most common route is to share, either by replacing someone in an established shared flat, or by a group of friends finding a place together.

As an individual looking for a group to share with, if word of mouth or Facebook fail you, Gumtree (www.gumtree.com) is an obvious starting point, at least for London and other cities. Other useful websites are listed in Appendix 2.

The Government's 'Rent.a.Room' scheme has also encouraged those with a spare room to take in what was once called a 'lodger' to supplement income and perhaps provide some company, if that is what you want.

'Sharers' usually end up with an AST – sometimes one per person, sometimes one for the group with all of you on the same tenancy. If the latter, remember you will each be liable for all of the rents so you will be vulnerable if one of you fails to pay.

As a group or couple looking together, there are lots of property websites on which to research - all have 'to let' sections, plus the traditional routes of letting agents, the local newspaper's property section and small ads in newsagents. Many letting agents focus on letting but others are 'add-ons' to established firms of selling agents.

The websites are useful in assessing what you can expect to get for your money in a particular area by filtering out properties that are too big or too small, too cheap or too expensive.

You will need to determine your budget – net income less known expenditure plus a margin for the unexpected – and your preferred location (and travel costs if you will be commuting).

Bear in mind:

1. you will be expected to provide a deposit of four or six weeks' rent;
2. the landlord will take up references for you, including a bank reference and/or a credit check and an employer reference;
3. when considering locations, and the individual properties within that area, factors should include:
    a. general standard of the area including security;
    b. 'commutability' – time v cost; frequency of train or underground or bus services; where they stop; is the property within 'black cab' range?
    c. availability of the amenities you need - shops, restaurants, pubs, sports or health clubs, churches, 'green space';
    d. the size of the space you need – how many bedrooms? single or double? how many bathrooms (more than three sharing a bathroom is painful)? entertaining space? a kitchen you can actually cook in?
    e. the condition and running costs of the specific property – avoid damp or condensation; or high heating bills or contributions to on-site facilities such as health clubs unless you are going to use them;
    f. the amount and quality/cleanliness of furniture including beds and storage;
    g. parking or storage for cars, bikes or motorbikes, if you need it;
    h. garden, if you want it;
    i. security, both around the property and inside it (fire and burglar alarms);
    j. noise (from roads, schools, pubs, clubs, upstairs).

This is a list similar to that you would have if you were buying, but of course you are only looking to commit for a temporary period of six or 12 months rather than making an investment, and you are not intending to solve any drawbacks by making improvements.

Whilst not all letting agents are 'rogues', bear in mind they need no qualifications or experience to set themselves up as letting agents.

You have some legal protection – under the Property Misdescriptions Act 1991 it is a criminal offence for those acting as estate agents or letting agents to make false or misleading statements, for example in letting particulars (including information on websites), and under the Estate Agents Act 1979 any monies paid to estate agents or letting agents should be kept separate as client monies.

Tenancy deposits should now be protected, as we explain below.

Under the Estate Agents Act, letting agents can be 'struck off' and banned from practising. All of those remedies are a deterrent to the unscrupulous, but despite this the Property Ombudsman reports that calls for help to his office about lettings have risen from 77 a week in 2008 to 129 a week in autumn 2009. It is clear, for example, from the Law Commission 2008 report 'Encouraging Responsible Letting', that the regulation of letting agents is inadequate and it is likely that the redress schemes and code of standards recently introduced for selling agents will be extended to letting agents in the near future.

One factor to bear in mind is that landlords and letting agents and management are subject to the UK's general anti-discrimination legislation. That means both the equality legislation as to how they choose tenants or advertise for them (so it is illegal to choose tenants on the basis of race, gender, religion, sexual orientation or age) and the disability discrimination legislation which stipulates when the landlord may have a duty to provide facilities for the disabled, which can include not only the physically disabled but also those with mental disabilities including schizophrenia and (very recently) autism.

A disabled person can require a landlord to make 'reasonable adjustments' to the property he/she occupies or allow the disabled person to do so, or to make changes to the common parts. For example, in *Williams v Richmond Court (Swansea) Limited* an old lady wanted to install a stairlift on the common staircase of a block of flats. The court refused to enforce this in this particular case on the basis of the effect on the other residents, but clearly in other circumstances a similar request could be enforced.

The Equality Act 2010, most of which is due to come into force in October 2010 once codes of practice have been published, will bring together and update all the various anti-discrimination legislation and will change some of the procedures and standards.

## The terms

When deciding whether or not to enter into any particular AST, and especially when reviewing the wording of the tenancy agreement (which, it goes without saying, you should read carefully before signing)[15] there will be a number of factors you should consider, including:

*The rent*

This will usually be a fixed amount, payable monthly in advance. VAT will not apply in respect of your rental payments. The landlord or letting agent may require proof that you are able to meet the rental payments before agreeing to enter into an AST with you, usually in the form of references from your employer, bank and any previous landlord.

*The deposit*

This is usually equal to four or six weeks' rent and is collected by the agent for the landlord's protection against you failing to pay rent, or causing damage to the property. There is now an important new Tenancy Deposit Protection Scheme which controls how the agent holds this money as we discuss below. As well as the amount of the deposit, you will need to agree what happens to the interest earned by the deposit during the rental period. The landlord often assumes that he will have the benefit of the interest (and historically, this usually happened) but this need not automatically be the case. The deposit is after all your money, not the landlord's, and when discussing the terms of the AST with the landlord (or the letting agent) you should be able to put forward a good argument that you should have the benefit of any interest. If this proves difficult to agree, it might be possible to agree to split the interest equally between you.

*The length of the tenancy*

This must be a minimum of six months, and a year is conventional. There is now no legal maximum. It is common for the agreement to specify that the tenant may terminate on two months' notice after the first six months, and often it may be possible to negotiate the right to extend or renew the tenancy on similar terms for another year or two, usually with a pre-agreed uplift in rent (say 5%, or in line with the Retail Price Index).

---

[15] Well, what else do you expect two lawyers to say?

It is important to identify clearly what is, and is not, included under the terms of the tenancy. Usually it will be obvious from the advertisement or initial details whether the property is to be let furnished or unfurnished. 'Unfurnished' is more common for family houses let for longer periods, but generally 'furnished' is the norm. Depending on the sophistication, location and price of the property, this may include only the most basic furniture from junk shops or the owner's family home, or high-design plasma TVs and top quality kitchen and bathroom fittings. More usually, the typical property is furnished from Ikea in a bland but functional style. When comparing the value to you of different future 'nests', do take into account the value to you of the quality and quantity of furnishing. Conversely, you may want the furnishing to be minimal as you may have some cherished or familiar items of your own to bring in and use, or at least store, pending the purchase of your own property. If viewing a property, check with the agent or landlord that what you see is what you will get, and that if anything is damaged or you simply cannot live with it, it will be replaced or removed. Landlords generally do expect some upgrading or replacement between one letting and the next. From a hygiene point of view, you may wish to insist on the mattresses and bedding (if provided – many tenants provide their own) being replaced.

## Legal responsibilities

What can you expect from your landlord before you start? Four concerns of a legal nature arise on any letting:

*Licensing*

Are the landlord and the letting agent licensed or members of any accreditation scheme or trade organisation? The Labour Government intended to introduce a licensing system for all private sector landlords, but this has not been implemented, and the Coalition Government has announced that it will not pursue this initiative.

There is a licensing scheme already in operation for 'houses in multiple occupation' or HMOs, under the Housing Act 2004, and in force from 6 July 2006.

The underlying purpose was to reduce the level of fire risk in multi-tenanted properties, and to ensure that high risk properties were identified and targeted for improvement – for example by improving fire protection such as using fire retardant materials, requiring smoke alarms and fire alarms and providing fire escape routes.

The owner or manager of an HMO must have a licence from the local authority, and that licence will contain conditions including a maximum number of residents.

An HMO is defined as a house or flat which:

1. is occupied by more than one household who share facilities such as a kitchen or bathroom;
2. is non self-contained bedsit accommodation occupied by sharers where there is no family relationship; or
3. is a converted building (as opposed to new build) occupied by more than one household unless each household has a self-contained flat; or
4. is a converted building comprising self-contained flats but where the conversion does not comply with Building Regulations (unless more than a third are owner occupied).

All properties with three or more storeys and occupied by five or more people in two or more households must be registered.

As well as improving fire safety, the licensing system is intended to 'weed out' those landlords who do not pass a 'fit and proper person' test.

Failure to obtain or comply with an HMO licence is a criminal offence.

Accommodation provided to students by a university (as opposed to accommodation provided to students by the private sector even if approved by the university) strictly speaking does not require an HMO licence, although equivalent fire safety regulations apply.

You should be aware that recent changes in planning law relating to HMOs – particularly aimed at so-called 'student ghettoes' in cities like Leeds, Sheffield and Nottingham – mean that planning permission is needed for 'multi-occupation' (here, confusingly, meaning three or more people rather than five or more). So your landlord may not be allowed by planning law to use the property in this way. Many people will ignore this change in law.

There are several landlord trade organisations – the National Landlords Association; the Residential Landlords Association, the National Federation of

Residential Landlords and the Guild of Residential Landlords all have accreditation schemes although the members of those organisations tend to be 'professional' rather than 'one-off' landlords. This form of self-regulation does not have much in the way of 'teeth' for an unhappy tenant, but it is useful to know up front whether your landlord is a member so that at least you have the possibility of complaining to the trade organisation if the landlord fails to comply with his obligations.

Perhaps more usefully, although still of limited value, a number of local authorities have established registers of landlords in their area, and those on the register have signed up to a code of practice for 'landlord good behaviour'. For an example, see the Sheffield Responsible Landlords Scheme at www.sheffield.gov.uk/rls, which includes over 330 landlords owning over 900 properties. There is a national accreditation scheme for agents, the National Approved Letting Scheme, www.nalscheme.co.uk. Again, however, there is little by way of direct legal sanction available to an unhappy tenant, except to complain to the local authority or the authorities who maintain the register so that the landlord in question may be removed from the register if it has breached the code of practice.

Most of these codes of practice encourage landlords to agree to a dispute resolution service which means that landlords and tenants can refer any dispute to a mediation service which will attempt to achieve an agreement without the cost, time or expense of going to court. In some cases (including Sheffield) local authorities employ tenancy protection officers who can take steps to prevent landlords taking unlawful action should this be necessary.

Letting Agents may belong to one of their own trade associations – the National Association of Letting Agents (which recently merged with the Association of Residential Letting Agents), or the UK Association of Letting Agents or the Association of Residential Managing Agents, or the Royal Institution of Chartered Surveyors. They may show the logo of the relevant organisation on their note paper. If not, ask whether they belong. If in doubt, you can check their answer on the website of the relevant organisation.

If the tenant has a later complaint about the way the agent acted, you can report it to the relevant trade association, which in the case of a serious allegation may take disciplinary action. These organisations are likely to take action if dishonesty or misuse of cash is involved, but less so if the agent is simply incompetent, unresponsive or slow. Those who are members are also subject to the complaints system run by the Property Ombudsman (see www.tpos.co.uk). The number of Ombudsman disputes involving letting agents increased by almost 50% from 2008 to 2009.

Unfortunately, the more recent 'standards' legislation which applies to agents selling property does not apply to agents letting it, so the extent of redress is limited.

*Energy Performance Certificates*
The landlord (and the agent) is required by law to provide an Energy Performance Certificate (EPC) to any potential tenant when marketing the property. An EPC is a brief report prepared by an energy assessor, which shows the energy efficiency of the property on a scale of A (good) to G (bad).

EPCs have been required for all lettings beginning on or after 1 October 2008.

The letting market has not adjusted to the fact that EPCs are needed on lettings as well as sales, but over time production of EPCs for lettings should become common practice.

*Tenancy Deposit Protection Scheme*
As mentioned above, there is now a system to protect tenants' deposits against the risk of the landlord or their agents holding on to the deposit (or even disappearing with it at the end of the tenancy). It is well known (at least in rumour if not always in fact) that landlords and their agents will use any excuse to hold on to the tenant's deposit at the end of the tenancy for as long as possible, setting off against it significant (and sometimes dubious) costs, and fight any attempt by the tenant to recover it. In turn, tenants have been known to retaliate by failing to pay the last month's rent, leaving the landlord to recover their rent from the deposit - understandable, but two wrongs of course do not make a right.

In fact, two protections exist.

**1. The Estate Agents Act 1979**

If the deposit is held by a letting agent (rather than the landlord) the agent is under a legal obligation under the Estate Agents Act 1979 to keep that deposit money in a separate client account (what Americans would call a trust account) with the name of the tenant identified. That means that the money does not belong to the agent or the landlord and the bank in which it is deposited has to be made aware of, and therefore to recognise, the right of the tenant to his or her deposit in the event of a problem arising. This separation is helpful at a practical level in tracking the money and ensuring that the agent has not spent it on something else, or paid it over to the landlord, and is helpful at a legal level if the agent itself disappears or becomes insolvent as the monies should then be in the bank and safe for the tenant to recover.

However, this legislation is not effective to protect deposits held by landlords rather than agents, or to prevent 'end of tenancy' disputes over deposits.

Research in 2006/7 suggested that 16% of deposits were not returned, and a further 20% were returned only in part. Over half of tenants who had all or part of their deposits withheld felt it had been withheld unjustifiably.

## 2. Compulsory tenancy deposit schemes

After various attempts at self-regulation through the landlord and agent representative bodies were considered to be ineffective (mainly because a large proportion of landlords and a fair proportion of letting agents do not belong to any representative bodies) a compulsory tenancy deposit scheme was introduced in 2007. This provides for the deposit to be either held by, or insured by, an independent third party approved by Government. This is instead of the system whereby deposits are held by the landlord or letting agency.

Since 6 April 2007, deposits taken by landlords and agents for assured shorthold tenancies in England and Wales must be protected with one of three authorised schemes.

1. The Tenancy Deposit Scheme is an insurance-based scheme where the tenant pays the deposit to the landlord or agent, which retains it and pays a premium to its insurer, Aviva. This scheme is run by The Dispute Service, which provides 'dispute resolution and complaints handling for the lettings industry'. This scheme claims to protect over £800 million of deposits. The website is www.thedisputeservice.co.uk.

2. My Deposits is a partnership between Hamilton Fraser Insurance and the National Landlords Association. Its members are mostly landlords, although tenants can also join, and this scheme claims to protect £330 million of deposits. The website is www.mydeposits.co.uk.

3. The Deposit Protection Service is the only scheme that takes custody of deposits rather than insuring them. It is free to use and open to all landlords and letting agents, and is funded from the interest earned from deposits held, which presently total £261 million. The website is www.depositprotection.com.

Whichever scheme applies, the landlord or agent must provide to the tenant within 14 days of receiving the deposit details of the relevant scheme, contact details and instructions on how to apply for release of the deposit and what to do if there is a dispute about it. The deposit must be returned to the tenant within 10 days after the tenancy ends, subject to any lawful deductions. If there is a dispute about how much should be deducted, the landlord must pay the tenant the amount that is not disputed, and pay the rest to the Tenancy Dispute Scheme or My Deposits, and the dispute is then settled under the scheme. In the case of the Deposit Protection Service, they hold the deposit until the dispute is settled by agreement or the courts, or mediation.

The deposit schemes are intended to ensure that tenants get all or part of their deposit back when they are entitled to it, to make any disputes easier to resolve and to encourage tenants and landlords to agree from the start of the tenancy the condition of the property and its contents so that disputes are minimised. They do not protect the landlord against the letting agent becoming insolvent – in which case the landlord is obliged to return the deposit to the tenant himself, and chase the agent for the deposit monies (unless they have been paid to the Deposit Protection Scheme).

There are serious sanctions where the landlord does not comply, including payment of a penalty of three times the deposit, and even a bar on the landlord recovering possession of the property from the tenant.

The Tenancy Deposit Scheme gave landlords rather a shock in April 2009 by limiting its cover to only those agents regulated by one of the specified landlord trade associations, and ceasing insurance cover to those who are not regulated. That has forced landlords either to make sure that their agents do join one of the regulatory bodies, or to move their deposits elsewhere. The regulatory bodies approved by the Tenancy Deposit Scheme are The Association of Residential Letting Agents, the National Approved Letting Scheme, the National Association of Estate Agents and the Royal Institution of Chartered Surveyors. Affected tenants have been notified of this change but it is a matter only the landlord can control. There is not much the tenant can do if the landlord or agent to refuses or is unable to correct the position.

It should be remembered that the deposit schemes only apply to ASTs so they do not apply to those 'tenancies' which are not ASTs – for example company lets, those at particularly low or high rents, or where the landlord shares the same property.

Press reports suggests that there are not many disputes under the tenancy deposit scheme, which indicates that it is having the desired effect. Problems no doubt remain with those landlords and agents who have not signed up to it.

The first case on the Scheme has been reported (*Draycott v Hannells Letting*) where the letting agents had put the deposit into the TDS but after the 14 day deadline, and were not penalised. However, there are appeals pending in other cases on the Scheme which may produce different results.

*Landlord's mortgage*

There have been a number of instances where tenants have found themselves homeless (often at very short notice) because the landlord has not been paying amounts due under his mortgage, and the landlord's lender has enforced its right to sell or take possession of the property and recover what it is owed by the landlord. It is likely that with the large increase in speculative buy-to-let buyers between 2002 and 2006, and the fall in property values from 2007 to 2009, and the difficulty in remortgaging, a number of buy-to-let investors are in mortgage difficulties and therefore their tenants are at risk. Some other landlords also will be 'accidental' or 'reluctant' landlords who are letting their property only because they cannot sell at a price they would accept – and some of those are likely to be letting in breach of their mortgage conditions. In both situations, the 'bad boy' is the borrower/landlord but the lender will win any legal battle and the tenant will lose out, both in respect of being allowed to continue to occupy the property (that is, the tenant is likely to be turfed out) and (probably) as regards recovering any money paid in advance to the landlord, including the deposit if not held by an agent or protected by the Tenancy Deposit Scheme. This seems, and is, extremely harsh on the tenant, particularly as the tenant may get little or no warning that legal enforcement action is being taken by the lender (since the lender may not know of the tenant's existence).

The court rules were changed with effect from 1 October 2009 so that lenders seeking to enforce through repossession are required to contact all occupiers, not just the borrower, and to allow a right for the occupiers to appear at the court possession hearing and to allow even unauthorised occupiers a short period (probably two months) to move out. This does not protect tenants in all circumstances, and a new law – The Mortgage Repossession (Protection of Tenants) Act 2010 – gives similar protection even to tenants where the owner/landlord has let unlawfully, that is, without his lender's consent or knowledge.

## How to reduce risk

So how can you protect yourself against such concerns? By asking three simple but firm questions to which you expect an answer, before you commit yourself:

1. Is the landlord, and the agent if there is one, part of any licensing scheme or trade organisation?
2. Which of the Tenancy Deposit Protection Schemes will apply?
3. Has the landlord's lender consented to the letting to you?

Conversely, the landlord will want to check you out. In practice this will usually be done by the landlord's agent. They will expect to meet you, to verify who you are (which may mean producing passport, driving licence etc) and seek to establish that you are respectable and can pay the rent, by getting references on you (which would normally include a bank reference, an employer's reference and, if you have previously rented, a reference from your previous landlord). They will also run a credit check on you through Experian or other credit reference agency to see if you have any outstanding judgments or County Court orders against you. If any of these proves less than satisfactory or simply cannot be provided (for example if you have not been in work, or have been abroad) then the landlord may be prepared to allow you to proceed if you provide a larger deposit to cover his greater risk, or if you can provide a guarantor (perhaps one of your parents - if they are prepared to take the risk!).

## Signing on the dotted line

Once you have agreed the rent, the deposit arrangements and the period of the tenancy, you have had satisfactory answers to your three questions, and the landlord has checked you out, you should be 'agreed' and ready to proceed. At this stage the landlord or agent should provide you with the final form of assured shorthold tenancy, and you should consider it carefully before signing it. Neither you nor the landlord is legally committed yet (negotiations to date should have been carried out 'subject to contract'), so either of you can back out if you so decide.

That is not the end of the process: you will need to consider carefully, agree and sign the tenancy agreement, pay the deposit, and usually the first month's rent, before you get the keys. You will also need to ensure that the landlord or the agent arranges and carries out an inventory of the contents (if the property is being let furnished) and notifies the various utility companies – electricity, gas, telephone, water, internet provider (if relevant) and the local authority for council tax purposes that you are moving in, and when, so that meters can be read and all the bills split accordingly. Normally, the landlord or agent should also arrange a pre-move clean for the whole property.

## The form of tenancy agreement

The tenancy agreement itself will be in relatively standard wording (it may even be a pre-printed form – but that does not mean that you can ignore it). It imposes important responsibilities on you. A well-drafted one will be clear and easy to read; many are not. If the latter, an alarm bell should ring.

In considering it, first look at the key items you have already agreed: the rent, the period of the tenancy, the right to break or extend and the amount of the deposit, and the deposit protection arrangements, and who gets the interest.

Then you need to look at the other provisions to ensure that they are consistent with what you expect. These will be a mixture of obligations that you have to comply with, and restrictions that prevent you from doing things.

*'To do'*

Typical examples of things you positively must do are as follows:

(a) keep the inside of the property clean and tidy and in good repair and condition. That will include replacing light bulbs, broken windows etc;
(b) pay for outgoings such as electricity, gas, water and telephone;
(c) pay council tax;
(d) insure the contents you bring in (for example, TV, laptop, clothes, credit cards, phone);
(e) use the burglar alarm properly; and
(f) maintain the garden (unless the landlord agrees to do so).

*'Not to do'*

Typical 'you shall not' restrictions include:

(a) no pets;
(b) no smoking;
(c) no sharing, except for family members (unless sharing is pre-agreed);
(d) no damage to furniture, furnishings and other contents;
(e) no use except as a private home (so no business use); and
(f) no changes to the property including redecoration.

## The landlord's obligations

In return, the landlord's obligations will be shorter and simpler:

(a) to allow the tenant to occupy;
(b) to insure the building and the contents provided by the landlord;
(c) to keep in repair the structure and exterior of the building including drains, gutters and external pipes, and the installations for water, gas, electricity and sanitation, and the heating/hot water system. The landlord does not usually explicitly take on responsibility for machinery such as washing machines or cookers but in practice these are normally treated as the landlord's responsibility. It would be worthwhile asking the landlord or letting agent to clarify the position when negotiating the terms of the agreement; and
(d) to maintain the garden (unless this is to be the responsibility of the tenant).

In addition the landlord will be liable to pay any costs that relate to the property which you do not explicitly agree to pay - for example ground rent and service charge if the property is leasehold, or any maintenance charge for shared facilities.

## Standard clauses

The tenancy will also include as standard a few provisions that are necessary but hopefully neither of you will want to implement in practice:

(a) a right for the landlord to enter and inspect the property, usually after 24 hours' prior notice, to check on its condition and to ensure that you are complying with your obligations;

(b) a right for the landlord to terminate the tenancy if you are in breach of its terms, or become bankrupt;

(c) an obligation for you to give back the property in good condition, including the contents of the inventory at the end of the tenancy;

(d) an address for service on the landlord of notice of legal proceedings.

## Future contact

An important point to check before moving in is who the contact point will be during the tenancy. You may find that either the landlord intends to manage the property itself or plans to use an agent (who may not be the same as the letting agent) to manage the property. You need to be clear from the beginning of the tenancy as to who the rent is to be paid to, and who to call if there is a problem with the property (such as a burst water pipe or a burglary). Bear in mind that if the landlord is managing the property directly, he or she may or may not be local, and you may want a more local point of contact in case of emergency. You may also prefer to keep at 'arm's length' from the landlord personally and deal through an agent rather than direct.

## Tenancy extensions

During the tenancy, assuming all goes well (that is the handover works effectively, you pay your rent on time, no disasters happen and you are happy), there is every chance that as the tenancy period approaches its end, you may be able to agree an extension to the tenancy even if you do not have that right explicitly in the tenancy agreement.

## What if there are problems?

If you do have a problem, such as difficulty in paying the rent or you have damaged the furniture (no doubt by accident) or experience problems with the property itself, or the neighbours, then we strongly recommend that you speak promptly to the landlord or letting agents or those responsible for management, and ensure that they understand the problem and, if the problem is down to you, how you propose to deal with it, or if there is a problem that is their responsibility, what you expect them to do in order to deal with it.

It is rare for problems about an assured shorthold tenancy to reach the courts, simply because the sums involved and the periods of time for most tenancies do not justify the cost and delay of court proceedings. If legal proceedings are initiated, it is usually because the rent has not been paid, or because tenants have overstayed at the end of the tenancy and failed to move. Sometimes, court proceedings are taken in order to demonstrate to the local housing authority that the tenant is 'unintentionally homeless' so as to allow them to be re-housed by the authority. Generally though, most disputes can be dealt with either through the dispute resolution service of any trade association the landlord or letting agent may belong to, or if it relates to a deposit, through the dispute resolution service for the relevant protection scheme.

For those on benefits, local housing allowance or LHA (the current version of 'housing benefit') may be available even for private sector renting. Unlike housing benefit, LHA is usually paid to the claimant, not to the landlord.

## What to do at the end of the tenancy?

If you and the landlord are well organised, there should be a smooth handover back to the landlord so that the landlord or the agent is able to carry out an inspection shortly before the end of the tenancy, you move out on or before the due date, taking all your possessions with you, you and the landlord (or agent) manage the reading of meters and splitting of the bills for the utilities and council tax as at the right date and, if all goes according to plan, your deposit is returned promptly (with interest, assuming you agreed that).

If there is an issue over handover arrangements for the property, or in relation to the deposit, then if one of the tenancy deposit protection schemes applies the dispute resolution mechanism under that should be triggered; if there is a problem around handover arrangements, or about the deposit where it is not protected under one of the schemes, then it is likely that the local authority or any trade association to which the landlord or letting agent belongs is the best bet.

# CHAPTER 3 BUYING A PROPERTY

## Buy or rent?

Chapter 1 has given you a basic introduction to the legal framework of the UK property system and its historical origin. Chapter 2 has put a framework around renting. This chapter is intended to give you a practical guide to buying your first home and thus reflects the conversation mentioned in the introduction. Broadly speaking, the points we make apply regardless of whether you are buying a freehold or leasehold property: where there are distinctions between the two, we make this clear.

The starting point is a young couple wanting to 'get on the housing ladder' and set up their first home together, that is, to live as a couple for the next three to five years. Although the couple would not be averse to their property rising in value during this time period, they are not primarily interested in making money from their purchase – they want to make a home.

A critical first decision for them will be whether they would be wiser to rent or to buy a property, or perhaps to combine the two with an assisted 'affordable housing' purchase. That decision will of course depend on a variety of factors, including the value of their savings, how much of those savings they wish to use in the purchase, how much they can borrow by way of a mortgage on the one hand, and the cost of renting on the other. (We talk about mortgages and how they work in Chapter 5.) A useful, if broad-brush, starting point is the comparison tables on www.rightmove.co.uk, or propertysupermarket.com, or the other mortgage providers' websites mentioned in Appendix 2. We have covered renting in Chapter 2, and we cover 'affordable housing' purchases in the last section of this chapter.

**How do I know how much I can get as a mortgage?**

The crucial factors in getting a mortgage are:

(a) your current and projected income(s);

(b) the 'loan to value' ratio: that is, what percentage of the value of the property to borrow (or put in another way, how much you are putting in as a deposit yourself);

(c) your credit rating (at least not having a poor one).

## BUYING A PROPERTY

Conventionally, until early 2008, a typical building society or bank would in principle be willing to offer four/five times your annual salary (the 'earnings multiple'), sometimes six times (though 30 years ago, most banks or building societies would generally only lend three times the applicant's salary by way of a mortgage). If you were a couple, they would calculate the sum they were willing to offer as a mortgage sum by reference to three times one salary and add the second salary. Sometimes, banks and building societies would be willing to offer 100% of the property value (as valued by them, not the price you had agreed to pay for the property). Sometimes, however, they would be willing to provide funds equal to a fraction of the property's value – in other words, the loan to value ratio – (say 80%) meaning that the applicant would have to find the balance of the purchase price themselves.

With the squeeze on loans following the onset of the Credit Crunch, these 'rules of thumb' no longer apply. Some lenders will still apply similar rules, others will require a higher deposit (or a lower loan to value ratio) and/or a lower earnings multiple. Bearing in mind that at least part of the reason for the Credit Crunch has been lenders lending too much to those who cannot afford to repay, aiming for an earnings multiple of over four or a loan to value of over 100% (which many lenders applied in 2006/2007) means you can easily become overstretched very quickly unless your income rises rapidly.

For first time buyers in particular, the consequence of the adoption of a more conservative approach to loan to value ratios by lenders (in mid-2009 75% or less was the maximum for many lenders, meaning the buyer needed to find at least 25% of the price in cash, plus costs) is that buying a property has for many become virtually impossible despite the overall fall in property values.

Putting this in cash terms, the amount a typical first time buyer had to find from their own resources in 2009 was £33,000, compared to £3,000 in 2006.

So, it is important to be realistic.

To find out how much you can borrow, carry out some basic online research about typical mortgage rates and fees. Then talk to a couple of banks or building societies – they have mortgage advisers in larger branches whose job it is to sell mortgages to people like you and there is plenty of competition between them – or go to a mortgage broker who (if he is an independent financial adviser, not a tied broker only selling one lender's products) will have access to a variety of mortgage providers and be able to advise you on what he thinks is right for you. Remember he may be on commission, and be clear before you start whether you are paying him a fee for his advice.

Also, do a credit check on yourself – via Experian or another credit checking agency - to ensure your record is clean before you start.

Your mortgage payments can vary depending on the movement in interest rates – as we explain in Chapter 5, some mortgages are offered at a fixed interest rate for a period of time to encourage people to take out loans, and to offer some measure of certainty to borrowers during the first years of their mortgage – but sooner or later such fixed interest rate periods come to an end, meaning that you will then revert to paying interest on your mortgage at the lender's mortgage interest rate, or be forced to look around for a new fixed interest rate mortgage. This latter option may however not be available, and even if it is, interest rate movements may mean that new fixed rate deals are set using interest rates which are higher than those in force when you first bought the property (and in any event, changing mortgages – though sometimes a smart financial move in the long run - almost invariably entails at least some expense, effort and inconvenience in the short run). In other words, you should consider carefully what fraction of your monthly (after tax) take home pay you can afford to spend on mortgage payments, and allow for a sensible margin just in case your mortgage payments go up. You should also make sure that you allow for sensible living costs and other likely expenses when deciding whether or not you can afford to pay the mortgage you are considering. Matters which you may want to take into account when carrying out this assessment include:

- food costs;
- cost of clothing;
- transport costs (including petrol, insurance and (if you have borrowed money to buy a car or other vehicle) loan repayments);
- social life;[16]
- pension and life assurance costs (if you have these);
- telephone/internet costs;
- utility costs.

---

[16] In the authors' experience, many people underestimate the costs of visiting the pub regularly.

Bear in mind also that properties are usually cheaper than you expect for a reason, maybe because of their condition or because they do not fit standard mortgage criteria, which are much tighter than they used to be. For example, many lenders will not give a mortgage on a flat above a shop, or high-rise blocks, or ex-council property, or even simply newly-built properties. Check your lender's criteria before you start looking.

## Research

Assuming you are satisfied that you can afford to take on the financial burden of buying a home and can get a mortgage at a price you can afford, it will be time to begin the buying process. This can be broken down into three phases: research; finding 'the one' and agreeing a price and finally, the legalities.

### House price reports

A good place to start your research is house price reports, both nationally and for the area(s) in which you are considering buying. You will frequently see reports in the press about house prices, or rental levels, falling or rising. These have a considerable effect on confidence and perception amongst the general public. They need to be recognised as inevitable generalisations of activity in the market, which may not be particularly relevant for your personal needs, or indeed in every location, but they do show trends. Each is based on subtly different information.

The six main monthly indices are:

*Hometrack* tends to show the 'front end' of the market because its information comes from estate agents' opinions about likely selling prices. It also tracks the number of new buyers registering, the average time a property is on the market, the percentage of the asking price being achieved and the number of sales agreed. Information is usually on a national basis, and although often quoted in newspapers is aimed at property professionals such as lenders and estate agents.[17]

---

[17] The monthly house price survey is accessible at www.hometrack.co.uk/community-and-analysis/survey.cfm.

| | |
|---|---|
| *RICS* | based on reports from RICS member surveyors on whether in their view prices are rising or falling, month by month – this includes a regional breakdown and comments from agents. |
| *Halifax* | the best known index: it records asking prices for properties on which the Halifax has agreed to lend month by month. There are breakdowns according to house type (all, new and existing) and buyer (all, first time buyers and movers) and regional indices. It is adjusted for changes in the mix of properties included, and seasonally adjusted, with the intention that it truly shows trends in the price of an average property. |
| *Nationwide* | similar to Halifax: based on Nationwide lending data for properties at the post survey approval stage, adjusted for changes in the mix of properties included, and seasonally adjusted. |
| *Council of Mortgage Lenders (CML)* | based on mortgage lending information from its members (which includes almost all active mortgage lenders in the UK) and shows lending figures, including a breakdown between new lending, remortgages and buy-to-let. |
| *Land Registry* | the Land Registry records all transactions as applications are registered there, once the transaction has taken place. It therefore includes only those that actually happen, and at the price at which they actually happen, not the asking price. It includes all transactions whether mortgage led or cash only. It is therefore the most accurate, although usually the last to show a trend. |

The various indices tend to follow a similar pattern with some timing differences. They are good for newspaper headlines; not so good for deciding what any particular house is worth now or will be worth in the future.

Before you start looking at properties, you need to carry out a careful analysis of the minimum requirements you want in a property and of your finances, to work out what you can afford. If you cannot get what you want for the amount you can afford, there is no point in wasting your and other peoples' time, money and emotions, and you will need either to wait and save hard to close the gap (do you really need the car, the holiday, the health club, the extra night out, the expensive clothes?), find another source of funds (the Bank of Mum and Dad?) or adjust your minimum requirements (can you live further out and commute further, do you really need a garden if there is a park nearby, is that second bedroom vital, can you buy cheaper and 'do it up' yourselves?).

## The Bank of Mum and Dad

Many first time buyers, of course, find that they are stuck in the vicious circle of rising rents draining away their cash, rising prices and shrinking mortgage offers, so that their first step on the housing ladder seems to be receding. So they turn to family to 'bridge the gap' in coming up with sufficient cash to fund that all important deposit.

We cover in this section some ways in which this can be done, while giving parents some protection.

Let's take a typical example. James is earning £30,000 pa, and is looking to buy a £150,000 flat, and has savings of £5,000. So he will need (say) £5,000 for purchase costs including furniture and some decoration. A typical building society will lend him up to 80% of the price – so £120,000. There is a shortfall of £30,000, of which £15,000 will be needed at exchange to fund the 10% deposit, and £15,000 will be needed to complete. Lower mortgage interest rates would be available if James could get the loan to value ratio below 70%.

His parents could:

1. give him £30,000
2. lend him £30,000
3. persuade the building society to increase their loan to value ratio to 90% so he gets £135,000 from them and the parents give or lend him £15,000.
4. the parents buy the property in their own name.

Factors to take into account (assuming his parents have that money in cash or can get it) are:

1. a gift is likely to be a potentially exempt transfer for inheritance tax purposes. Depending on the parents' circumstances and other previous gifts, this may trigger IHT now, or affect the amount payable later.

2. a loan should be documented to be clear in what circumstances it is to be repaid – maybe in instalments, maybe on a fixed date, only when the property is sold and whether interest is payable, and if so when and at what rate. If the parents don't charge interest, that may be treated as a gift in itself and potentially subject to inheritance tax although the parents' annual exempt gift allowances may apply. A common arrangement would be to roll up interest to be added to the repayment of the loan when the property is sold.

3. a loan could be secured by a second mortgage on the property – although we suspect most parents would see that as overkill. Whether or not it is, it may need to be declared to the building society.

If the parents don't have the necessary cash to lend, but do have the equity in their family home (that is, it is worth significantly more than any loans outstanding on it) then they could raise the cash by taking out a second mortgage on their own home, and then give or lend it to James.

To persuade the building society to increase its loan to value ratio, the simple answer is for the parents to guarantee the mortgage. This will only be acceptable to the building society if one or both of the parents is still earning and has an acceptable credit history. There are obvious risks to the parents in this if James does not or cannot make the mortgage payments, for example if he is ill or loses his job. It does limit the parents' ability to borrow for themselves too.

An alternative recently offered by Lloyds TSB which addresses these concerns is their 'Lend a Hand' mortgage scheme, under which the borrower (James) provides 5% of the purchase price, and the parents put at least 20% of the purchase price into a deposit account with Lloyds, as security for the loan. This means that the parents retain their cash, and James gets a mortgage at a significantly lower interest rate than it would be at 95% loan-to-value, if he could get one at all.

This all gets more complicated if James is planning to buy with a partner, because the parents are likely to consider more carefully the risks to their cash if the relationship breaks down and James and his partner want to go their separate ways. If James and his partner marry or enter into a civil partnership, the allocation of the value of the property and whether it is sold or not will be in the discretion of the courts. If James and his partner buy in joint names, but do not marry or enter into a civil partnership, then the 'joint tenancy/tenancy-in-common' rules come into play and the allocation of the value of the property is likely to be uncertain and therefore may lead to a dispute on break-up. Issues such as who made the mortgage payments may become relevant. This can get emotional, particularly where there is an imbalance in earnings or wealth. We give some examples on page 104.

A partial answer may be to borrow the purchase costs – legal fees and stamp duty – from a new scheme promoted by James Caan of Dragon's Den[18], but don't forget that any loan has to be repaid.

Best advice (which in fairness the authors did not themselves take) is that legal advice should be taken and the parents' contribution documented as a loan to James, and for James and his partner to sign a written 'co-ownership agreement' or 'co-habitation agreement' which records the couple's original contributions to the purchase cost, and sets out what would happen to the property if the couple separated. www.firstrungnow.com has a free sample of such an agreement.

## What do I want?

Having worked out how much money you can afford to spend on a property, you will have to make a decision as regards the type of property you want to buy. Of course, you may already have a pretty clear idea what you want, but you may need to refine that depending on the properties available within your price range and within the area (or areas) within which you want to live. Then too, deciding the type of property you would like to buy is a very personal matter; what appeals to you may not appeal to another person, and vice versa. Nevertheless, there are a number of questions you can ask yourself to help you identify the property you want.

*Location*

Clearly, you will want to buy your property in an area that suits you. Issues that may be relevant to you when deciding where you should buy include:

- whether the property is near transport links (or is it too near – and hence too noisy)?

---

[18] www.look4aproperty.com.

- is it accessible to current and future workplaces (for both of you)?
- will it mean you will have a long commute?
- is it within reach of shops or other needs, such as family (of course you may not want this!), sports clubs, churches or other places of worship, doctors and dentists, pubs and restaurants, cinemas and clubs or green spaces?

*Type of property*

Are you looking for a property that is:

- a flat or a house?
- new or old?
- purpose built or a conversion?
- ex-council?
- above a shop?
- ground floor (higher risk of burglary) or upper floors (is there a lift)?
- in a quiet neighbourhood?
- in an area where prices are rising or may fall? (For example, if public transport is set to improve in the area, this may lead to an increase in local house prices. On the other hand, closure of a large local business may lead to falling demand for housing and therefore falling house prices in the future.)

Other factors that you may want to take into account could include:

- does the property have a garden?
- does it include a garage or another form of off-road parking (important if you have a 'special' car or motorbike)?
- is it in a residents' parking zone or congestion charge zone (or likely to be)?
- is the property suitable for any pets you may have (or want to get)?
- is it suitable for your 'activities' (for example, if you play a musical instrument, you may want to avoid flats with poor sound insulation, if only to avoid endless disputes with neighbours)?
- speaking of neighbours, are they likely to be a source of annoyance to you? This can be difficult to ascertain, and generally involves you asking questions of the existing owners and their agents (but being somewhat wary of the replies you receive unless they can be independently verified). Some potential purchasers visit the property's location at different times of day and on different days of the week so as to try to get an overall picture of local noise levels (noisy neighbours may not be obvious if you are

visiting a property mid-morning on a weekday; however, if they are given to holding noisy parties at weekends, this may become obvious if you walk past the property on a Saturday evening).

*Do you need (or want):*

- one bedroom or more?
- a property that you can 'do up' or one that you can move into immediately?
- more than one bathroom?
- a large or a small kitchen?
- are the rooms generally large enough for you? Many recent flat developments have very small rooms; on the other hand, some older properties with high ceilings can have large heating bills.
- is it suitable for visitors (including aged granny, young children or dogs)?

So, following this analysis, you might, for example, decide that you want a two-bedroomed flat with a separate sitting room, a kitchen big enough for two, no garden, off-street parking and within 10 minutes of food shops, pubs and a railway/underground station.

Finally, think about how long you intend to stay in the property, and what events might make you change your view – for example, becoming one of a couple, a baby, a job change, your income increasing?

Recommendation: distinguish between and write down your 'must haves' and your 'nice to haves'.

## Finding 'The One'

So you have analysed your own financial position, and your own needs and wants. What next?

Assuming you have an approximate idea of the area you want to live in and the price you can afford, there are four main ways to focus your search upon those properties worth going to see:

1. Use the web-based search sites (listed on page 361). Each of these acts as a collective advertising site for properties being sold by a large number of agents. They have useful search facilities so that you can, for example, trawl for two-bedroomed flats within a particular town or post code, and within a particular price bracket. This is a great way of testing whether the

kind of property you want is likely to be available in the area you want at a price you can afford. They do overlap and repeat to a considerable extent, so that the same properties will appear on several sites (although zoopla may mop up some of its rivals, having already bought propertyfinder.com and ThinkProperty.com). As an indicator, rightmove may have 23 million visits a month, findaproperty 3.6 million, primelocation 2.8 million, propertyfinder 2.4 million, globrix 700,000, homes and property 300,000 and homes 24 250,000 visits[19].

As with all internet-based searches you get what you ask for, and you will miss any properties that are marginally outside your area or price bracket, so it is a good idea to search fairly widely and then narrow it down. Bear in mind also that the properties advertised are generally sorted by asking price, whereas your budget is based on the price you achieve after negotiation and, depending on the desirability of a particular property, you may have scope for negotiating down the advertised price (particularly in a falling or stagnant market), so in the scope of your search you should include properties up to maybe 10% above your target price.

The national and London newspapers also have their own websites, as does Sarah Beeny of TV's 'Property Ladder' (www.tepilo.com). Tesco and one of the larger firms of estate agents, Spicer Haart, are trialling a website (isold.com). Google now has a search function linked to GoogleMaps, which is useful if you know where you want to buy, and want to track down property on sale in that area.[20] There is a similar service (including an iPhone app) on www.propertynearme.com.

2. Read the local newspaper in your chosen area (the paid-for one, as well as the free one, if there is one). This will show you the range of properties currently available, and who the active local estate agents are, from their advertisements. In bigger cities, most local agents tend to focus on quite small areas, and to operate within a particular price bracket, so you can assess from the local paper whether if, say, you are looking for a two-bedroomed flat for £150,000 you are wasting your time with an agent who mostly sells family houses for over £500,000 or vice versa. Some but not all

[19] Source - Statbrain.com

[20] Go to GoogleMaps, then choose the 'Properties' link from the 'More' menu.

local papers have online property advertising: many will be happy for you to subscribe to their paper for perhaps three months so that the paper is delivered to you – useful if you are based elsewhere. In addition to the usual estate agents' advertisements, you may find a few properties advertised in the local newspaper in the 'small ads' by individual sellers.

3. Visit local estate agents; look at the properties advertised in their windows – again to make sure that they sell the type and price range of property you are looking for; talk to them, and get your name on their distribution list for details as they receive new instructions. Many agents now, of course, have online advertising on which the details of the properties they are selling are posted. The usability and sophistication of these websites varies, particularly as regards search facilities. Generally the national firms of agents have the most effective websites, although that does not, of course, necessarily mean that they have the right properties for you.

   Judging by our own experience, you will find that even if you are crystal clear about your particular requirements and search criteria (say, a two-bedroomed flat for up to £175,000 within 10 minutes' walk from of station), the agent will send you details of five-bedroomed houses for £1 million in the country, and sometimes forget to send you details of a property fitting your needs which appears on their websites. Grit your teeth, and keep reminding them of your existence and your needs.

   If you come across to them as disinterested, or just fishing, they will lose interest in you within a few weeks. If you come across to them as definite as to what you want, and show that you are ready to move - for example, you have sold your property or have nowhere to sell and have an 'in principle' mortgage agreed (they are very keen on prospective customers who have in principle mortgages because it suggests that the buying process is unlikely be delayed on the part of the buyer by problems in obtaining a mortgage) then you will be at or close to the top of the list of those they call when a suitable property comes to them. From your point of view, you will want 'first go' at properties within your range. With the relatively new procedures for home improvement packs, which require a number of items to be prepared before the property can be marketed, there is often a time lag of a couple of weeks between the agent being instructed, and the agent being able to market formally through websites or written details, so you may be able to get ahead of the rest if you are (as the agents call it) 'hot to trot'. From an agent's point of view, the ideal transaction is one involving minimum effort, so if he or she can link a willing seller and a willing buyer without needing to print and issue details and pay for newspaper or online advertising, they are in estate agent heaven.

You will want to register with several agents – the number depends on how many in the relevant area actively sell the kind of property you want. It costs nothing to register, so go for more rather than fewer. (Individual agents themselves may be less than keen for you to register with other agents, but that's just tough. One thing we should stress here and now is that agents generally do not work for you, the buyer, but rather for the seller. So, in your dealings with them as a buyer, you should have no hesitation in ensuring that you act in your own best interests.)

If you are after a property with particular characteristics – a river or sea view, or for letting potential, or high value or in central London – consider registering with specialist as well as local and national agents.

For some particularly desirable and narrow categories of properties, or where the buyer is abroad or being sponsored by an employer, it is possible, although not common, to have an agent acting on your behalf, which in the case of an individual would normally be a property finder, and in the case of an employer-backed move would be a relocation agent.[21] These will charge you, or your employer, a fee.

4. Once you are focussed on a particular area, drive, cycle or walk around it, to get the feel of it and to identify any properties with 'for sale' or 'to let' or 'sold' boards on the outside. This again will help you to identify which agents are local specialists. You will also start to see the advantages and disadvantages of particular roads and properties within that area – for example, where traffic clogs the road, where parking is impossible, where

---

[21] Such agents are not fulfilling the normal role of estate agent as it is usually understood: that is, they will be trying to find you a property (or a range of properties) within the parameters you specify, rather than trying to sell properties placed on the market by a variety of sellers. Unlike 'normal' estate agents, they will (or at least should) be 'on your side'.

there is noise from a railway or pub or takeaway food shop, where children congregate after school (which can be surprisingly annoying, but informative about the local school).

Using this research, you can refine your list of needs and wants, judge whether you are being realistic about achieving your goal at a price you can afford and, if not, whether you wait and save for a higher value property, or adjust your criteria.

Once you are down to a relatively short list of properties, you can also use Google Earth and Streetview to track down and visualise properties and the local neighbourhood, to help you decide whether to bother viewing them.

Whether on paper or on line, property details should include the address of the property, photos, a verbal description and floor plans. Agents are only human, and the quality and level of property details vary. Although 'porkies' are rare (and illegal under the Property Misdescriptions Act 1991) the photos and description will inevitably show you the most attractive features, not the bad ones, and the sizes shown on the floor plans may be on the optimistic side.

*Viewing*

However you approach your search, electronically or on foot, you will want to view any property you are interested in from the inside. Photographs and floor plans and imaginative descriptions are all very well, but they are not the same as seeing the real thing. There is also nothing better for helping you decide what you do and don't like. So, it is worth seeing a number of properties, including a few which don't quite match your list of criteria – for example, a three-bedroomed flat or one slightly outside your chosen area or price bracket – as part of the scouting process.

You can arrange viewings via the estate agents selling the property, and usually, although not always, someone from the agents will show you around, rather than the owner him/herself. There is an odd vibe to having the owner show you around – you may be distracted by considering whether you like the person rather than the property, and you will find it difficult to avoid making complimentary but probably insincere remarks about the features or decorative style the seller points out. It is better to be non-committal, with either the seller or the agent, and to concentrate on taking mental snapshots of the key features - the location, aspect, size, parking, kitchen and bathroom facilities and garden if there is one. Try to look through the seller's taste in decoration and furniture to the skeleton of the property underneath. The size and shape of rooms, the positions of windows and radiators and the extent of storage space will all be of more practical use to you. Keep notes – even if only a few scribbles on the agent's written details – so you can remember, after viewing other similar properties, which is which. Remember that the furniture and clutter will usually go with the seller and that you will almost certainly redecorate as your way of making this place your own.

Unless you take an instant dislike to a property, it is better to let the agent know your response a day or two later. Be clear with them whether this is a 'possible', a 'definitely not' or a 'don't know'. Unless the property is unique or the market is exceptionally hot, you should restrain yourself from being too enthusiastic – don't forget it is the agent's job to negotiate the best possible price for the seller, and you weaken your position by appearing to be too keen. We have often found that our initial opinion of a property's suitability changes as we see other properties and discuss and compare them afterwards, and both good and bad points become clearer, so your initial reaction can be misleading.

There is no rule as to how many or how few properties you need to see in order to make a decision; we have bought at different times, after seeing only a couple of properties, or after seeing dozens over 18 months or more. Obviously, the differences between alternatives that are relatively standard (such as two-bedroomed flats in purpose built blocks in the suburbs) are likely to be less significant than those between more 'one-off' properties such as rural five-bedroomed houses.

When considering the asking price for a particular property, it can be very useful to use price comparisons, which are now available to you through 'nosy neighbour' websites (listed at page 362). They will tell you the date and the price at which nearby property has actually been sold and, if the property you are looking at has changed hands recently, the price paid then. These sites get their information from the Land Registry, so the prices they show are the actual prices paid, not the asking prices. The dates they show are the dates when the transfer was registered, which is normally two or three months after the price was actually agreed. You can also get suggestions from these sites as to how the market has performed in that area recently, so you can see whether prices generally are rising or falling, and how fast. Bear in mind that this information may be deceptively convincing. In quiet times it is based on very little sales activity, but it can still be quite good negotiating material. It is important that if you are going to use any of this information in negotiations with the selling agent, you check it carefully and at least superficially look at the other houses or flats that you are going to use as comparisons. For example, even in a terrace of houses, some may have advantages such as a garage or a loft conversion, which you should take into account in comparing prices with the property you are considering. Some of these websites also give useful information about nearby facilities such as pubs, restaurants, schools and transport.

When looking at property details, either online or on paper, look carefully at floorplans to help you envisage where you will put furniture, particularly large items like beds, wardrobes and sofas – then check whether windows, radiators, or electrical or aerial or internet points get in the way. On the floorplans, look carefully at the dimensions and take these with a pinch of salt – check on site yourself. (Also consider size – houses, and particularly flats, are now often compared by floor area as much as by number of bedrooms.

*Dealing with estate agents*

As you embark on your first property purchase, you will probably read or hear horror stories about fraudulent or unscrupulous estate agents ripping off innocent and unsuspecting buyers like yourself. When you meet a real estate agent, you may be pleasantly surprised to find that he or she does not have horns and a forked tail.

The image provided by the media, as with so many, is based on a small number of extreme cases. There have been, and no doubt still are, some rogue estate agents. However, both the agents through their professional bodies and the Government want consumers to be protected by setting best practice standards and having effective regulation.

Although no definitive statistics exist, it is thought there are about 14,500 estate agent offices in the UK, of which perhaps 4,500 belong to the NAEA and a similar number belong to the corporate networks.

Many agency offices selling residential property are now part of large chains - either national firms of agents such as Savills, Knight Frank, Chesterton Humberts, Countrywide (which operates under many names including

Bairstow Eves and John D Wood, and has recently bought Hamptons International), Reeds Rains or YourMove and so on, most of which are still owned by the senior partners of the firm, or a network owned by a bank or insurance company such as Halifax Estate Agency (owned until recently by Lloyds/HBOS) and Connells (owned by Skipton Building Society). In most areas, there are also smaller local firms that have been established for many years and pride themselves on knowing their local area and being part of the local community in a way that employees of the larger national agencies or networks can never be.

Property search websites do, in one sense, create a network because they collect together information from a number of agents, but that does not mean that the agents themselves are connected in management or financial terms. Those websites are simply a way of joint marketing in the same way as advertising through newspapers. Some are owned jointly by firms of agents but operate as independent businesses.

As with any business, the employees within the office you contact will vary in age and level of experience, and the more basic task such as arranging viewings will often fall to the most junior member of staff. In the bigger agencies, the more senior staff tend to focus on management and to be concentrated in the bigger city offices. In the local agents the owner of the agency often sits within the branch. It is worth pushing to meet more senior staff, particularly at the beginning of your search, so you get an experienced and realistic view as to what your budget price will get you in that area, what type of housing stock is available there, and what parts of their 'patch' are on the way up, or down.

The more senior people tend to belong to their own professional organisation, The Royal Institution of Chartered Surveyors. Those who do (it now involves a fairly rigorous vocational training and examination process) are entitled to use the letters MRICS or FRICS after their names.

Many smaller agencies, and the branches of the insurance company-owned chains, tend to belong to the National Association of Estate Agents instead of the RICS – this is more of a trade body, with a shared set of best practice standards and a disputes resolution service, rather than a formal educational qualification. Members are entitled to use the letters MNAEA or FNAEA after their names.

*Regulation of estate agents*

In terms of formal legal regulation of estate agents, there are three key Acts of Parliament.

**The Estate Agents Act 1979** – which sets out rules for agents about holding clients' monies and makes breach of those rules a criminal offence. This tends to protect sellers and landlords, rather than buyers. Agents usually hold money in the form of preliminary deposits on sales, or by collecting deposits or rents on lettings. The Act provides for professional standards on billing clients and explaining terms of business, services to purchasers and disclosing personal interests in transactions, and enables the banning of individual 'rogues' from acting as estate agents.

**The Property Misdescriptions Act 1991** – which makes it a criminal offence for agents to publish misleading information, for both sales and lettings.

**The Consumer, Estate Agents and Redress Act 2007** – which does not directly licence or regulate estate agents but does require them to sign up to one of two redress schemes, either that supervised by The Property Ombudsman Service (www.tpos.co.uk) (formerly the Ombudsman for Estate Agents) or the Surveyors' Ombudsman Service (www.surveyors-ombudsman.org.uk). Failure to sign up to one of these by 1 October 2008 means that the firm is practising illegally, and subject to a fixed penalty of £1,000. Before that date, Ombudsman schemes existed, but on a voluntary basis. As this requirement is only fairly recent, the impact is not clearly visible, but it should prevent the rogue agent from setting up and practising in your local high street or on the internet. There are three important limitations: it does not apply to letting agents (who are reportedly more likely to be rogues than selling agents), to those selling property outside the UK, or to those selling commercial property. The Ombudsman services are available to those complaining about letting agents but only on a voluntary rather than compulsory basis.

2007 research by *Which* suggested that (at least in the opinion of the consumers they questioned) 70% of estate agents 'frequently' gave misleading information, 14% of agents described the property incorrectly and 9% of those questioned thought the agent acted unethically.

Both the RICS and the NAEA have said, during the passing of the 2007 Act and since, that there should be a full regulatory system so that all selling and letting estate agents would be registered and therefore subject to a code of best practice. However, the redress scheme deals only with penalising those who have failed to behave, after the event.

The RICS and NAEA have jointly produced a new code of standards for all residential selling agents, published in July 2009 and known as the 'Blue Book'. This does not yet apply to letting agents.

There may be further change: three reports published in June 2008, August 2008 and January 2009 (the first a review of the residential property market by Sir Brian Carsberg, commissioned by the RICS, NAEA and ARLA, the second 'Encouraging Responsible Letting' by The Law Commission, and the third by Professor Colin Jones 'Regulation and Redress in the UK Housing Market', commissioned by the Government), all call for greater regulation than the 2007 Act provided, particularly for letting agents. The Office of Fair Trading published a further study into Home Buying and Selling in February 2010 looking particularly at competitiveness of estate agents but it is unlikely that any further legislation will follow, except for regulation of letting agents. The OFT considered, but did not recommend, introducing a licensing system for selling agents.

This is all great in theory, but rather distant from day-to-day habits.

If, as a buyer (or indeed as a tenant), you have a complaint about the behaviour of an estate agent, all you can do is check whether the individual, or other members of the firm of agents you are dealing with, are members of the RICS or NAEA, and whether the firm has signed up to one of the redress schemes, and if the firm does not deal with your complaint, use that to complain to the relevant Ombudsman so that the situation is properly investigated.

If money held by the agent has gone missing or there has been a material misdescription, or if the agent is not a member of one of the redress schemes, you should approach the local authority trading standards officer for advice. They have the power to enforce the rules. They are also likely to know whether there have been other complaints about the same agency, and the outcome of those complaints.

## Making an offer

With the benefit of your analysis, your financial position and your availability of funds, your research on the availability of properties and previous local transactions, you are fully armed to make your offer on your chosen property.

If markets are hot and the property you want is in demand, you may need to offer the asking price, occasionally more. If markets are less hot or falling, you may succeed with a low offer. During 2008 it was generally thought to be the case that the only people selling were those who had to sell - perhaps for one of the 'D reasons' we cover in Chapter 6 – so that a 'cheeky' offer of, say, 20% below the asking price was worth making: occasionally it succeeded. Those times are unusual, but it is always worth establishing how long the property has been on the market, why it is on the market, and whether the seller has already found somewhere else to move to before finalising your offer, and also whether there have been any other previous offers which have not proceeded. Conversely, the firmer your own position, the better - it is good to be a cash buyer such as a first time buyer, or at least to know that your existing property is either sold or on the market, and that you have your mortgage finance arranged. On the other hand, if you are desperate to buy a home (for example, a baby is on the way or school term dates are looming) and the market is such that sellers have the upper hand, you may find that your scope for aggressive negotiation as a buyer is limited.

Even during 2008, for some properties the asking price or more was achieved when the property was particularly desirable; as the market has turned and started to recover in mid-2009 the scope for bidding under the asking price has narrowed. This is in part because asking prices, according to most market information available, dropped 10-30% from their 2007 levels.

As with any negotiation, you should be clear in your own mind as to your preferred price – carefully calculated allowing for all your budgeted costs – and the maximum you cannot go beyond.

The agent is duty-bound to put any offer you make to the seller: you can often gauge from the agent's reaction to your proposal whether the agent will recommend it to the seller, but you can never be sure. All offers should be made 'subject to contract' if made in writing – if those three magic words are used then the offer can be accepted by the seller without creating a legal contract to sell and buy. If not, you could be stuck with buying the property at that price whether or not the legal or mortgaging process throws up any problems.

Usually the buyer pays a 'preliminary deposit' of £500 or £1,000 to the agent when the offer is accepted, as a sign of commitment. This should be refunded if the purchase does not proceed.

*Sealed bids*

If the market is hot or an individual property is particularly desirable so there is more than one bidder, agents may suggest the seller makes its decision between them, and achieves the sale at the best price, by prompting 'sealed bids'. If so, the agent will set a deadline to bid by, you make your bid (still subject to contract) in a sealed envelope and the agent or seller (often both together) open the bids at the appointed time. Usually, the seller does not commit to sell to the highest bidder, so spelling out that you are ready to move is worthwhile. 'Referential' bids (say, £500 more than the next highest bid) are often prohibited.

*Home Information Packs*

The seller and the agent, are required to complete and make available to potential buyers a home information pack (HIP) which is intended to provide various information necessary for the buyer to make a decision whether to buy the property.[22] The key elements are legal information about the ownership of the property, responses to questionnaires giving practical information, and an Energy Performance Certificate, or EPC, describing how energy efficient the property is and suggestions for improvement.

*Fixtures and fittings*

It is important in finalising the detail of your offer to be clear what is included in the sale and what is not. This will be helped by the fixtures and fittings list in the home information pack, which will be the seller's check list of what is included and what is not. Conventionally, when buying an existing property, the seller can take with him or her everything that can be removed without

---

[22] The requirement on sellers to provide a HIP was suspended (but not formally abolished) with effect from 21 May 2010. It will be abolished once legislation is passed, later in 2010. The requirement to provide an EPC continues.

affecting the fabric of the property unless it is specifically agreed that a particular item will be left behind. This will include carpets and curtains, furniture and detachable equipment such as washing machines, dryers, fridges and dishwashers, but not fixed equipment such as boilers, baths and showers, basins and sinks, curtain rails, floor and wall tiles, fire places, door handles and so on. There can be plenty of scope for argument about what falls on one side of the line or the other – the most notorious case involved extremely heavy statues which were removed from a stately home, which the court found should not have happened. Most differences of opinion turn out to be relatively minor and do not end up in the courts, but are annoying and upsetting for those affected.

The clarity of the law is not helped by the fact that 'fixtures' means different things to different people in different circumstances. Strictly, on buying and selling a property, it means those things that have become part of the property, such as the boiler, and therefore should not be removed on sale. However, agents often refer to 'fixtures and fittings' as the items which will go with the owner. It is desirable to agree with the seller which items are left. Some may be included in the sale price, others may be extra. You can allocate part of the overall price to the items. This is particularly useful when carpets or kitchen white goods are fitted and awkward to replace. It can save money to allocate part of the price to 'fixtures and fittings' where the overall price is a little above the stamp duty thresholds of £150,000, £250,000 or £500,000 or (from 2011) £1 million, so as to bring down the price for the house to or just below that level, paying for the contents separately. The temptation to overdo this should be resisted because HMRC are well aware that this habit can be abused, and may investigate if they are suspicious.

Expectations about what is taken and what is left vary across the world and in particular in the US the seller normally would take everything with them, down to the door handles and light bulbs, as one of us found once when buying from an American, leading to a nasty surprise on moving day – we had not planned to spend the day replacing bulbs and handles!

If the property is listed, particularly Grade I, it may be a criminal offence to remove items such as fireplaces, which form part of the fabric of the building.

The extent of what is included is likely to be different on buying a new property; most, in particular, now include the kitchen white goods, and it is common for carpets and curtains to be included as an incentive, even if it is not the show home.

## Buying from new

Buying a new property from a developer presents some rather different opportunities and challenges.

Usually, you will not be able to see the particular property you want, except maybe in shell form, and you will be offered plans and an artist's impression of the finished product, as well as a tour of the show flat or house.

You will need to take the plans and drawings with a pinch of salt – a show flat or house will usually be the best laid out, and there are some subtle developer's tricks to be aware of – slightly undersized furniture, to make the room look bigger, especially double beds; extras which are in the show property but not in the written specification; the orientation of the show property may not match the one you are offered so that the light will fall differently; noise levels from roads, neighbours or lifts will not be obvious.

However, buying a new property from a developer can have advantages: obviously everything is new and you do not need to replace decorations or kitchens or bathrooms or worry about repairs such as a new roof or boiler; if you time things right, you may be able to design adaptations to suit your lifestyle – making a bathroom en suite, or combining a kitchen or breakfast room, or upgrading kitchen equipment or showers, although you will pay for this. The developer will take on responsibility for snagging items for a limited period after completion, which a seller of older property will not. The structure of the property will be guaranteed by a warranty from either the NHBC or another insurance-backed provider to cover major building defects for 10 years.

There are, of course, some downsides:

There will inevitably be some snagging items; developers vary in their enthusiasm to deal with these quickly and properly, but most buyers find these particularly irritating. Unless these are very serious, the NHBC or other warranty will not cover these snagging items and you will have to complain directly with the developer.

Some parts of the development may not be finished when you move in, particularly landscaping and gardens, and if it is a big or phased scheme then construction work may continue elsewhere for some time after you have moved in.

Timing is unpredictable. A good developer will keep you informed as to expected completion timing but however good the developer is, weather or delivery problems can disrupt finishing off. This is particularly difficult to cope with if you are not a first time buyer and you are trying to co-ordinate this purchase with a simultaneous sale – you may need to have a very understanding buyer.

Conversely, when the property is ready and you get the completion notice, you will have only five or 10 days to get your act together to complete, both on the money side (and often your mortgage lender is not used to moving that fast) and on the practical moving side (you tend to live in half-packed limbo for several weeks).

Minor but irritating: the practical things (curtain rails, clothes hooks, extra cupboards) are down to you, rather than already being there as they usually would be with a second-hand property. Very recently the NHBC and other warranty providers have produced and imposed a Consumer Code of Conduct for 'Home Builders' (effective from 1 April 2010) which is intended to make new build contracts fairer and encourage builders to manage after-sales complaints better. This will be useful ammunition for buyers.

## Buying at auction

Buying at auction is an interesting alternative to the conventional estate agency route, and can be a quick way to a bargain, or a disaster.

A number of firms of agents hold auctions of residential properties, usually five or six times a year. Examples are Jones Lang LaSalle, Allsop, Clive Emson and Strettons. Some of them also hold auctions of commercial or investment properties, but usually separately. A couple of online auction platforms have recently been created, for example, www.bidprop.co.uk or www.mustbesold.com, and Zoopla ran its first online auction in February 2010.

Some websites track all the property auctions as well as enthusing about the bargains available at them (beware the hard sell…) but many enable you to identify which are relevant for you. See the list on page 362.

Properties are placed in auctions by sellers either because they have not sold through normal channels – perhaps they are in very poor condition or are unusual buildings such as redundant chapels, lock-up garages or small development sites – or because the sale is caused by a dispute of some kind, for example if it has been repossessed by a mortgage company, or if the owner is bankrupt, or if there is a family dispute. Alternatively, it may be placed at auction because the seller is a charity or trustee or a local authority that needs to demonstrate they have achieved full market price for the sale.

The auction houses are, at the time of writing, complaining about the lack of stock – the number of repossessions sold at auction dropped from 7,413 in 2008/9 to 3,196 in 2009/10. A factor is that many mortgage lenders have introduced restrictions on lending on repossessed property.

Forthcoming dates for auctions can be obtained from the websites for the various firms, and they are also advertised in property trade magazines such as Property Week and Estates Gazette. Auction catalogues, both paper and online, are usually produced four to six weeks before the auction date. In the run-up to the auction day, buyers must do all the necessary preparation, including organising surveys and finance and all legal work including searches etc.

The auction catalogue will, in its small print, contain legal details of each property and general and specific conditions of sale.

In most cases, the catalogue contains a guide price to assist buyers (this is not the same as a reserve price, which is the price below which the seller has decided not to sell).

At the auction, the successful bid – signified by the fall of the hammer – means that, in effect, contracts are exchanged and the deposit (usually 10%) is payable to the auction firm on that day before the end of the auction. This is usually required to be in the form of a banker's draft or building society cheque, rather than a personal cheque. Completion is normally four weeks later.

Properties are always sold 'as is', which includes their legal status – for example, the existence and terms of any tenancy – as well as their physical condition. Hence it is vitally important for would-be buyers under an auction process to ensure that all their surveys and legal investigations are carried out beforehand.

You need to know before bidding that you have your funds available to complete: if you are unable to complete you will lose your deposit. So, if you will need a mortgage it should be pre-arranged.

Prices at auctions tend to appear to be less than on conventional sales of comparable property sold by conventional means, but that is because the property usually has some kind of problem that the buyer is taking on.

So, you can catch a bargain, but you can snag a disaster.

There is a sub-culture of investors and developers who habitually attend, and buy and often sell, at auctions and they can be quite entertaining in themselves, as can the auctioneers. If you are thinking of finding a property through an auction we strongly recommend you attend one or two by way of rehearsal, before you think of identifying a property to buy, or bidding.

As with any auction, the thrill of the moment can be dangerous. We recommend you set yourself a maximum price before you go, and take a calm and assertive friend to hold you down as the bidding goes above that level.

Occasionally, particularly if it is a special property or in a rural area, there will be a local auction of a single property. The same ground rules apply.

## Valuations and surveys

Especially when buying a property for the first time, or to 'do up', you will be concerned about the physical condition of the property and the cost of any necessary repairs.

From a purely financial point of view, you and your mortgage provider will both be interested in obtaining a professional opinion as to what the property is 'worth' and whether it is structurally sound.

Before you get to 'offer' stage, you can save yourself time, money and heartache if you can spot significant problems. Even new properties have the potential for expensive maintenance or worse. Not on a first visit but once you have shortlisted a property, look at it critically.

Ten top things to look out for are:

1 Cracks. Some cracks are superficial and easily hidden by painting – a new house will always 'shrink' so that gaps develop over the first few months along skirting boards and door frames - but more serious cracks may

indicate subsidence which is a whole different ball game. Look out for separation between a home and an extension, and for cracks following a line of bricks on the outside. If in doubt get a surveyor's advice.

2 Damp (rising). Damp is common and costly to fix. Look down, for darker patches in corners, for recent painting, and warped skirting boards.

3 Damp (creeping). Check for a damp-proof course (a thin dark horizontal layer just above ground level, which should be visible on the outside of the external walls). Check whether earth has accumulated above the damp-proof layer, for example if there are flower beds or shrubs alongside the walls.

4 Damp (gutters). Check that both gutters and downpipes work (make sure you see the property when it is raining) and look for signs of staining on the walls, under the gutters or behind the downpipes. Guttering is often blocked by leaves or tennis balls and if left overflow can damage roof timbers and soak though walls.

5 Damp (drains). Driveway or garden improvements are often one of the selling points for a house. But both DIYers and builders tend to forget to allow for drainage so that they build over drainage points, or don't allow for rainwater to drain away from the house. Driveways, paths and patios can throw water towards the house rather than away from it.

6 Roof (outside). One of the most common survey comments is the need for a new roof – and this is expensive. Victorian and Edwardian houses are likely to need re-roofing if they have not been re-roofed to date; check the roofline to see if it is horizontal (if not, the supporting timbers may need renewing) and the tiles, and the flashings around the edges and any chimneys, for broken tiles and curled flashings which may have allowed rain in. A new roof is not always good news – modern tiles are much heavier than slate, so the supporting timbers may have needed reinforcement. Compare other houses nearby.

7 Roof (inside). If you are serious about a house, get your head into the loft to see whether the roof timbers look sound, and the depth (and age) of insulation. Also, if there are pipes or tanks in the loft above the insulation they are at risk of freezing and bursting, especially if you improve the

insulation (to save on heating!). Also, look at where the external walls meet the roof - if the gap is filled in with softwood (common in new houses) this will be subject to weathering, and access for replacement will be difficult.

8 Windows. Old wood framed windows are vulnerable to rot. Try pushing a pencil into the underside of the windowsill. Sash windows are often 'destringed'. Check whether all the windows open (and stay open). Older windows are usually a route for significant heat loss. Newer UPVC window frames may be better for heat loss but in due course, because the plastic becomes brittle with exposure to sun, will require replacement - both the window and the frame - which is a major task.

9 Plumbing. Look for leaks – at the back of the dishwasher or washing machine, under the bath, and discolouration (or recent re-painting) of ceilings, even distorted ceiling panels. Try all the toilets to make sure they work, and ask about the central heating.

10 Electrics. Flick all the switches to make sure everything works - lighting, heaters, kitchen appliances, electric showers.

Think planned maintenance. It is tough to do this when you are stretching your finances to the limit to buy, but think in terms of spending 1% of the value of the property each year in maintenance – so, on a £250,000 property, £2,500 per year. As a rule of thumb, you can expect to replace the roof every 20 years, the plumbing every 15, the electrics every 12 and the boiler every 10. If these are imminent, reconsider the price you are willing to pay for the property.

Once you get past choosing the property and agreeing the price, you and your mortgage provider will want a valuation and/or survey.

There are three levels of report: a valuation report, which simply assesses the value of the property for mortgage purposes and gives a little context around that; a full structural survey which will give a detailed report on the condition and method of construction of the property and identify any repairs or more serious defects; and a HomeBuyer Report.

A mortgage valuation will be carried out by either an employee of the mortgage lender or a qualified surveyor from a firm on their panel. You will pay for this valuation, usually at the same time as you apply for the mortgage and pay the mortgage provider his fee, according to a scale imposed by the mortgage provider. The price will vary according to the amount you intend to borrow. The valuer will carry out only a limited inspection of the property from the outside and, after some research with local estate agents as to the value of other properties and the state of the market in that area, will give a value figure to the mortgage company, which the mortgage company will use to assess how much it should properly lend by applying its loan to value ratio to this figure. You may be able to get a copy of the mortgage valuation, although you will have to ask for it and may have to pay a little more. The mortgage valuer will tend to take a conservative view of value at the best of times (after all, his or her job is to protect the interests of the bank or building society, not the borrower), but especially during a falling or 'stuck' market such as that in late 2008 and early 2009, because the available valuation information will be out of date and prices have dropped and may drop further.

The mortgage valuer is also likely to be cautious because in fairly similar market circumstances in the early 1990s, a number were (successfully) sued for negligence by mortgage lenders, and they will not want to take that risk again.

If the mortgage provider's valuation means that the amount you wanted to borrow to buy the property is reduced, you will have a shortfall in funds, which may lead you to seek a reduction in the price you will pay for the property if you can negotiate that with the seller, and if not, you may have to withdraw.

The mortgage valuation will not give you any assurance as to the condition of the property or whether there are significant defects to be remedied or repairs to be carried out.

At the opposite extreme, a structural survey (usually commissioned by the buyer rather than the mortgage provider), will provide a much more detailed inspection of the property and produce a much more detailed written report – may be up to 20 or 30 pages. Such a structural survey is strongly recommended for older properties and those obviously in need of repair, or if you intend to carry out significant renovation or extensions, or if you have any suspicion of serious structural problems, such as subsidence, damp, wet or dry rot or woodworm or other infestation. The structural survey does not replace the mortgage valuation because the structural surveyor will not normally express a view as to the market value of the property. Lists of structural surveyors are available from the RICS or through their website.

Again, if the outcome of the structural survey is that you will have to spend significant amounts of money, for example, on a new damp proof course, or remedying damp, or underpinning to cure subsidence, or replacing the roof, you should obtain costings from building contractors and consider whether some or all of this cost should be deducted from the sale price so that it is, in effect, paid by the seller.

If there are significant structural problems, it is likely the mortgage lender will either reduce the amount of the loan or impose a retention from the amount of the loan until the remedial works are done.

Occasionally the structural surveyor will recommend further investigations – such as more detailed testing for damp or dry rot, or investigation for the structural integrity of, for example, previous extensions to the building – if he is unsure from his own examination of the building. Such a recommendation should ring loud alarm bells for you. If you decide to proceed despite that warning the further investigations should be followed through carefully.

The halfway house, if you will pardon the pun, between the mortgage valuation, which is too superficial, and a thorough structural survey, which is too detailed unless there is a good reason for it, is the HomeBuyer's Report (previously called the Home Buyer Survey and Valuation). You can usually ask the mortgage company's surveyor to carry this out on your behalf and it is a useful and usually reassuring check that there are no obvious defects in the property that will require repair or remedial work, as well as an opinion on value. This will give the property a colour-coded condition rating on various elements of the building – green for good reports, amber if further investigation is recommended, or red if the property needs urgent attention. A HomeBuyer's Report is, for most people, sufficient if the property they are buying is of standard construction and built since 1919 – brick or stone, with a tile or slate roof, and in a terrace or semi-detached, or a flat in a block. The HomeBuyer's Report is an 8 to 20 page report as opposed to the 20 to 50 page detailed report from a structural survey.

For comparison purposes, using Yorkshire prices as an example, a valuation for a £300,000 house would typically cost £200, a HomeBuyer's Report would typically cost £375 and a full building survey £725.

The HomeBuyer's Report or structural survey will usually also give a value for building insurance purposes, this is a valuation of the amount which you need to insure the building in the event of fire or other damage, which is derived from the projected cost of rebuilding, not from what the house is worth on the open market. It is a good idea to ask for this when you commission the Report or survey, rather than incur another fee later.

Bear in mind that if you are buying a flat within a larger building, the risks of serious problems or future expenditure are likely to relate to the whole building, not just the individual flat you are buying – whether subsidence, or the need to replace the roof, or boilers or lifts - and it is wise both to look at these yourself, at least to judge the age of them, and to ask your solicitor or licensed conveyancer to ask about past and/or future repair or replacement expenditure, and to ask the surveyor to consider whether the block is generally in good condition or likely to require significant work. In most blocks of flats, the cost of any repairs of renewal will fall to the tenants. Assessing a risk is not just a question of cost, but also convenience – in one case we know involving a flat in a large block, the process of changing an aging collective oil fired heating system to individual gas fired boilers in each flat involved 12 months of building works throughout the block, and reduced the size of each flat's kitchen significantly, although in the longer term it did reduce the heating bills dramatically.

## The chain

A chain arises when there are a series of inter-connected, interdependent sales and purchases.

A typical example is where you, as a first time buyer, are buying a flat from a couple who are moving to a small house; the sellers of the small house are themselves buying a larger house; and the seller of that larger house is selling to buy a smaller place for retirement.

Usually, the seller and buyer forming each link in the chain will want to exchange each transaction on the same day to ensure that they are neither homeless nor bankrupt, and likewise to complete each transaction on the same day.

Your single simple purchase is connected to, and dependent upon, those three other purchases in which you have no part, and no control. So if there is a problem with any of them, from the survey or title investigation, or mortgage offer, or simply if any of the other parties change their minds or get a better offer before you have exchanged, then your purchase is at risk. Even if nothing so serious happens, it is inevitable that all the transactions will move towards exchange at the speed of the slowest, and that much time and effort will be expended between lawyers in co-ordinating the timing of exchange and completion. Simple obstacles such as the absence of one legal advisor through illness or holiday can impact on all of the linked transactions.

The operation of the chain is further complicated if the person at the far end of it is moving to a new build property, because even if they have exchanged, the completion date will be uncertain until close to the date, and the period for them between completion notice and completion date will be short, usually five or 10 working days, so co-ordinating that with other links in the chain is difficult.

If time slippage occurs because of delays in the chain, other problems can arise, such as a mortgage offer expiring, or local searches being 'out of date', which may need renewal, causing further delay and the risk of unsatisfactory results.

Chains also create logistical problems at key moments; often the seller of a property in the chain will need to use the 10% deposit paid by 'his' buyer as part of the (larger) deposit he has to pay on 'his' purchase; this is usually agreed between solicitors provided that funds are 'tagged' and held by another solicitor.

Logistics for completion arrangements on chains are usually complex because of the need for several sets of individuals to physically move on the same day, and the challenge of moving monies from you to your seller (including mortgage monies), to his/her seller (including more mortgage monies), to his/her seller, including more mortgage monies, etc – all within one banking day.

Experienced legal advisors can, of course, cope with these challenges, provided all those representing the other links in the chain are willing and able to cope too.

So can you break the chain? Apart from avoiding a chain by buying a new build property or finding a seller who is not buying at the same time, it is almost impossible for the first time buyer to do so; it is only sellers who can break the chain by selling without buying simultaneously, perhaps by moving to temporary accommodation such as a hotel or the home of family or friends, or by moving into rented accommodation for a longer period. This, however, can be extremely stressful and something that most people seek to avoid if they possibly can. Those who are buying and selling at the same time do have the possibility of 'bridging', that is, borrowing to buy without selling at the same time. This is high risk, and scary, because you will have two sets of loan payments to make, and no certainty as to when the sale will go through. Banks and building societies are reluctant to lend unless there is simply a timing difference, that is, you exchange contracts on both your purchase and your sale but the completion date for your purchase is before the sale completion date, so you won't have the cash from the sale when you need it for the purchase. Possible, but nerve-wracking!

If you are in a chain that is stuck, bear in mind that the selling agent may (for once) be your ally. He or she will be financially motivated to get the transaction through because otherwise his or her commission disappears; they may be able to talk to the seller or to other agents further up the chain, who will be similarly motivated, and to get more open information than will tend to pass through the lawyers, and to suggest alternative solutions, such as one seller renting, or a series of price adjustments along the chain. They are also generally better at assessing whether 'chain problems' are real, or are a cover for someone further up the chain getting cold feet.

## Choosing and using a legal adviser

In order to ensure that you buy your property in a legally secure way, that your mortgage is properly documented, and that both your purchase and your mortgage are properly documented at the Land Registry, you will need a solicitor or licensed conveyancer to carry out those tasks on your behalf.

The role of the solicitor or conveyancer will be to ensure that you get good title to the property when you buy, that he or she gets replies to certain key questions before you commit yourself (mostly 'there isn't a problem, is there?' questions), and the mortgage and the transfer to your property documented so that when you come to sell again that process will be as straightforward as it can be. The solicitor or conveyancer does not usually negotiate the price, but may negotiate other important conditions on your behalf, such as the timing of completion, and obtaining any consents needed from third parties.

All solicitors are members of the Law Society, which is their professional organisation: they are subject to regulation by the Solicitors Regulation Authority (SRA). There are over 100,000 qualified solicitors in England and Wales, but many of those specialise in areas other than residential house buying. If you wish to use a solicitor, you will therefore need to find one who specialises in residential conveyancing.

Instead of using a solicitor, you can use a licensed conveyancer, who will be a conveyancing specialist. These belong to and are regulated by The Council for Licensed Conveyancers and there are approximately 1,000 of them in England and Wales, although the majority work within solicitors' firms. There are less stringent educational requirements for becoming a licensed conveyancer – for example, it is not necessary to have a degree.[23] A licensed conveyancer tends to do nothing but residential conveyancing and have less experience of other kinds of legal practice.

Both solicitors and licensed conveyancers are required by their professional rules to have professional indemnity insurance to protect their clients against the consequences of negligent mistakes. The minimum cover for both solicitors and independent licensed conveyancers is £2 million – although many have much higher amounts of cover.

It is very rare, although not unheard of, for unqualified people to set up as solicitors or licensed conveyancers, despite the fact it is a criminal offence to do so. If you are concerned, you can double check the websites of the Law Society[24]

---

[23]Strictly speaking, it is possible to become a solicitor without possessing a degree as well, but this is very rare.
[24] www.lawsociety.org.uk

or Council for Licensed Conveyancers[25] in order to confirm that your chosen solicitor or conveyancer is 'legitimate'.[26]

A solicitor or licensed conveyancer cannot properly act for both you and the seller unless both of you agree. We would not recommend this, as you should always have independent advice.

So how do you find the best one for you?

Solicitors tend to arrange themselves either in large firms – the largest international heavyweight law firms have hundreds of partners and thousands of staff, but they will not want to buy your house or flat for you (and given their charge-out rates, you would not want them to either) – or smaller local firms, often in your high street, maybe 'one-man bands'; or specialists, including some conveyancing warehouses heavily dependent on standardised processes and unqualified staff, rather like a call centre.

If you develop a good relationship with a selling estate agent then he or she may be able to recommend a solicitor, particularly if the agent is the principal of a well-established local firm of agents (although he or she is likely to recommend his or her mate from the Rotary Club or the golf club). The Law Society and the Council for Licensed Conveyancers have lists of conveyancers available on their websites. The Daily Telegraph also offers access to solicitors who specialise in conveyancing, and also other areas of law, called the Telegraph Solicitor Network.

The factors you need to consider are:

Price – you should expect a clear written explanation of the full cost of the services to be provided, including VAT and all ancillary costs such as the cost of local searches, SDLT (stamp duty) and land registration fees. Solicitors are required by the professional rules to provide this – quote 'Rule 15' at them if they are reluctant or slow to do so.

At the time of writing, typical pricing is in the range of £350 to £500 for a freehold purchase at, say, £200,000. This is the figure for the solicitor's own

---

[25] www.conveyancer.org.uk

[26] In the professional sense, that is.

costs (and there will be VAT on that amount) but there will be important additional charges that you will have to pay, such as:

| Cost category | Explanation | Approximate likely cost |
|---|---|---|
| Bank Transfer Fee | A fee solicitors charge when a CHAPS transfer is required for one of a number of purposes, for example, to pay off a mortgage, to send monies to the seller's solicitor or to transfer the net proceeds from a sale to your bank account. | £20 per transfer |
| Bankruptcy Search Fee* | If you are funding your purchase by a mortgage, your lender will require the solicitor to check whether you are or have been bankrupt. | £2 per name |
| Chancel Liability Search Fee | A search to establish whether there is a risk of the property falling within a parish where the house owner faces a potential liability to contribute towards the repairs of the chancel/local parish. | £17 |
| Disbursements | 'Disbursements' are amounts that solicitors pay others on your behalf in the course of your transaction. The disbursements that most people incur are indicated in the table by an asterisk. | |
| Water & Drainage Search* | The solicitor will need to make a drainage search to check whether the property you are buying is connected to public water supply and drains. | £45 |
| Environmental Search Fee | An environmental search may be necessary if there are concerns over environmental issues such as subsidence, flooding, industrial contamination or radon. | £40 |
| Land Registry Document Fee* | Authenticated copies of your title from the Land Registry. | £6-12 |

| Cost category | Explanation | Approximate likely cost |
|---|---|---|
| Land Registration Fee* | After your purchase is complete, the solicitor will register you as owner of the property at the Land Registry and any mortgage charge. The Land Registry fee is paid to the Land Registry for the work they do in registering your ownership and/or mortgage charge. | £220 |
| Land Registry Search Fee* | Following exchange of contracts a priority search of the title register is made to check that the state of the register has not changed and to ensure that the buyer has priority for a period of 30 working days over any other application to change the register that is lodged during that time. | £3 |
| Local Authority Search Fee* | A local authority search should reveal whether there is anything adverse recorded against the property with the local council. The council is asked to reply to a long list of questions by the solicitors. Some conveyancers will use a search company to undertake this work and the fees can vary substantially. | £40-500 |
| Mortgage Fees - Sale | If your present house is subject to a mortgage, it will be necessary for the solicitor to pay the lender the money due on the mortgage and cancel the registration of the mortgage against your property. | £50-75 |
| SDLT Completion Fee* | An additional fee for completing the Stamp Duty Land Tax return form, which has to be submitted to HM Revenue & Customs in almost all cases | £25 |

| Cost category | Explanation | | Approximate likely cost |
|---|---|---|---|
| | following completion of the purchase, along with any payment due. | | |
| Search Fees | Online conveyancers may charge this fee as an additional Legal Fee for performing the required searches. Solicitors tend to include this work within the quote for Legal Fees as the searches are almost always required. | | £80-140 |
| Stamp Duty Land Tax | This is a tax payable to the Government calculated on the value of the house to be purchased.<br>Stamp duty rates are:[27] | | |
| | Up to £125,000 =<br>£125,001-250,000 =<br>£250,001 - 500,000 =<br>£500,001 + =<br>(£1 million +)[28] | 0%<br>1%<br>3%<br>4%<br>(5%) | |
| VAT | VAT is payable on the solicitors' fees at the rate applicable at the time of the bill, which is currently 17.5%, but will rise to 20% on 4 January 2011. | | |
| | Prices are as at 30 June 2010. | | |

Expect to pay more for a leasehold purchase, because there will be more documentation to review. Some solicitors will charge extra for the work involved in a mortgage.

---

[27] Following the 2010 Budget first time buyers can claim relief from SDLT on residential transactions up to £250,000 between 25 March 2010 and 25 March 2012. The Coalition Government has said it will review the effectiveness of this before deciding whether to retain or extend it.

[28] Proposed in 2010 budget but not due to be introduced until 2011.

*Quality of service*

Establish, before committing yourself, exactly who will be doing the work and (assuming it is delegated by the senior solicitor to a junior) what level of supervision he or she will get, and what level of attention you will get. In particular, many solicitors tend to tell you what is going on only when pushed, and to be available only during their standard office hours of 9-5.30, Monday to Friday, when you may be working yourself. Conveyancing specialists and warehouses now tend to have online updating and alerting systems so that you can monitor progress online at a time convenient for you. However, these are only as efficient as the people operating them, and telephone contact can be more frustrating.

When assessing firms, ask them how they will communicate with you, and how long they expect the whole process to take, up to exchange.

With smaller and local firms, you would expect to meet the solicitor dealing with the purchase to go through the results of his or her review of the title and enquiries and searches, and then sign the contract to provide the deposit monies. For conveyancing warehouses, the service may be less personal. In either case, you should receive a written report a few days before exchange telling you the outcome of those investigations, and summarising the terms of the purchase contract.

*Location*

It is useful, if practical, to use a solicitor or licensed conveyancer who is local to the property. There are still local and regional peculiarities to which properties are subject – examples include subsidence in former coalmining or brine extraction areas, radon contamination where certain geological conditions exist, contaminated land where former industrial sites have been developed, proposals for new development that are at early stages so not obvious. A local solicitor or licensed conveyancer should be aware of these, one from another town or city may not be.

*Panels*

Looking ahead, the loan and mortgage arrangements will require legal input on behalf of the lender. The traditional building society and bank lenders will usually be happy to allow your solicitor or licensed conveyancer to carry out the necessary documentation on their behalf, provided the solicitor or licensed conveyancer's firm is on their panel list. Large commercial firms tend not to be on those panels, because they do not generally do this kind of work, and very small firms (one- or two-man bands) tend not to be because the building societies and banks consider they are high risk. So, assuming you know your mortgage provider by the time you choose your solicitor or licensed conveyancer, check whether the solicitor or licensed conveyancer is on that lender's panel. If not, you may incur a double cost because the lender will insist on instructing his own solicitor to oversee and check the work yours does, and to ensure that the mortgage documents are correctly signed and registered. This can also lead to delay.

If you are borrowing from more than one lender, it is likely the second or later lenders will insist on using their own solicitors instead of yours in any event.

*When do you instruct?*

It is a good idea to identify the solicitor or licensed conveyancer you intend to use either before or immediately after you make your offer to purchase a particular property, and to make sure they are aware of the fact that you have made an offer. Once you have made your offer and it has been accepted, the first formal step will be for the agent to write a letter confirming the property, the price, the names of the seller and buyer, and those of the seller's and buyer's solicitors or licensed conveyancers, and any special conditions. That letter should act as a trigger for the first formal step in the legal process, which is the seller's solicitor sending out a pack of information to the buyers. So it is helpful to have that name and address ready. Time lost at this stage is time lost overall.

It is also sensible to tell your solicitor or licensed conveyancer when you have agreed a price and given him or her the name of the agent, otherwise the agent's confirming letter will land on their desk with no prior warning. It will also be useful to the solicitor if you pass on the HIP to them at that stage, assuming you have received and read it yourself.

Since buying property is a well-known way of laundering the proceeds of criminal activity, solicitors and licensed conveyancers are subject to strict professional rules requiring them to look out for money laundering. In practice, this means that you will be expected to meet them before they start working for you, and you will need to produce some proof of your identity, such as a passport and driving licence or utility bills in your name showing your current address. Don't take it personally: this is their protection against being caught out later and the rules apply to all their clients. This procedure should only be necessary the first time you use that firm. Bear in mind that if you are buying jointly with your partner, both of you will need to satisfy these requirements.

During the progress of the transaction, you will want to be updated regularly as to what is happening, and more particularly what is not happening, so you can take steps to rectify that. Our suggestion would be to make regular phone calls or email requests of the solicitor (in the middle of the week rather than on Mondays or Fridays which tend to be their busiest days), to keep abreast of progress and to make sure that they have your file at the top of their list. Bearing in mind that most solicitors carry caseloads of several dozen matters at once, all of which, for the relevant client, is the most important matter in the world, and it is not surprising that it is those who are polite but firm who tend to get the best treatment.

## The legals

### Up to exchange of contracts

So, you have made your offer and it has been accepted (offers should always be made 'subject to contract' – that is, subject to the parties entering a legally binding contract; either party can thus pull out before signing (and exchanging) contracts generally with no penalty). Your solicitor[29] is instructed, and you have passed the HIP to him or her. What next?

The 'legals' fall into two stages: the period up to exchange of contracts, and the period from exchange to completion.

The period up to exchange of contracts is the anxious time, because you know it can all still go wrong - some problem could arise on the mortgage valuation or survey, the seller could change his/her mind or get a better offer (although the seller may well be worried that you might change your mind), your solicitor may find some title problem or dispute which means that you should not buy. Most of all, you are anxious because so far you have been busy and in control,

---

[29] You may of course have decided to instruct a conveyancer, but for the sake of clarity we will simply refer to your 'solicitor' from this point on. The points we make in relation to your solicitor will also apply to any conveyancer you may appoint.

with your analysis and research and viewings and negotiation, but from now on everything is in the hands of others, and you are just waiting for them. This is also when the dreaded 'chain' makes its mark (see page 85).

First, do what you have to do: make sure that your solicitor knows the details of your offer - not just the price, but what contents are included, and your preferred timing, including any periods when you will be uncontactable or available to sign documents. In particular, if you are planning to make any improvements to the property, make sure the solicitor knows that, as it may affect his or her advice later. To get the mortgage lender working, make sure you have completed all their procedures and forms and paid all the fees; be clear whether you want their surveyor to do a homebuyer's report; if you want a structural survey arrange that too.

Make sure the selling agent knows that you are doing these things – he or she will have to arrange access for the valuer, for example – so you come across as committed to buying. This may be important later.

Keep in regular contact with each of the solicitor, the mortgage lender and the agent, to make sure that you are aware of their progress, and resolve any reasons for delay.

*What else can you usefully do?*

Depending on your current living arrangements, you may have a property to sell, a tenancy to terminate or a room to vacate. If you are selling, see Chapter 4. If you have a tenancy to terminate, you would be wise to wait until contracts are exchanged and you have a definite moving date before formally giving notice, but it may be helpful to give informal notice (most completions on purchases are three to four weeks after exchange, and most notice periods to terminate tenancies are two months so if you can give 'advance' notice you may save yourself a month's rent). On the other hand, if you can afford it, a gradual move can give you the opportunity to decorate or fix up the new place before you move in.

You can visit the property again to check details more carefully, and to measure up for furniture, carpets and curtains – and perhaps agree with the seller to buy some of the carpets, curtains or white goods, if you want.

You may choose to take the risk of ordering new furniture before exchange (beds and sofas often have six to twelve week order times) but at pre-contract stage you are still taking a risk in doing so.

You can also consider what repairs or alterations or redecoration you may want to carry out before or soon after you move in, and locate builders or tradesmen, and get them to quote to do the work. Again, it is premature to commit yourself but you can save time later by getting ready.

As exchange approaches, you should get quotes and timescales from removal firms, unless you plan to do it yourself. You can start packing or throwing away or recycling stuff, and working out what furniture will go into which room in the new place. You usually need to put in place building insurance from exchange of contracts because (depending on the small print of the contract) the buyer buys the property in the condition it is in at the date of the contract, not the date of completion, so will be legally bound to proceed with completion even if the property burns to the ground, so you should research insurance cover and prices in advance, although again do not commit ahead of exchange. Most importantly, make sure that you have available the amount of money required to exchange contracts – the deposit is normally 10% of the purchase price - and that you are confident in your ability to pull together the cash required for completion, to the extent that it is not covered by the mortgage.

Meanwhile, what is happening with the legals? The traditional process (before the introduction of HIPs) was a stately waltz of exchange of information between the seller's and buyer's solicitors or licensed conveyancers. The process generally started with the seller's solicitor, who once instructed would issue a draft contract and a copy of the seller's title to the property (including the lease if leasehold) to the buyer's solicitor, who would study these documents, raise 'pre-contract enquiries', lodge searches at the local and other relevant authorities and then wait for responses; once the responses were all received, and (if the buyer was getting a mortgage) the mortgage lender had formally confirmed the mortgage offer and the mortgage valuer had confirmed the valuation, the buyer's solicitor would read the contract, mark it up with any necessary changes and send it back to the seller's solicitor. Those changes would be agreed between the lawyers (hopefully acting on the instructions of their respective clients), and once retyped the contract would be ready for the buyer and the seller to sign. The buyer would meet his or her solicitor to go through the results of his/her review of the title, enquiries and searches, sign the contract, provide the solicitor with a cheque for the 10% deposit, and then once the seller had signed and the deposit monies were cleared through the solicitor's account, contracts would be exchanged. At that point the completion date would also be fixed.

All this would usually take four to six weeks if run efficiently on both sides, assuming there was no chain to cause delays.

When HIPs were introduced in 2007, the early part of this process should at least in theory have started more quickly, because the HIP would include the seller's title, a recent local search and replies to some basic enquiries. This supposed increase in the speed of the process was one of the main justifications by the Government for the introduction of HIPs in the teeth of widespread criticism from many experienced property professionals.

With the suspension and intended abolition of HIPs, this trigger for the seller and the seller's solicitor to prepare in advance for a sale has gone; it will take time before we know whether sellers and their solicitors have changed their habits to be more prepared earlier, or will revert to the stately waltz.

Whilst it is often unfair to blame the lawyers for every single delay in the conveyancing process,[30] if you feel that matters *are* proceeding too slowly, telephone your solicitor and ask him or her if they can suggest any way that the process can be speeded up – sometimes all that is required for a file to miraculously reappear at the top of an in-tray is for a gentle call to be made from one side to another asking how matters are proceeding.

The normal period between exchange and completion is four weeks, although this can be negotiated to suit seller or buyer. Simultaneous exchange and completion is possible but only if all of the money arrangements and final searches have been set up in advance. Two weeks is the usual minimum. It is possible to have a 'floating' date, for example if the seller is awaiting

[30] Of course we would say that, it is difficult to resist that temptation. Solicitors are not always great communicators (present company excepted).

completion of a new property, when completion would take place say, 10 days after the seller gives notice that they are ready.

Legally, a contract to buy or sell property must be in writing, and contain all the relevant terms. A verbal contract is not binding in law although it may amount to a 'moral' obligation. Many buyers and sellers unfortunately do not recognise those.

One last thing before exchange: choose your completion date carefully. Most of you will want to complete on a Friday, particularly before a long bank holiday weekend. Avoid that if possible: the removal firms will be booked up, the solicitors will be busy, and the bank money transfer system will be overloaded. If something goes wrong on the day, you are stuck for a weekend rather than just overnight so choose a Wednesday or Thursday instead; the day itself will often be less stressful as a consequence.

## After exchange of contracts

So, you have passed exchange, you have a completion date, what next?

Formally, you will need to sign any mortgage documents and related forms, perhaps for life insurance or mortgage protection. You may need to sign the Land Registry transfer but only if you are taking on (or repeating) obligations affecting the land. If you are buying a new build leasehold property, you will need to sign the lease.

You can now give formal notice on your existing tenancy (or tell your parents the good news). We also strongly recommend that you make a will, since you will now have a significant asset to pass on, and if you are buying jointly with someone else, it is important to document your co-ownership arrangement, to make sure you treat each other fairly during your ownership and if the relationship breaks down. For more information see Chapter 6: Looking Ahead. As part of the Land Registry transfer, where you are buying in joint names, you will have to make a decision whether to own as 'tenants in common' or 'joint tenants'. The difference is important, not least for inheritance tax purposes. For an explanation of these terms see page 103.

Once you have exchanged contracts, you can't change your mind. A contract is a contract, and even if your mortgage offer is withdrawn, or your personal circumstances change, or the value of the property falls – tough! Those buyers who have come up with ingenious reasons why they should not have to buy the over-priced (they say) off-plan flats out of which they hoped to make a fortune have, to date, failed to evade their responsibilities under their contracts.[31]

Practically, you will need to firm up your removal arrangements, whether you are employing a removal firm or following the 'van and mates' route. If you are providing any of the completion monies, that is, if you have a less than 90% mortgage, you must ensure that the necessary funds are in the solicitors' account, with enough to cover their fees, the SDLT (see page 160) and Land Registry fees in good time before the completion date. Occasionally, particularly in the case of leasehold property, there may be some adjustments (known as 'apportionments') to be made for amounts the seller has already paid towards ground rent, buildings insurance or service charges, so make sure that, with your solicitor's help, you make allowance for these.

You may also need to line up furniture deliveries, decoration and so on for immediately after completion. Don't assume you will get the keys before completion has legally happened, which is likely to be in the afternoon.

Arrange, through the Post Office, for redirection of the post from your current address.

Take photos and check measurements for bringing furniture in.

Throw away or recycle everything you can – it's now or never!

If you think somebody might want what you don't need try freecycle (www.freecycle.org).

Pack – which takes much longer than you think.

Prepare change of address cards or emails.

Arrange to farm out pets or children for the day itself.

Double check that all your furniture will fit, (a) through the front door, (b) up the stairs, (c) in the room you want it, and label it clearly room by destination room.

---

31 Reportedly, eight developers have sued 300 flat buyers to force completion. One (Ballymore, developer of Pan Peninsula in London's Docklands) has sued 130.

Arrange internet and satellite TV connections, and land line phone connections if these have been cut off.

Buy cleaning materials and make sure you have (or hire or borrow) a good vacuum cleaner.

## Completion day

On the day you will need to have pulled together (we suggest in a distinctive box or folder) and have to hand at all times during the day:

- some cash;
- mobile phone;
- crucial phone numbers, including the agent, the seller, your solicitor, the removal firm and your mortgage company;
- labels and pen and paper;
- blackberry or other email device;
- knife and scissors;
- cleaning materials; and
- screwdrivers and light bulbs.

Make sure that there are at least two, preferably three of you - one to clear out of your existing place, and stay behind until everything has gone, one to arrive at the new place and check things in, and one to provide transport in between.

Make your exit carefully, including checking and noting down meter readings.

Take a proper break for lunch – the removal firm will do so, and the bank money transfer system will do so too, usually between 1.00 and 2.15.

Allow your seller time to move out - if the new place is bigger than your old one they probably have more stuff than you do – but if practical get a set of keys from them so you can clean up before your possessions arrive.

Be ready to do a lot of cleaning very quickly.

Check meter readings, and make a written note of the readings, and that the sellers have left all the contents they said they would (if there is a problem, it is much easier to deal with this on the day of the move than later).

Keep in touch with the agent and your solicitor, but do not 'phone every five minutes; it does not help.

Usually, the selling agent will hold the set of keys until the moment of completion. Completion will happen when the seller's solicitor has received all the monies needed to make up the purchase price, including paying off the seller's mortgage: for you, the formal moment of handover will be when the agents release the keys to you.

## After completion

Congratulations! So you have completed, what is left to do?

Formally, your solicitor will receive the Land Registry transfer and the release of the seller's mortgage, the lease, if leasehold, and any remaining title deeds from the seller's solicitor. Your solicitor will notify the mortgage lender and the landlord (if any) that completion has happened; your solicitor will file the SDLT return and pay the SDLT due, and once that is acknowledged, apply to the Land Registry for registration of the transfer to you, cancellation of the seller's mortgage and registration of your new mortgage. The SDLT return (which the solicitor may ask you to sign) and the payment must be made within 30 days of completion, otherwise a penalty may be payable. It is acknowledged by HMRC who stamp and return an SDLT return form, which is needed to make the Land Registry application. Registration at the Land Registry usually takes two to four weeks from the date of application, although if the property is newly built, or leasehold, or was previously unregistered, it may take longer than registration of a simple transfer of an existing title, to allow time for the Land Registry to prepare and verify plans. The original documents will go to your mortgage company, but ask your solicitor for a copy, both for your own interest and as a starting point for the HIP should you decide to sell the property in the future.

Notify the utilities and the local authority that you have bought the property, including the date and meter readings.

Arrange contents insurance. Unfortunately, burglary is particularly common in the few days after a buyer moves in.

Send out the change of address cards or emails. Make sure you notify all those you rely on – banks and building societies, your employer, magazines and clubs and organisations you subscribe to, savings organisations, insurances, the DVLA for any car or motorbike (this is a legal obligation), and generally anyone who sends you letters, particularly remembering those you do not hear from often.

If you have bought a new build, complete and send off guarantee cards for all equipment provided. You should also keep a careful note of all snagging items and defects, and make sure the developer knows about them. It is more effective to give the developer a more comprehensive list once you have 'road tested' the property for a little while than to tell them the snagging items individually as they arise, but make sure that you tell the right person, and confirm it in writing or email, and comply with any time limits that you agreed to in the contract.

You can of course now carry out whatever decorations or improvements you intend… but that is another chapter.

## Post transaction review

After you have been living in your new property for a month or so, it is worth sitting down and considering what you have learned and what you would do differently next time, and keeping a note of that. For example, you might ask yourself:

Was I happy with the agent, surveyor/solicitor/mortgage provider? Would I use them again or recommend them to others?

Was my analysis of my own needs and wants accurate, or did I miss something?

Did I stick to my budget? If not, where did I go wrong?

What financial reserves do I need to build up, for mortgage and other outgoings, for future improvements or for a future move?

What can I do now or in the future to improve this property for my own use?

In the short term: decoration, new carpets and curtains, better insulation.

In the longer term, a new kitchen or bathroom, loft extension, rear extension, basement extension.

If it is leasehold, can I buy the freehold (or extend the lease)?

If it is subject to covenants, can I buy those off or get insurance?

And MAKE A WILL!

## Joint tenants and tenants in common

When you are buying jointly with someone else - whether husband/wife or unmarried couple, brother and sister or just friends, some special rules can apply and it is essential for you to decide, and your legal advisers to know, who will own the property and on what basis.

By far the most common arrangement is to buy the property in joint names, although there may be good reasons not to: for example, if one or other is independently wealthy and/or there are inheritance tax considerations to be taken into account.

If two or more people buy property together, the co-owners will usually own through an (automatic) 'trust for land', which means that they own together (strictly speaking, they are 'trustees' for one another) and neither can sell the property on their own. There are two ways of holding the value of the property, either as 'joint tenants' or as 'tenants in common'. The choice between these alternatives should be made carefully, and must be recorded on the transfer to you when you buy, so a decision is needed before then.

'Joint tenants' is the conventional way for husband and wife or civil partners to jointly own property: it means that if one dies while owning the property, the other automatically receives the benefit of the other's share and becomes the sole legal and beneficial owner. In other words, the deceased person's share of the property does not pass under his or her will (or in the absence of a will, under the rules of intestacy).[32]

'Tenants in common' means that each owner owns a distinct share in the property (usually 50:50 but not necessarily so) and if one dies while owning the property their share does not automatically pass to the owner, but instead passes under the will (or intestacy if there is no will) according to the instructions contained in the will or the intestacy rules. This is sometimes more suitable for inheritance tax reasons, even between husband and wife or civil partners, and is more usual for joint owners who are not couples.

It is possible to convert ownership as 'joint tenants' into ownership as 'tenants in common' by one owner serving a 'notice of severance' on the other. It is not possible to reverse the process, that is simply to convert 'tenants in common' to 'joint tenants', without some reasonably complex (and hence expensive) legal manoeuvrings.

---

[32] To repeat ourselves, you should always make sure that you have a valid will once you have bought a property.

The decision whether to own as 'joint tenants' or 'tenants in common' depends on individual circumstances and you should always take tax advice before making a decision, which your solicitor or legal adviser should be able to provide. The default option is 'joint tenants'.

The financial consequences of failing to consider this are much more significant than most people realise, particularly for an unmarried couple.

In *Stack v Dowden* [2007], an unmarried couple purchased a property in joint names. Each contributed financially to the purchase of the property but did not expressly declare their respective beneficial interests in the transfer document.

Unusually, the House of Lords held that the presumption of joint legal and beneficial interests had been rebutted and awarded a higher share to the woman.

The House of Lords established the following key principles for determining the respective beneficial interests in this, and similar, cases:

A conveyance into joint names will result in a legal and beneficial joint tenancy unless the contrary is shown.

If this is disputed, the court must ascertain the parties' shared intentions in the context of the whole course of their conduct relating to the property. Factors to consider include:

- any advice or discussions at the time of the transfer that indicates the parties' intentions at that time;
- the reasons why the parties purchased the property jointly;
- the purpose for which the property was acquired;
- the nature of the parties' relationship;
- whether the couple had children for whom they both had responsibility to provide a home;
- how the purchase was financed, both initially and subsequently;
- how the parties arranged their finances, for example, whether their accounts were held
- Separately, together or a combination of both; and
- how the couple discharged their outgoings on the property and other household expenses.

In *Kernott v Jones* [2010] an unmarried couple purchased a property as joint tenants. The relationship ended. The man moved out and purchased a house in his name, for which he was solely responsible. The woman remained in occupation of the property and was solely responsible for it. After 12 years separation, the man severed the joint tenancy and a 50% his share in the property.

The Court of Appeal held that there was no evidence to displace the presumption of equal shares. It was not possible to infer a joint intention from the parties' conduct since their separation that their equal shares should be varied. It declared that the parties held the property as tenants in common in equal shares.

This decision shows how difficult it is to rebut the presumption of 50/50 joint beneficial interests, and the consequences of not addressing this when you buy, or if you separate. It also illustrates the importance for cohabitants of entering into a written agreement as to their shares in the value of a property.

## Special schemes for first time buyers

The very substantial price increases for most housing during the period 2002 to 2006 have caused a special affordability challenge for first time buyers. For those who believe the statistics, the affordability ratio (calculated by comparing average house prices to average earnings) soared from under three to over six during that period, meaning that the average house price equated to more than six years' worth of average earnings. Whilst the downturn in 2008 into 2009 has reversed this process to an extent, and the ratio at the time of writing is now down to roughly four, that is still higher than the long term average, which is why some forecasters continue to predict further significant house price falls. For first time buyers in particular, the mortgage famine in 2008-2009, above all the lenders' reduction in loan to value ratios forcing buyers to put in a larger proportion of the price as their own cash, has made it even more challenging for first time buyers to buy, despite the general fall in market values. As we have already said, the cash a first-time buyer needed in 2009 averaged £33,000.

All of this means that 'affordable' housing has become even more important for first time buyers. There are several Government-promoted initiatives intended to help. Unfortunately, these are not particularly easy to find, or to understand, with the result that the overall picture is patchy and confusing. We will do our best to explain and point you in the right direction. We apologise in advance for the jargon and acronyms: they are not of our making!

First, a little background. During the boom times, planning permission for most larger developments was granted subject to a requirement for a proportion of 'social housing' to be provided alongside private housing. In some areas this was up to 50% of the residential content of the scheme. Usually, the private sector developer built both the private and the social housing buildings and sold the social housing part of the scheme to a housing association during or at the end of the construction period, and housing associations, usually in conjunction with the local authority, allocated the social housing to appropriate occupiers. 'Social housing' does not just mean housing for rent, as we think of 'council housing'. It also includes various forms of part-sale, collectively called 'intermediate housing' or 'low cost home ownership' (LCHO).

There is no question but that the UK has a serious shortfall in housing generally, and 'social housing' in particular. The trade body for housing associations, the National Housing Federation (NHF) estimated in late 2008 that the overall existing stock of affordable homes was 3.9 million units (houses or flats) and that there is unsatisfied demand for another 1.67 million households to move into affordable homes, which they predicted would rise to 5 million households by the end of 2010. The rise in the nation's population is making this worse.

Conversely, only 205,000 affordable homes were built between 1999 and 2007, but more than twice as many affordable homes, previously council housing, were sold in the same period through the 'Right to Buy' scheme - 440,000 - with the result that the total affordable housing stock fell by 200,000 in that period.

To make matters worse, the supply of affordable homes through planning requirements imposed on private sector developments is drying up as those development schemes stall or are mothballed, and new schemes do not start because they are not financially viable.

The Government's agency for housing provision, the Homes and Communities Agency (HCA), which replaced the Housing Corporation on 1 December 2008, identified just over 27,000 completions of units for social renting in the year to 1 April 2009, and just under 20,000 LCHO completions, but the number of new social housing starts dropped to 44,000.

The HCA is therefore promoting the development of new social housing and LCHO. Part of that involves finishing off existing public sector schemes, part involves new public sector build and part starting to invest in private sector developments that which would not otherwise proceed (known as Kickstart Housing Delivery).

The key providers of LCHO or intermediate housing are housing associations (known as Registered Social Landlords, or RSLs) who provide 'affordable housing' to buy, as well as to rent, under various schemes.

The two main routes are shared ownership and shared equity. Both of these are useful for first time buyers who have some resources but not enough to buy outright in the open market.

Shared ownership involves an RSL, or sometimes a private developer, selling to you a share of the ownership of the property (known as the equity) and simultaneously granting a lease to you to enable you to occupy. So you pay out now for, say, 50% of the value of the property, using normal mortgage finance, and pay a rent which is 50% of the market rent of the property. Through a system known as 'staircasing', you can then buy chunks of the equity of the property as you can afford them, and the rent will go down in proportion. Usually, over a number of years you can buy up to 100% of the equity of the property and so then own the whole of it, meaning a full leasehold interest in the case of a flat or the freehold in the case of a house. However, in some areas, particularly rural areas, where affordable housing is in short supply and difficult to replace once 'used up', the RSL may wish to hold on to ownership of the property. This means that either the maximum share you could buy is 80% or that when you come to sell you have to sell it back to the RSL. Either restriction may affect the market value of the property. Some 13,000 towns and villages fall into 'protected areas' where these rules apply.

Shared equity means that you buy the whole property with a mortgage from a conventional mortgage lender of 50-75% of the value, and in addition you get an interest-free loan for the rest, or most of it, from a housing association or the developer.

## 'Home Buy'

The Government's initiative to support these arrangements is known as 'Home Buy' and offers four alternatives:

*Open Market HomeBuy* – shared equity by another name – which supports outright purchases on the open market by providing a loan. The loan is usually interest-free for a time, often five years. It can be repaid early, and must be repaid on sale.

*New Build HomeBuy* – shared ownership by another name – also known as 'HomeBuy Direct', which offers the opportunity to part-buy, part-rent newly built property either from an RSL or from a developer.

*Social HomeBuy* – which offers existing social tenants the opportunity to part-buy a minimum share of 25% in their existing home at a discount, paying rent on the outstanding proportion.

*Rent to HomeBuy* (introduced as a pilot scheme in July 2008) – particularly aimed at first time buyers who are unable to buy a share of a property through the New Build HomeBuy scheme because they cannot raise the necessary mortgage finance (many lenders, particularly in 2008, perceived such loans as 'sub prime' and therefore higher risk). The first time buyer will rent the property at less than market rent (typically 80% of what you would normally pay) for a fixed period of up to five years, and during or at the end of the period the buyer will have the right, but not an obligation, to buy a share in the property through the New Build HomeBuy scheme. The hope is that the buyer can save up enough during the reduced rent period to achieve a mortgage offer later.

*London Wide Initiative* - an initiative by the HCA to build 5,000 homes across London for key workers, to be available on a shared equity basis.

These well-intentioned schemes have received some but not universal publicity, and are varied in their effectiveness. In particular, it has been reported that only 251 people had benefited from the 'Rent to HomeBuy' scheme between July 2008 and July 2009, although developers claimed that more were in the pipeline.

The HomeBuy schemes give priority for assistance to:

- existing tenants of social housing;
- those on housing waiting lists for social rented housing who are nominated by the local council as being in housing need;
- public sector key workers (such as police, firemen, nurses);

- other priority first time buyers designated locally;
- first time buyers with an annual income of under £60,000.

This last category was added only in May 2008, and widens the catchment for the schemes very significantly but as the figures above suggest, the message has only slowly got through to those who need it.

Schemes with confusingly similar names include:

*My Choice HomeBuy* – similar to Open Market HomeBuy, run by a consortium of housing associations.

*Own Home* – also similar to Open Market HomeBuy – run by 'Places for People', one of the larger housing associations.

Other names for 'Rent To HomeBuy' include 'Try Before You Buy', 'Up To You' and 'Rent Now Buy Later'.

Terms such as interest rate and length of loan vary from scheme to scheme, so check and compare details carefully. An important difference between some of the RSL schemes and some of the private developer schemes, buried in the small print, is whether the price for buying additional percentages of the equity in the property is fixed at the time you first sign up, or is recalculated at the time you decide to buy the extra percentage, so that if values rise you will pay more.

Unfortunately there appears to be no single website that pulls all this information together.

To find schemes which are eligible for these support arrangements in your chosen area, try the housing department in the local council (they cannot advise you, but can point you in the right direction); or find the local HomeBuy agent via the HCA[33], or in London the Housing Options website.[34].

Housing associations active in this sector are listed on page 362.

A number of private sector developers are working in partnership with housing associations and the delivery of schemes, and they are also listed on page 362.

---

[33] www.homesandcommunities.co.uk/homebuy

[34] www.housingoptions.co.uk

The great obstacle to any of these schemes is mortgage finance. The number of mortgage lenders who are willing to lend on affordable housing, even through HomeBuy Direct, is limited. There are some specialist mortgage brokers for affordable housing, including SPF Sherwins (linked to Savills) (www.spfsherwins.co.uk), Censeo (linked to Genesis Homes) (www.censeo-financial.com) and SharetoBuy (linked to Britannia Building Society)(www.sharetobuy.com).

Judging by newspaper advertisements, at least in London, many of the new developments on which HomeBuy alternatives are being promoted are one-bedroomed flats in large clusters in inner or distant outer London boroughs. It is likely that as the HCA invests its funds in stalled schemes these will be for larger scale developments. An 'ideal home' three-bedroomed semi-detached house in a leafy suburb is unlikely to be achievable in these larger developments, but there are and will be smaller schemes – often the social housing element within a private sector scheme – in more desirable areas, so research this carefully. Demand will be higher for the most attractive and attractively-priced schemes, some of which may come down to a ballot to choose buyers. In any event, you are likely to be interviewed by the housing association or private sector developer to ensure you have the necessary funds.

Bear in mind that even 'affordable housing' has significant costs attached: you are likely to require a 10% deposit on the share in which you are taking out a mortgage, and will still need cash to pay costs and fees in addition to that. One significant advantage of shared ownership as opposed to shared equity is that you will not pay SDLT until the proportion of the value of the home that you own reaches 80% but it does follow that if you are 'staircasing' up to that level, SDLT eventually becomes payable. One other advantage of social housing is that the housing associations, both for their own ideals and through government encouragement, are more effective at adopting 'eco standards' for housing. So, many schemes will be ahead of the game in terms of energy efficiency, with many projects providing the kind of insulation standards and green features you will be hard pushed to find in older houses.

One concern about affordable housing, particularly shared ownership, may be the kind of neighbours you will have. Most housing associations were originally created with the laudable objective of providing housing for those who were and remain unable to buy themselves, and to take over the role of local authorities in managing 'council housing'. Housing associations have evolved and many are now more sensitive to market pressures. Those eligible for either shared ownership or shared equity will be in work and with incomes able to support the financing arrangements. Until 2007, most affordable shared ownership schemes were aimed at key workers, particularly those in the emergency services and teaching, but with the relaxation in mid-2008 of the criteria and acceptance of those with an annual salary of up to £60,000, the picture has changed. Information on applicants for affordable housing is difficult to obtain, but Genesis Homes, one of the larger London-based housing associations, published an analysis of its applications in 2008, which showed that a large majority were white collar professionals; more than 20% classified themselves as managers and another 15% worked with finance, marketing or publishing. Just 1.7% worked in emergency services and 5.6% in education. Male/female applicants were split 50/50, and 81% of applicants were below the age of 40. 48% of applicants were existing private or social tenants, and 40% lived with friends or family.

The burst of HCA activity and funding in 2008-10, which played an important part in keeping the house builders afloat and first-time buyer properties available, has not survived the change of Government and the HCA has had to reduce its budget for 2010-11 and beyond. In particular, the Kickstart initiative for new schemes has stopped, leaving 108 schemes in limbo.

## Right to buy

Whilst this book is not specifically aimed at those likely to exercise the 'right to buy' from a council or Registered Social Landlord, many properties have come into private ownership through the 'right to buy' schemes and it may be helpful to give some background by way of summary.

Local housing authorities have for many years been able to sell council-owned homes, with Government approval, but seldom did so. Following the Housing Act 1980, public sector tenants were given a statutory right to buy their homes at a discount to market value, subject to various conditions. It has been estimated that more than 1.5 million homes were sold through right to buy between 1980 and 1990, and that over 400,000 more have been sold since then.

The original right to buy benefited most tenants of a local authority, provided the tenant had lived in that property for more than two years. There were certain exceptions, for example properties adapted for use by the disabled, or the elderly. If the property is one the landlord intends to demolish for redevelopment, the landlord can exclude the right to buy. If the property is in certain rural areas or a National Park etc. the landlord can limit who the property can be sold to. The local authority can also seek to suspend the right to buy if the tenant has engaged in anti-social behaviour.

If the property is a house, the freehold will be sold. If the property is a flat, a 125-year lease will be sold, with a ground rent of £10 per annum or less. There will usually be an ongoing service charge arrangement with the landlord responsible for repair of the structure and outside of the property, and the tenant responsible to pay a fair proportion of those costs. In some cases disputes have arisen about the scale of these costs.

A 'rent to mortgage' scheme was introduced in 1993 to extend the scope of the scheme further, but this was abolished in 2005.

The discount to market value varies depending whether the dwelling is a house or a flat, and how long the tenant has lived there.

The discount rises year by year from 32% to 60% for houses, or from 44% to 70% for flats.

In return for the discount the tenant benefits from, the landlord is entitled to repayment of part of the discount if the property is sold (originally within three years, now within five years). This is often protected by a second charge on the property in favour of the local authority or Registered Social Landlord. The landlord can also require the property to be offered back if the tenant decides to sell within 10 years.

The procedures for right to buy are technical and need to be followed carefully by anyone seeking to exercise the right, and advice should be sought. The 1980 Act rules (now in the Housing Act 1985, as amended) still apply where the landlord is a local housing authority.

These rights do not apply to a tenant of a Registered Social Landlord that is a charity (as most are). For tenants of a Registered Social Landlord different rules apply.

By the Housing Act 1996, the tenant's right to buy was extended to include Registered Social Landlords (to whom many former council properties had by then been transferred) but only for properties built, or bought, with public money after 1997. Some of the exceptions mentioned above do not apply.

RSLs have also sold a number of properties to tenants voluntarily rather than through the formal 'right to buy' procedure.

There are reports that private companies have been encouraging council or RSL tenants to exercise the right to buy, get the discount and agree to sell the property immediately to the company in return for a 20-year lease at no rent. The Government sought to prevent this abuse of the system in 2004 by making such an arrangement a trigger for repaying the discount immediately, although it may be difficult for local authorities to enforce this.

From the point of view of a buyer of a former council or RSL property where the seller has bought the property through 'right to buy', you need to be aware that, if the property has been bought only in the last five years, the seller will have to pay part of the price back to the council or RSL (and there may be a second charge on the property to secure this) and if it has been bought in the last 10 years, the seller may have to offer it back to the council or RSL, which puts the sale at risk. So it would be wise to establish upfront that the seller understands this and has already made the necessary arrangements.

As we mentioned on page 23, a particular risk with ex-council properties, especially flats, is the backlog of major repairs which turn into large service charge costs for buyers – so surveys are essential.

## 'Squatters' rights'

Two very different sets of circumstances fall within this media label.

First, there are the situations where squatters move into an empty house, or camp on a piece of open ground, much to the fury of its owner.

Secondly, there are situations where someone has occupied a piece of land for so long that, as a matter of law, it becomes his (or hers). Lawyers call this 'adverse possession'. This is usually a neglected or abandoned piece of land, perhaps left over from a previous development scheme. It is very rare for ownership of a house to be acquired in this way although the media seize on it when it happens.[35]

The underlying legal principles are the same for both situations, but the circumstances are usually very different.

In the first situation, the owner is entitled to evict the squatters and recover possession, but must do so (assuming the squatters are physically still there) through court action. As a matter of public policy he/she would be committing a criminal offence if he/she took matters into his/her own hands by using force or damaging the property.

The squatters may have committed a criminal offence by breaking and entering the property, but unless there are witnesses to the entry who can identify those who did so, which is unlikely, the police are powerless. On open land or highway land (such as a lay-by) there will be no breaking and entering to prosecute. Simply occupying without the landlord's permission is not a criminal offence. Recognising the difficulty for landowners caused by squatters, the courts have an accelerated procedure (known as the Part 55 procedure, previously Order 113) which is likely to take two-four weeks from court application to court order; the court rules also allow for the fact that it will usually be impossible to identify some or all of the squatters. They also give the local authority power to pursue court action in relation to land occupied by squatters where it is not clear who the land is owned by, or it is part of the highway.

Obviously, it is usually a waste of time pursuing the squatters for the legal costs incurred or the damage caused to the property, or clearing up costs, so squatters have a considerable nuisance value. Developers therefore tend to apply higher security standards to vulnerable sites, and to disable all utility services in empty property awaiting redevelopment; some employ 'live-in' security guards.

Moving to the second situation, adverse possession, namely where a person who is not the legal owner of land can become the legal owner by possessing the land for a specified period of time.

---

[35] According to Sweet & Maxwell, there were ten such cases in 2008, two in 2007, one in 2006 and none in 2005.

Until 2003, the rule was simple in principle, although not always easy to apply in practice. If a person was in physical possession of land for a continuous period of 12 years without objection from the legal owner, then the person possessing became the owner even if the legal owner later objected. The person in possession would have to show that they had occupied the property as their own during the 12 years, for example that they were not occupying with the legal owner's permission. Common indicators of treating the property as one's own would be maintaining the boundary fences of the land or the access to it, or cutting grass etc. Often the land would simply be 'folded into' the garden of the person in possession of it. So the person in possession could quite easily claim land without the 'paper' owner being aware he was doing so.

The legal position was reviewed by the Law Commission and the Land Registry and, in view of the accessibility and increased coverage of the land registration system, the system changed with effect from 13 October 2003 for registered land. The old rules still apply to land that is unregistered – a diminishing commodity – or where the adverse possession relied upon was for a period of at least 12 years ending before 13 October 2003. For land that is registered, the person in possession will be entitled to apply for registration as owner of the land after being in 'adverse possession' for a continuous period of 10 years (which can include time before 13 October 2003). However, there is a crucial procedural difference: the Land Registry will give the existing registered owner (and any registered mortgagee) notice of the application by the person in possession for registration, so that the registered owner has the opportunity to object. If the registered owner objects, the application will be rejected unless the applicant can justify his claim, which is difficult to do.

If the application is rejected but the person in possession stays in possession for a further two years (giving the registered owner time to prove his title by taking court proceedings for possession) the person in possession can apply to the Land Registry again, and will be registered as legal owner even if the registered owner then objects again.

So, it has been in practice considerably more difficult to succeed in a claim for ownership by adverse possession of registered land since 13 October 2003 because the registered owner has been able to (and usually will) object, and assert his rights.

The first reported case on the interpretation of the new rules since 2003 is *Baxter v Mannion* where the 'paper owner' complained after the person (allegedly) in possession had been registered that he did not receive notice of the application from the Land Registry. The 'paper owner' succeeded on the particular facts. If the address on his paper title had been correct, so that he received the Land Registry's notice, he would have objected and the case would never have arisen. A lesson to be vigilant on details.

There was an attempt (*JA Pye (Oxford) Limited v Graham*) to argue that an adverse possession claim breached the rights of the 'paper' owner under the European Convention on Human Rights because enforcement of the adverse possession claim would deprive the 'paper'owner of its property. After a long running battle that went as far as the Grand Chamber of the European Court of Human Rights (after both the Court of Appeal and the EHCR had found in favour of the paper owner) the paper owner lost. Not surprisingly, the land in question was worth fighting over because it had valuable development potential.

# CHAPTER 4 SELLING A PROPERTY

## The right approach

In theory, selling a property is the mirror image of buying one, so once you have bought, you should be able to sell without thinking about it too hard. In practice, selling is often more stressful than buying, and of course the most stressful experience of all is when you aim to do both at the same time.

As with buying, timing makes a huge difference: if you get it right and have the kind of property people want, when they want it, you may have multiple bidders so that you can choose, and have a back-up offer if needed. At other times, and perhaps with a property which is less instantly attractive, maybe because it is quirky or in a location that not everyone would prefer, or maybe because there are six others just like it on the market at the same time, you may struggle to find anyone even to view it, let alone to make an offer. The ups and downs of the market over the last few years have illustrated this perfectly: in 2006 almost anything would sell, even the worst; in 2008 almost nothing would sell, even the best.

So what can you do to reduce the stress and improve your chances of a successful sale and move?

## Choosing your timing

It may be too much of a cliché to describe selling a house as a military operation requiring the same level of preparation, but there is something to that.

You can analyse selling a property as falling into five stages:

1. Marketing
2. Deciding
3. Getting to exchange
4. Getting to completion
5. Completing

## Stage 1 - Marketing

The property market is, to some extent, driven by fashion and sentiment, and to a large extent is seasonal. In most years, the peak viewing season is from Easter to the end of June, with another flurry of activity in September. This is driven partly by the weather and summer holidays but also many buyers have a deadline to work to, which is either moving in before the new school or academic year starts in September, or being 'in for Christmas'. It is rational for them to look to find the right property roughly three months before those deadlines so they have time for the transaction to go through, and to settle in, beforehand. Seasonality is perhaps less of an issue for city centre properties than it is for suburban or rural properties but it is a significant factor nevertheless. A more subtle influence is that spring time is when the property supplements tend to start making optimistic predictions about house price rises over the coming months, and for those who have half-decided to move this may influence them to commit themselves, so that they don't 'miss the boat'.

Sentiment and fashion are much more difficult to predict, but again the contrast between 2006 and 2008 illustrates the power of, on the one hand 'if I don't buy now I probably won't be able to afford it next year' or 'I don't want to buy now because it will be cheaper next year' on the other.

It is easy to become part of this thinking rather than an observer of it; in our view (in fact one of the themes of this book) your reasons for buying, or for moving, should be your desire for a home, and your need for a better or different space or facilities, rather than a short term desire for profit - in other words in choosing your timing. Think five years ahead rather than one.

That may help you to decide whether it is better to take advantage of a general 'rush to buy' a little earlier than you would have chosen to move, or to wait a year or two before deciding to move, so as to miss the 'best not to move' part of the cycle. You may even, as so many have done during 2008 and 2009, consider adapting your existing property rather than moving, and if so Chapter 9, on property development, is for you.

So, unless you are under non-negotiable time pressures such as a job move, a baby arriving or estate agents' 3Ds (Death, Debt or Divorce) you can attempt to be master of your destiny by choosing your time to move rationally rather than emotionally.

## Choosing an agent and setting a price

In choosing which estate agent to use, your purpose is to ensure that your property has the maximum possible exposure to those buyers who are most likely to buy it. In most urban and suburban areas you will have a choice between small local agents, who specialise in that area only, and the branches of larger national or regional agents. In rural areas it is likely that 'trophy properties' – those likely to go into *Country Life* – will need national exposure through one of the major agents specialising in that kind of property, such as Savills or Knight Frank, but smaller properties would be beneath their radar and will need to be marketed through a local agent. For some specialist properties (riverside or seaside properties) there may be specialist agents who focus on buyers looking for that special feature. Local agents tend to operate within a pretty closely defined area, and to some extent within a defined price bracket or size of house,[36] and you need to make sure you pitch your property through the right agent at the right market both in terms of area and price. The obvious routes for finding an agent are:

- word of mouth (if you have reached that stage, the school gate is a very useful source of information);
- walking, cycling or driving around your local area and seeing whose 'for sale' boards predominate;
- looking at the local paper (the paid-for one as well as the free one if there are both) to see which agents are advertising properties in the same area and price bracket as yours.

As we mentioned in Chapter 3, Tesco are trialling an online sales website. It is conceivable that this will radically change the way properties are sold in England and Wales (although, naturally, estate agents pooh-pooh that idea). For an ambitious attempt to find a new free web-based way of selling property, see Sarah Beeny's tepilo.com.

Before talking to any agents, it is useful to get some sense of pricing. Several 'nosy neighbour' websites can be very helpful for this because they give you information on recent sales close to your property (listed on page 362): all have very useful information with which you can compare your house to other recent sales (it may be worth looking at the houses in question yourself to establish whether they are in fact similar: for example, do they have a loft extension or garage or are they detached rather than terraced?).

---

36 Try reading the adverts in the local papers in Wimbledon for an example.

You can also gauge the level of interest in the market generally by considering the house price indices (how much have prices risen, or fallen) but bear in mind the limitations of those indices we mention in Chapter 3.

You can also search the property listing websites (listed on page 361) to see what else is currently on the market in your area and how similar it is to yours: that is, what your competition will be.

Once you have identified who are the most likely agents you will appoint, look at their websites to see what else they have on the market and how similar it is to yours. Several tend to keep properties on their websites even when they are under offer, and that can provide a useful hint as to how successful they have been in selling those houses (although you may find they last rather longer on the websites than you might think, to give the impression of activity).

Then we suggest you make a short list of agents and visit the local offices of, say, three. It is useful to see the set-up of their offices and get the feel of how lively their own place is. Then get all three to visit the house and give you an idea of the selling price they think you should ask, and what realistically they think you will achieve.

This also gives you the opportunity to ask some pertinent questions, such as who will be your primary point of contact (the advantage of the local agent may be that you are dealing with someone on a day-to-day basis who is senior in the organisation rather than a school leaver, but they may be less available); how many other properties of a similar type they have on the market; what other prices they have achieved recently (which you can verify with the comparison websites such as www.upmystreet.com etc); how long those other properties took to sell and what advertising they plan to do, including what listing websites they will put it on. For higher value properties, a brochure will be essential, and for the very top end properties more extreme forms of marketing may be required – *Country Life* or the glossy colour property supplements of the broadsheet newspapers. Also take the opportunity to ask their advice about how best to present the property and what its best features are, and whether any changes should be made before you market. From all of these questions you get a sense of whether you think the agent is competent, and whether you can work with them. It is not essential to like your estate agent as a person. As a group, they get a pretty rough deal in the press and some of that is justified. It does help if you think they know what they are doing.

Setting the price - with the benefit of your research on the 'nosy neighbour' websites and advice from the three agents about pricing, you can now set realistic expectations about the price at which to start marketing the property, the price you will achieve, and how long it is likely to take to find a buyer who is in a position to proceed. At that moment, before committing yourself to any agent or any marketing we suggest you stop and think whether if you sell at the price they suggest is achievable, or perhaps a little below, and after allowing for all the costs of moving, you will have enough money available to buy the next property you are aiming to get. If not, you are wasting your time and it is better to stop now.

## Agency terms

Agents are usually employed either as:

1. sole agents, which means they have the exclusive right to market and sell the property[37]; or
2. joint agents, which means that they are not alone and another agent you choose - sometimes more than one – is also instructed to market the property; or
3. rather confusingly, what agents sometimes call joint sole agents: that is, more than one agent is instructed but the second agent is recommended by the first. This may suit where the property is to be marketed both locally and nationally, so a large national agent may bring in a local agent to get the best of both worlds when selling a larger or higher value property which deserves both local and wider marketing.

Agents prefer sole agency both because it makes them feel better (bigger) and because they can charge a higher fee, and receive all of it. Normal agent's fees for sole agency are in the order of 1.5-2.5% although this does vary by area and by how desperate they are for business. Remember there is VAT on top of any fees. Fees may be negotiable, particularly when agents are keen to increase their turnover.

---

[37] Some agents use the phrase 'sole selling rights' which means they get their fee even if you find the buyer yourself.

Fees for joint agency tend to be slightly higher in aggregate, although obviously split between more people.

'Joint Sole Agency' is usually suggested by the agents rather than by you. They will deal with the allocation between themselves so you only pay one fee. This is likely to be in the range of 2.5-4% plus VAT.

Fees may be higher in percentage terms at the bottom end of the value scale, and lower in percentage terms at the higher end of the scale. Beware of extras being added on top, such as the cost of a 'for sale' sign, newspaper advertisements or internet listings, brochures, photography etc. These are reasonable if pre-agreed but can be a nasty surprise if they are not drawn to your attention up front (the agent should do this but it may be in the small print).

A couple of agents were so desperate for business in late 2008 that they offered to drop commission-based fees altogether in return for a one-off upfront fee of £999 (instead of the average commission of £8,000). This was, not surprisingly, unpopular with their competitors and, as far as we know, the offer has not been repeated. However, Tesco are proposing a range of fixed fees on their website.

The appointment of the agent is normally for a fixed period, with a right for the owner to extend. What is the right period depends on the kind of property, the kind of market it is in and the time of year. It may be reasonable to limit the appointment of a sole agent of a desirable house in a good market, starting at Easter, to four weeks so that you have a second chance during the peak season; if you are marketing a rural or 'ordinary' property in September it may be reasonable to commit yourself for six months.

Although agents don't like it, you are perfectly entitled to stop using them at the end of the fixed period and go to a different agent on a sole agency basis. It is more common to go on to a joint agency or joint sole agency basis, keeping the existing agent but adding another one, after the fixed period has expired. You can only judge this by assessing the number and seriousness of potential buyers the first agent brings to view the property, and by keeping an eye on what is happening in your local area about agents' boards, and in the local paper etc. during the time when your property is being marketed.

Two final (related) thoughts: do not necessarily go with the agent who gives you the highest 'valuation' or the lowest percentage fee; some agents have been notorious for using those ploys to get you on their books and then, when they cannot generate enough interest, persuading you to accept a lower asking price or a higher fee at a later stage. It is unfair to name names in this respect but they do not all start with F!

## Selling at auction

The traditional property auction houses operate alongside estate agency firms, and most are divisions of such firms. Examples are Allsop and Barnard Marcus. Most sellers through auctions are 'in the trade' such as banks or building societies selling repossessed properties, or receivers, or developers under pressure, or those who need to demonstrate they have achieved market value, such as local authorities or family or charity trustees. Generally speaking, the sellers are not owner-occupiers with any emotional attachment to the property, it is just something they have to sell. Often the properties themselves are in some way less than perfect.

Conversely, the buyers at auctions are normally trade or private bargain-hunters, so for a 'normal' property it is unlikely you would get the best price. Consequently, it is unlikely you would use this route for a conventional sale, even though the 'instant' nature of it – contracts are exchanged on the fall of the auctioneer's hammer and completion is usually four weeks later – may be superficially attractive.

Auctions are sometimes used for 'one-off' properties such as a beach hut, or a 'lordship of the manor', or a large and unique country house.

Online auctions are becoming available, such as www.mustbesold.com or www.bidprop.co.uk, but again these are for the 'distressed' seller.

## Presenting the property

First impressions really matter when buyers come to view your property. You do know this. When you were looking at properties yourself, how many did you reject at first sight because the front gate was broken, or the front garden overgrown, or the paint on the front door was peeling, or the hall was cluttered with children's toys or the kitchen smelt, or the dog yapped at you, or you couldn't stand the Laura Ashley curtains, or the avocado bathroom suite? Most of these flaws are, of course, superficial, and you as buyer have trained yourself to look at the true attractions of the property you might buy, rather than the superficial disadvantages, but buyers who view may not be as sophisticated as you. It is difficult to stand back and take an objective view of the good and bad points of your own house, but that is what the agent is doing when he comes round to give you a view on value. It is therefore worth using him or her as a kind of rehearsal. Rather than tell the agent that you will clear up, and that you will fix the gate, do it before he or she comes.

If, when you have looked objectively at your property, something more drastic than tidying up is needed, a weekend or two spent redecorating or taking stuff to the dump or even putting it into self-storage could well pay off.

When taking the agents around, it is worth asking for (and acting on) their advice as to both the good and bad points of your house, and the things that will attract or deter buyers, particularly those things which you can solve simply. You cannot change the fact that your house is north facing or that there is a bus stop nearby, but you can make sure in particular that the front looks tidy, the house is clean and clean smelling and that the back garden is under control if not neat. Agents will also tell you that most houses are over-furnished. It may be hard to get rid of your grandmother's wardrobe and that extra set of chairs, particularly if you are aiming to upsize to a larger house, but it may be worth getting them out of the way for the time being. Conversely, agents hate showing buyers around empty houses; the scars of use tend to be all too obvious, and the sense of being 'lived in' – the nest we are all looking for – is lost, even if the spaces seem larger. So, ask yourself, and the agent, and perhaps a critical friend, to advise on how to de-clutter and, to a degree, standardise your house.

It is worth spending some time and money clearing up and freshening up the garden. Consider re-laying the lawn, improving privacy by replacing fences, repairing or relaying paths and patios or decking. Think about your target market. Families with children will want open play space. Young professionals will want low maintenance entertaining space. Older couples may be attracted by a pretty flower bed.

Bear in mind also the impact of the surroundings of your house. If the roadside verge outside is a mess, tidy it up, if your neighbour's garden or front hedge is a mess, offer to do something about it. If it is really desperate, perhaps you and other neighbours or in extreme cases the local council can insist on your neighbour doing something about it.

## Viewings

Once you have appointed your agent(s), their job is to seduce potential buyers into coming round to view the property and, you hope, to fall in love with it. You need to set out clearly with the agent in advance the ground rules for viewings: will the senior agent you have been dealing with actually come round with the buyers, or at least send the office boy or girl? How much notice will you get in advance (be realistic)? Are there times or days you will not allow viewings? Bear in mind that most buyers will want to view at weekends or (in cities) the evenings. Will you stay in the property whilst the buyers are coming round (this can be awkward for both seller and buyer)? Can you arrange to have your children, dog etc out of the way when needed (difficult with teenage children on weekend mornings)? Can you keep the nosy neighbour away? Is parking difficult - can you make it easier by reserving a space?

It is worth rehearsing with the agent how he or she will show potential buyers around the house. You may be surprised to know that there is an art to showing the rooms in the right order, emphasising the good points, and glossing over the disadvantages, and dealing with awkward questions about noise or neighbours or your own circumstances, reasons for selling and so on. Sooner or later you will probably end up showing someone around yourself, perhaps on their second visit, and it will help you to know how the agent would handle things.

On these occasions, your body language is going to be analysed by the buyer – how desperate are you to sell, what are you trying to cover up? It is surprising how often buying decisions are influenced by whether the buyer likes the seller as a person, or thinks that their lifestyles are similar. If there are competing offers, the seller is also likely to prefer the buyer with whom he or she is more at ease.

Don't try *too* hard. Most buyers will see through the smell of baking in the kitchen on a Saturday morning, as a sign either that the seller has read too many magazines or is too desperate to sell.

In our experience, provided you have an agent, it is better not to discuss price direct with the buyer. It is always easier to go through a third party. It can be useful, however to discuss timing and the extent to which your sale is dependent on you buying another property and the buyer's ability to purchase is dependent on them selling, or on mortgage finance etc, and how far they are through those processes. If either of you has particular dates to achieve such as school starting dates, then it is better to get those understood sooner rather than later.

There was an important change to the selling process, and therefore to the sequence of events, with the introduction of Housing Information Packs (HIPs) in 2007. These were launched with the laudable intention of speeding up the house buying and selling process, although both the estate agency world and the legal profession who were on the front line in implementing these changes squealed long and hard about the change in habits they required and (perhaps with more justification) about the chaotic way in which the Labour Government introduced the HIPs requirement in stages. As so often happens with Government initiatives, the gap between a good theory in abstract and an effective mechanism in practice is illustrated by the HIPs saga, and whatever benefit might have been achieved if the theory was correct has been dissipated by the incompetence of the introduction of it, and the numerous and unexpected changes of detail.

The requirement for the seller to have a survey of the property carried out, which was originally to be part of the HIP, was dropped during implementation as a consequence of protests by estate agents and others that this requirement was an expensive waste of time.

All that is now history. The requirement on sellers to provide a HIP was suspended with effect from 21 May 2010. Despite this suspension, it is a good idea to 'get your house in order' in terms of paperwork for the sale, and instruct your lawyer in advance, to save wasted time later.

You do still need an Energy Performance Certificate (EPC), and that can only be carried out by an EPC inspector. A new industry of HIP providers has developed, who your agent will offer you. You need an energy assessor for the EPC but the rest can be done through your solicitor. The purpose of the EPC is to identify the level of energy performance, in other words how much energy the property uses, which is dependent on its construction, the extent of effective insulation, the type and effectiveness of the space and water heating systems, and the existence and effectiveness of any green 'features'. This will produce a brief one or two-page summary, with a rating between bands A (very good) to G (dreadful) for your house, an estimate of the annual heating cost and recommendations as to how to improve energy performance. It is standard for them to recommend improving loft insulation and switching to low-energy light bulbs if you have not done so already (so you could improve the rating significantly before the inspector calls, by doing this yourself). It is common for the recommendations to include replacing the central heating boiler with a newer condenser type, and installing cavity wall insulation if practical, but these may be expensive or messy and are unlikely to add value immediately.

One can see the worthiness of the principle of encouraging all house owners to be more aware of the extent to which their homes are energy efficient, and through that to encourage them to implement changes to make them more so, but it is unlikely that most buyers will take any notice.

You need to arrange the EPC before exchange takes place. Unlike the HIP requirement, you do not need the EPC before any marketing takes place. The EPC is likely to cost £85-£100 plus VAT.

A few things to bear in mind:

1. Unless you have followed our advice at the end of Chapter 3 and kept copies of all the key documents such as the Land Registry documents and the lease, or your solicitor has, he will usually write to your lender to obtain the title documents. To do this he will need details of your lender, including the mortgage reference or roll number. You need to allow at least a couple of weeks for this request to be dealt with. You may also want to tell your mortgage provider why this is required. They may require your written authorisation before releasing the title deeds to your solicitor, which can cause further delay. They may also chase for copies if they will not release the originals at this stage. Most but not all of the key title documents (if your property is requested at the Land Registry) will be obtainable from the Land Registry for a small fee. You can save your solicitor (and therefore yourself) time if you know the title number.
2. The requirement to produce an EPC applies, whether or not you use an estate agent. So if you plan to sell your property through word of mouth, or the internet, or a small ad in a newspaper or via a website, you still need an EPC. It applies to all sales, including those by executors.

3. The EPC requirement also applies equally to lettings (see Chapter 7), so if in a difficult market for selling, you end up letting instead, the EPC will not be wasted. However, the potential tenant is even less likely to care about the contents than a potential buyer.

## Choosing and instructing a solicitor

You usually need to choose and instruct your solicitor about the sale at roughly the same time you are choosing the estate agent. He/she will need to co-ordinate with the estate agent to ensure that all three of you are ready at the right time.

Of course, if you used a solicitor at the time of buying the property, and were happy with him or her, the obvious thing is to go back to the same person or firm. Details of your particular property may well have slipped their mind among the hundreds of similar transactions they have dealt with since, but if there are any peculiarities it may have stuck.

If, however, you did not get on with the solicitor at the time of buying, or they have retired or moved or are not available for any other reason, you will need to find another. Whilst it is useful to have a solicitor who is local to your property and therefore more accessible to you, it is not as important that they are aware of local nuances as it would be for a purchase, so if you are moving to a different area and are not committed to a particular solicitor, it may be worth considering choosing someone with local knowledge at the buying end rather than the selling end. If not, then it is worth asking the estate agent for recommendations (it is in their interest to recommend the most efficient, so that the transaction happens and the fees get paid, rather than the cheapest but then that is probably what you want) or use word of mouth at the school gate or elsewhere. It is both conventional and sensible to use the same solicitor for the sale and any simultaneous purchase, because one of the key factors in keeping the process as smooth as it can be is the co-ordination of the timing for both exchange of contracts and completion. You do not want to be a message carrier at the most critical stage of the sequence.

You can of course compare prices for solicitors; be careful to ensure that you also compare add-on costs such as disbursements – some charge for photocopying, couriers etc, whilst others do not. Some will charge for a sale which falls through and others will not. VAT will be payable on all charges.

It may not be particularly important to have day-to-day physical accessibility to your solicitor (particularly if you work normal office working hours which will be similar to his or hers) but you do need accessibility by phone or email or in the case of the bulk conveyancing firms by an on-line updating system which they call transaction management.

The need for personal attention increases with the value and complexity of the property, and your circumstances, particularly if there is Death, Debt, Dementia or Divorce involved (see Chapter 6).

## Instructing your solicitor

You will usually contact the solicitor, tell him or her you are selling and want to instruct them, and then to provide various pieces of information to the solicitor so they can be ready to draft a sale contract when a buyer comes along. The first and most important thing they need is access to the title deeds which (if you have a mortgage) will be held by the lender. As mentioned above, that may need specific authorisation to the mortgage lender from you, and certainly will need identification in the form of a mortgage account or roll number. If you have second or third mortgages, the title deeds will be with the first lender, but it is probably tactful to tell all the lenders that you are marketing the property at the same time, particularly if you are under pressure from them.

An experienced conveyancing solicitor will be part of the Law Society's TransAction Scheme, which sets out a protocol on how solicitors deal with each other through the conveyancing process, which can allow some short cuts. Membership of the TransAction Scheme will usually be apparent from their website or notepaper.

Part of the TransAction process will be for you to complete two sets of replies to questionnaires. The first of these is in the form of a checklist, a fittings and contents questionnaire which forces you to be clear as to what is included in the sale by identifying what you will leave behind, what you will take with you, and what does not exist in your case (see the section on Fixtures and Fittings/Contents for guidance). The second is a more detailed questionnaire called a Seller's Property Information Form, which prompts you to find and produce to your solicitor a number of other pieces of information, for example the band the property is in for council tax purposes, details of your buildings insurance, any service contracts (such as burglar alarm or boiler maintenance), connections you have for telephones and telecoms, and anything more specific to the property such as planning permissions or building regulation approvals or tree preservation orders or consents you or any previous owners have obtained in the past to authorise changes. To the extent that they pre-date the time when you bought the property, copies of these documents should have been obtained at the time you bought (which is a good reason for going back to the same solicitor because their file should contain these) but this does not always happen. For a leasehold property, additional information will be required over and above the copy of the lease, such as copies of any consents you have obtained for carrying out alterations to the flat, anything relating to the ownership of the freehold, or a residents' association, proof you have paid the ground rent, and details of any service charges including any upcoming expenditure which you have not paid for yet.

Whilst this may be tiresome to gather and provide, bear in mind that this is all the information that you would want, or at least your solicitor would, if you were buying your property.

The reason for these questions is the underlying principle of English law of 'caveat emptor', Latin for 'buyer beware'. In other words, it is for the buyer to ask questions and you to give truthful answers, rather than for you to decide what the buyer needs to know and tell him so. That does mean that if you give false or inadequate answers you can be sued for damages, or if the errors are major then in extreme cases the contract to buy could be set aside. So, you have a duty to do the best you can in giving answers. However, if a question is not asked then you do not have to answer it. The Law Society is consulting on a number of changes in the conveyancing process, one of which would be to shift this balance so that sellers have a duty to disclose relevant information, rather than buyers having the opportunity to ask it.

Areas of difficulty in answering questions can be about 'disputes'. It can be difficult to be precise whether an argument over the garden fence about little Johnny breaking a window in your neighbour's conservatory is a dispute, but court proceedings about moving a boundary six inches one way or the other, or the height of trees, or objections to a planning application for an extension probably are. You may need advice from your solicitor as to what is appropriate to disclose.

Some buyer's solicitors did have the habit in the past of asking questions which were almost impossible to answer sensibly such as 'have there ever been trees on the property?'[38] or 'is there anything else about the property you should tell us?', but guidance from the Law Society and the adoption of standard form enquiries, particularly through the TransAction Scheme, has curbed this over-enthusiasm.

Bear in mind that if something changes in the answers given, either in the period up to exchange of contracts or between exchange and completion, you are bound to tell your solicitor about that and it is likely that he will be bound to tell the buyer's solicitor, because your answers (which have been treated as effective at the point of exchange) should not be wrong or misleading as at that point. Conventionally, and as part of the TransAction Scheme, the questions are repeated and the answers repeated immediately before completion so that any changes since you first answered the questions should be notified to your solicitor who, in turn, should tell the buyer's solicitor about any changes.

One point to bear in mind when instructing a solicitor who has not acted for you before, or indeed a solicitor who is now more aware of the Anti-Money Laundering Rules than he or she used to be, is that you are likely to be asked for evidence of your identity such as your passport, utility bills etc, and perhaps to meet face to face in a way which was not required when you bought.

The other element of the solicitor's work, apart from managing the transaction so that it actually happens, is to draft the sale contract, and the Land Registry transfer which is required at completion, and to liaise with your mortgage lender(s) so that they provide the necessary releases when they get repaid at the time of sale.

But we are getting ahead of ourselves: you don't have a buyer yet!

## Stage 2 – Deciding

### Offers and how to assess them

Offers will usually be made via your estate agent following one or two visits by the potential buyer to view the property. Your estate agent is duty-bound by his contract with you to tell you of any offers. You will expect his advice on

---

[38] Answer – according to the Domesday Book, yes.

how reasonable they are and whether they are final offers or could be improved. Depending upon the state of the market generally and the level of other viewings for your property in particular, you may wish to negotiate or to hold off responding.

There is an entire academic discipline denoted to the art of negotiation and tactics and strategies that may be adopted. However, it is unlikely that you are a professional negotiator, nor do you want to become one. Realistically, in most circumstances, the offer you receive will be close to but below the asking price. You need to decide is whether the margin is acceptable to you and leaves you with sufficient funds to purchase what you want. Of course, during 2008 the market strongly favoured buyers and it was all too easy for them to 'stick in a cheeky offer and see what happens'. Conversely, in 2005/2006, and at other times when the market is strong generally or a property is particularly desirable, there may be bids up to or even over the asking price, and competitive bids. If you are fortunate enough to be in this situation, it is increasingly common to go for 'sealed bids' where the bidders are given a time to bid by, they make their bids in a sealed envelope and then (usually) you and the agent open them together to determine who is the highest and best bidder.

It is important to establish, whether you have a single bid or multiple bids, how secure each of these may be: that is, whether the offer is dependent upon a mortgage offer, or the potential buyer selling their own property, and what the prospects of success are for that. Again, the agent should investigate and advise you on this so you are making a choice between bids, the strength of which you know.

You will also have your own opinion on the personalities of the bidders and the likelihood of them following through or backing out if you have met them yourself.

## Decision time!

It is important to be clear about what you are accepting and any conditions you may want to impose: for example, you may accept a price only on the basis that exchange takes place within a particular timescale; you may find that the offer is subject to you carrying out some repair work; it will almost always be subject to survey or a survey and valuation.

Again, your agent should advise you on the significance of all these points.

It is conventional, and important, for the offer to be accepted in writing even if it is not made in writing and again, your agent should deal with this. This should be 'subject to contract' so that neither you nor the buyer is bound at this stage legally. It follows that either of you can back out or re-negotiate the price or other terms at any time up to exchange of contracts.

If you have received competitive bids, and particularly if you have gone to sealed bids, you should ensure that those who are not successful are treated tactfully, as it is possible you may need to come back to them.

At this stage, you will need to be clear with your agent and with the buyer whether you are taking the property off the market. It is likely that the 'for sale' sign will stay up outside the property (although it may have 'under offer' on it), and the agent may mark it as being under offer on their own website. It is not uncommon (and annoying for the buyer) for the property details, including the asking price, to stay up on the various property websites it may have appeared on for weeks or months after their offer has been accepted.

Conversely, if you are not convinced about the ability or willingness of the buyer to deliver (perhaps because the buyer's offer is dependent on him/her selling their own property) it is reasonable to keep your property on the market until the buyer has a greater level of certainty in delivery.

At this stage, you will want to alert your solicitor so that he or she moves on with the sale process with the buyer's lawyer. A good test of the buyer's seriousness is to get their solicitor's details, which the agent should do at the time of sending out the confirmatory letter.

If you have not fully dealt with the paperwork side of the sales exercise, particularly the fixtures and fittings/contents list and the Seller's Property Information Form, now is the time to do so.

What if you are not using an agent, or you are working through a website? Simply put, you will receive and consider the offer yourself, and will make your own decision as to whether it represents full value, check the timing and conditions and confirm it in writing. It is vital to use the 'subject to contract' phrase, otherwise you could find you are inadvertently committed, at least to pay the buyer's costs, if you change your mind.

It is worth mentioning 'flirting' websites, where a buyer can make an offer on a 'what if' basis for a property whether or not it is on the market, and conversely a potential seller can put a suggested price on their house which might persuade them to sell. Examples are www.propertyhat.com or www.getanoffer.co.uk.

From a seller's point of view, bear in mind that if a buyer is using these routes to contact you, they will almost certainly have looked at one of the 'nosey neighbour' websites (listed on page 362) to get a sense of other prices in the neighbourhood of properties similar to yours.

## Exchanges of property

There are times when two buyers and sellers coincide, and find that they can meet each others' needs. For example, a couple with a growing family may want to move from a small house to a larger house with a garden and more bedrooms, at the same time as an 'empty-nester' couple may want to move out of their big detached family house to something smaller. The growing family would pay an amount to balance up the values of the two properties. This can work within a family, or it may by chance (or through the lateral thinking of a clever estate agent) happen between those who did not previously know each other.

Clearly, if both families find in this exchange what they are looking for, the buying and selling will be easier, and managing the timing of the move should be simpler.

Just to be clear, though, there is no tax advantage. For SDLT purposes the exchange will be treated as two separate transactions, at the values for each property bought. In the past, there was a tax advantage to exchanges like this, because tax was only due on the difference between the two values, but that is no longer the case.

## Exclusivity or lock out agreement?

As we have said, because sale and purchase transactions are 'subject to contract' during the period after a price has been agreed and before a contract is signed while the lawyers argue over detail, and surveys and mortgage arrangements are made, either party can still back out with no financial consequences. During the 'hot' market of 2006 into 2007, it became increasingly common for buyers to protect themselves by requiring a lock out or exclusivity agreement, which embodies a promise by the seller to stop marketing the property and not to accept any other offers for it, for a limited period of time. This tended to arise only on higher value or especially desirable properties but could if agreed apply to any property. It is an import from the commercial property world and before that from the world of buying and selling companies. Sometimes a non-returnable payment would be made for a period of exclusivity.

With the change in the market, these agreements are less common, but if the market becomes 'hot' again or a particular property is special and there is likely to be competition for it, then they will revive.

Some people assume that such agreements force the seller to exchange contracts at the defined price with that buyer. They do not: all they do is to create an agreement not to negotiate with or agree a price with or proceed with somebody else, so the measure of damages a buyer can get if the seller does in fact breach it is limited to the wasted costs the buyer incurs, which will normally be only survey and legal costs, including searches etc. From a buyer's point of view, such an agreement imposes a moral obligation not to proceed with anyone else, which most sellers would recognise and comply with, but not all. Conversely, there is little advantage from a seller's point of view in entering into such an agreement, because the buyer is not committed to proceed. The agreement may contain obligations on the buyer to instruct his lawyers to proceed and to make his mortgage arrangements and to instruct surveyors, but there is little practical enforceability in these. In reality, the pressure on the buyer under such an agreement comes from the length of the exclusivity period and the deadline that the end of it represents, rather than from any obligations the buyer has within it.

## Stage 3 – Getting to exchange

### Managing the process

Once you have accepted an offer, you have moved on to the third of the five stages of selling, getting to exchange. This stage is perhaps the most nerve-wracking because matters are in the hands of others – your solicitors, the buyer's solicitors, the mortgage provider and surveyor, and the buyers themselves (not to mention others in other parts of the chain, which we deal with in the next section). It is inevitable that time will pass with nothing appearing to happen, which can be extremely frustrating.

Things you can do to ensure that this painful period (which is likely, if there is no chain, to be six to eight weeks from the date of the agent's letter confirming the offer; if there is a chain, the period is entirely unpredictable) by making sure that you are 'on your game':

1. Make sure that your agent is aware of the timescale you want to work to, particularly if you have a timescale driven by your purchase and you want them to be simultaneous. If you have other time pressures like job start dates, family holidays or school term dates, ensure he or she is aware of those too.
2. Similarly, make sure your solicitor knows that the offer has been accepted, and the timescales and constraints on your own time that you may be working to.
3. Make sure the solicitor has all the necessary paperwork from you, including the details and addresses he needs to get information from others, such as your mortgage lenders and, if the property is leasehold, details of the managing agents and landlord to whom the ground rent, service charge, and insurance premiums are paid.
4. If your property is leasehold, particularly in a block of flats, and you have contact with the landlord or the residents' association or the managing agents, contact them to make sure that they know you are selling and are ready to answer the inevitable questions from your solicitor about service charges, insurance arrangements, upcoming works and payment of the ground rent.
5. If you have agreed to do any repair works, do them now rather than waiting – you do not want to do them under time pressure between exchange and completion, and you are likely to have to do them either for your own benefit or for any other buyer if this one falls through.
6. Be ready to arrange to allow the buyer's valuer and surveyor to look at the property, which they will need to do.
7. Be polite to the agent, your solicitor and the buyers if they are in contact, but not soft – you want to be helpful but you want the transaction to go through. With your solicitor, bear in mind that he or she has dozens of other people for whom their transaction is the most important event in the world, as well as you. He or she has a responsibility to keep you informed, and to make sure that your matter proceeds as fast as it can, but phoning

him or her every day is only going to be annoying. On the other hand, making no contact for weeks on end gives him or her the impression that you don't care. Assuming his or her main business is conveyancing, the busy times will be Fridays (when most completions happen) and Monday mornings (when an avalanche of post and emails tends to arrive, including new instructions from transactions agreed over the weekend) so arrange to be in touch at a convenient time midweek, once a week, to make sure you and he/she are both monitoring progress. Make the calls short.

8. If you sense that the buyer is slowing down (symptoms may be a delay in the buyer giving details to its solicitor, or that nothing happens about arranging surveys for a week or two) don't panic, but make sure the agent is aware of your concern; since they have a fee riding on the outcome they are likely to be motivated to push the buyer and can do so in a more dispassionate fashion than you can. They may also know the buyer's solicitor personally and can use that connection to assess how serious the buyer is or whether the buyer has problems (for example in getting mortgage finance) that the buyer has not disclosed to you direct.

## The legals

In formal terms, the process between the date you accept the offer and the date when you exchange is that:

1. Your solicitor drafts and issues the contract to the buyer's solicitor who will review and comment on it.
2. You will, through your solicitor, provide the replies to the pre-contract enquiries from the buyer's solicitor.
3. The buyer's solicitor may raise some additional points.
4. Various searches are carried out. The most significant and time consuming of these will be the local authority search. As seller, you can get your solicitor to do this and send it to the buyer's solicitors as part of the sales pack (as you would have done in the days of HIPs), so that the excuse commonly given by buyer's solicitors that they are waiting for the result of their local search will no longer wash. These used to take several weeks, even months in the case of a few councils which disagreed with the principle of house owning for ideological reasons or were exceptionally incompetent.[39]

---

[39] Surprisingly, it appears that Kensington and Chelsea is the slowest in England and Wales at present.

5. The buyer's solicitor will also review the Land Registry information proving your title to the property, and any other matters within it such as restrictive covenants or rights in favour of adjoining owners.
6. The buyer should finalise mortgage arrangements which will include their mortgage provider's valuation of the property which may well produce a figure lower than the price the buyer has agreed with you.
7. A well-advised buyer will also instruct a structural survey to be carried out, which (as we explained in the section on buying in Chapter 3) will test whether your property is sound and is likely to need short term or long term significant expenditure to keep it in good condition.

What if the mortgage valuation or the survey shows up problems? It will be pretty common for the mortgage valuer to apply caution to his or her valuation of the property and as a consequence for the buyer's mortgage company to limit its offer. This was particularly the case during 2008 when the market was falling. This may lead to a price re-negotiation.

Because the sale is still 'subject to contract', it is open to either you as seller or your buyer to re-negotiate the price, or withdraw altogether, and (subject to the terms of any exclusivity agreement, which may apply in relation to costs) the other cannot do anything about that, legally.

So, if the buyer's survey report throws up a problem (for example, damp, or the need for a new roof) which has not been allowed for in the originally agreed price, then the buyer is likely to seek an equivalent price reduction. Likewise, if the buyer's mortgage valuation shows a lower value than the buyer has agreed to pay so that the amount of the buyer's mortgage is reduced, the buyer may look to re-negotiate the price.

But there does not need to be a good reason for a change in the price the buyer is willing to pay, or the seller is willing to sell at. If the market is moving up fast, as it was in 2006, and the property is a desirable one, another buyer may come along and make a better offer; you as seller then have a moral decision to make whether you accept that higher offer – accepting that the new buyer is probably less ready to proceed than the first buyer – or offer the first buyer the opportunity to re-bid and maybe match the second bidder's higher price, or refuse to entertain late bids. Much will depend on your view of the morality of 'gazumping' as it is called, your confidence in either the first or the second bidder actually completing, and on whether you are being 'gazumped' yourself on the property you are buying.

Conversely, at a time when the market is falling and there are fewer buyers (as in 2008, for example) some brave or cheeky buyers reduced their prices as exchange of contracts approached, to snatch a bargain – 'gazundering'. From a seller's point of view, if this happens to you, you have a difficult choice between accepting a lower price now or maybe waiting for a long and uncertain time until another buyer comes along, with values falling further in the meantime.

These situations can be very painful, and are one of the main criticisms of the English conveyancing system.

However, the Office of Fair Trading has no better answer. According to their February 2010 market study on house buying and selling, roughly 20% of sales fall through between the time when an offer is accepted, and exchange of contracts, but they did not offer any improvements to the system.

## The chain

We have described the agony of the chain in Chapter 3 (see page 85) and we will not distress you by repeating that. If you sell and buy at the same time, the chances are that you will be in a chain. The only crumb of comfort is that as a seller you do have the option of completing on the sale (to achieve that certainty) and moving into rented accommodation temporarily while you either finish the process of buying the property you've already found, or find the property you really want.

We do not recommend the situation one of the co-authors found himself in, moving his family including two toddlers and a baby into a friend's house and all their furniture and goods into storage at three days notice because his sellers[40] reneged on their promise to sign, exchange and move out immediately. But it worked out in the end.

Assuming you get past this stage, you will need to prepare yourself for the move, on the assumption that the whole thing will go through smoothly;

[40] The three executors of an assassinated African dictator – based in three different countries and in hiding to avoid a similar fate – it's a long story.

presumably you will also be managing your purchase at the same time. If you are, you are likely to be focussed on that but there are things that you can usefully be doing in relation to the sale at the same time. In particular, clearing any clutter, which will be a bigger job than you expect (the last time we moved we finally threw away the spare nappies we bought for our now teenager). Lofts, garages and sheds are repositories for an astonishing amount of useless rubbish. Bear in mind you need to comply with legal requirements when disposing of certain items such as fridges, oil, batteries or gas canisters.

It is at this stage that lists become important – lists of things you are taking with you, lists of things you are leaving behind, lists of things you are going to throw away, lists of people to notify for official reasons when you move, lists of friends and family you need to tell about your new address, and lists of lists.

Subject to the pain of chains and the timing of any new purchase, the contract for the sale of your property will need signing with your solicitor say, four weeks after the agent's confirming letter. This should be the mirror image of the contract at the time of your purchase. There are unlikely to be many unusual obligations, although there will be a list of things you agree to leave behind, which you should check carefully, whether or not these are included in the price; there may be a couple of items you have agreed to do but have not yet done (that damned gate), and the key component to be agreed, which is the completion date.

Once signed, your solicitor will be able to exchange the agreement with the buyer when the buyer is ready and has also signed – and has their mortgage offer.

## Stage 4 – Getting to completion

Now your lists need to be refined and put into effect so that you:

1. arrange the removals;
2. dispose of everything you don't need (if you can get away with one skip you are doing better than we did);
3. arrange for the meters to be read on the day of completion;
4. gather, and label, all the keys;
5. make arrangements for moving day, including farming out children and pets;

6. (if you are anything like us) realise that the dishwasher you insisted on taking with you will not fit in the new house;
7. prepare the 'we have moved' address list for cards or email addresses for everyone, for each of the family;
8. read and digest the check list provided by the removers; and
9. pack everything you possibly can into packing cases before the big day. If you are not employing removers, hire a van and press-gang strong mates to help on the day.

Once contracts are exchanged, you and the buyer are both legally bound to complete – you to sell and to leave, the buyer to buy and to pay you. It is relatively rare for something to go wrong between exchange and completion, although there can be slippage as to a day or two on timing for some bureaucratic reason. Without wishing to depress you, things that can go wrong are:

1. there is a condition on a contract that needs to be satisfied. For example, on leasehold blocks of flats it is unusual but possible that the consent of the landlord is needed to transfer the lease. The timing of this may not be within your control and may cause delay; even less usually it might be refused if the buyer is not as respectable as you thought they were. You may have agreed to pay for indemnity insurance for a restrictive covenant: again, this could be delayed or, very unusually, refused. Something might come up on the final Land Registry search (in the days before the land registration system became widespread this was quite common but now is much less so) but if it does you are likely to have to make sure your solicitor deals with it before completion can take place;
2. rarely (but it did sometimes happen during 2008) the buyer's mortgage offer may be withdrawn leaving them without the funds to complete; or
3. (being really gloomy) the buyer could die or decide to split from his or her partner between exchange and completion. The chances are small but it does happen, and is extremely difficult for a seller to deal with.

## Stage 5 - The Great Moving Day

We have covered 'moving in' as part of Chapter 3 – see page 100. 'Moving out', and particularly 'moving in' and 'moving out' on the same day, is more of the same, so we will not repeat ourselves, but by way of emphasis, our 10 top tips are:

1. In advance, de-clutter, then de-clutter again, then de-clutter again. Be brutal. Freecycle.
2. Make sure with your lawyer you have signed everything and they have enough money for completion, and your mobile number(s).
3. Pack carefully and in advance.
4. Farm out children, pets and grandmas for the day.
5. Get your 'moving pack' together and keep it to hand.
6. Buy rubber gloves.
7. Have enough (grown-up) people around.
8. Exit in the am, eat lunch, enter in the pm.
9. Don't forget to read the meters (at both ends).
10. Afterwards, work out what you will do differently next time.

Depending on how nice a person you are, you might also think about what would make life easier for your buyer, such as:

- cleaning up, as much as you can;
- leaving a bottle of wine to help their move;
- leaving some large stamped, addressed envelopes with your new address;
- useful information such as guarantees for appliances, the days of refuse collection, the 'phone number of your decorator, doctor, dentist, hairdresser, etc; and
- the names of the neighbours.

# CHAPTER 5 MORTGAGES, TAXES AND PENSIONS

## Mortgages – origins and growth

One inescapable fact of modern life is that property in the UK is expensive. House prices generally have been rising for many years, and despite occasional periods of static or even falling prices, to purchase even a relatively modest property now presents most buyers – and particularly first time buyers - with a formidable financial challenge. In order to obtain a rough and ready insight into the magnitude of the problem, you simply need to compare an estimate of the average house price with that of the average salary: in October 2009, the Land Registry issued figures indicating that the average house price in the UK was £159,546 (house prices having fallen from a peak in January 2008, when the average house price was £184,203). Compare this figure with the average salary in the UK, which was approximately £26,000 for full-time workers,[41] and it can be seen that the average house cost approximately six times the average full-time worker's (gross) salary. Unsurprisingly therefore, most people contemplating a house purchase are obliged to borrow money, that is, to take out a mortgage, in order to be able to do so – and first time buyers in particular (who have not yet had an opportunity to build up equity in a home) often face the additional problem of raising a sufficiently large deposit as a pre-requisite to finding a lender willing to lend to them. The difficulties faced by would-be first time buyers constitute an increasingly serious social and economic problem, and we comment further on this issue below.

The concept of borrowing money by way of a mortgage in order to purchase property or otherwise raise funds is in fact an old one: landowners and property developers generally have been doing so for centuries. However,

[41] Figures released by the Office for National Statistics in November 2009 indicated that the median gross annual earnings for full-time employees for the tax year ending 5 April 2009 was £25,800. Of course, you have to be a little careful when quoting average figures: salary and house price figures vary considerably across different parts of the country (for example, in Cornwall, the average house costs eleven times the average full-time worker's salary in that county). But the principle is clear – for most people, houses cost many multiples of their salaries.

during most of that time, most people did not own land (and in practice had little or no opportunity of doing so). The idea that 'ordinary' people could own their own homes purchased by means of mortgages really only emerged into the popular imagination during the nineteenth century (and even then, it tended to be restricted to the middle classes and – as the century progressed – the better paid amongst the working classes) and was reflected by the explosion of domestic urban and suburban house building that occurred during the second half of that century and during the first decade of the twentieth. Having said that, it should be noted that even as late as 1900, 90% of all houses in the UK were rented from private landlords rather than occupied by their owners. Today, in contrast, approximately 70% of households are comprised of owner-occupiers, a far higher figure of home ownership than is found in many of our continental neighbours, where the tradition of lifetime property renting remains strong, and a ratio that most Victorians would have found staggering.

Tied to the process of increasing home ownership was the development of what became the building societies of the twentieth century, that is, financial organisations (originally generally local in scope and often temporary in duration, established to raise and lend mortgage funds to 'responsible borrowers'. As the twentieth century progressed, more and more people sought to purchase their own property, and mortgage lending rose accordingly. Towards the end of the century, building societies started to compete with, and even became, banks.

Today, mortgage funding is available in a wide variety of forms, and an understanding of the various types of mortgages, and their various advantages and disadvantages is vital to anyone contemplating a property purchase.

## The basic mortgage

A mortgage is, at its most basic, a form of lending whereby the borrower (known as the mortgagor), in exchange for the loan of money, grants to the lender (or mortgagee) certain legal rights – often referred to as a charge or security – over property, usually (but not necessarily) property that will be purchased using the borrowed funds. This is an area that can be legally complex, but essentially the security granted provides a degree of reassurance to the lender (usually a bank or a building society) that the money that has been loaned will be repaid in due course in accordance with the terms of the mortgage offer. Failure by the borrower to comply with the repayment terms can ultimately lead to the lender seeking to foreclose on the property: that is, the lender in such circumstances would have the right under the terms of the mortgage charge to take control of the property and to sell it, recouping its loan from the sale proceeds. Any balance of the sale proceeds in excess of the loan amount (and, typically, any outstanding interest and the expenses of the lender in seeking to enforce its charge) would be repayable to the borrower. Conversely, if the sale proceeds are less than the amount of the outstanding loan, the lender would usually have the right to pursue the borrower for the unpaid balance. Mortgages therefore should not be taken lightly; foreclosure by the lender can potentially lead to borrowers suffering substantial capital losses. In addition, a default on a mortgage can damage a borrower's credit rating and make it difficult for him or her to borrow money in the future.

## Mortgages and interest rates

Banks and building societies do not of course simply lend money by way of a mortgage out of the goodness of their hearts; they expect to make money by charging interest on the amount they lend until it has been repaid (and the mortgage 'redeemed'). Generally, the rates of interest charged in respect of a mortgage (a 'secured loan') will be lower than the interest rates charged in respect of unsecured borrowings (for example personal loans from a bank or a building society). There are various approaches that can be adopted in respect of mortgage interest rates; the types you are most likely to encounter include:

*Variable rate*

In the case of a variable rate mortgage, the interest rate charged is set by the lender by reference to its 'standard variable rate' – or SVR – which in turn is determined by reference to the Bank of England's base lending rate which is set at regular intervals by the Bank's monetary policy committee. Unsurprisingly however, SVRs are usually somewhat higher than the base lending rate (historically 2% higher than the base lending rate but since 2009 a 4% or even greater difference between the two has been more common). In theory, if there is a change in the base lending rate, this should be reflected in a change in the SVR. In practice, banks and building societies have been criticised for being slower to reduce their SVRs when the base lending rate falls than increasing their SVRs when the base lending rate rises. Indeed, recently some building societies have been criticised for announcing *increases* in their SVRs even though base lending rates have not changed.

Variable rate mortgages may in one sense be regarded as the default type of mortgage at least as far as interest rates are concerned; if you have a mortgage under which for a specific term, the interest rate is calculated by another mechanism (for example, a fixed rate mortgage as discussed below), then when that term comes to an end, the mortgage interest rate will usually revert to a variable rate automatically unless you proactively seek out a new mortgage deal.

*Tracker rate*

Tracker rate mortgages may be regarded as a variation of the variable rate mortgage; in this case, the interest rate tracks a specified standard rate (usually the Bank of England's base lending rate). The key aspect of a tracker rate is that (unlike a variable rate mortgage) it will change automatically as the base interest rate changes. The tracker rate will generally be set higher than the base rate by a specific amount – over recent years, as the base lending rate has fallen, the 'gap' between the tracker rate and the base rate has increased until now a gap of 2% or more is not uncommon. A few years ago, however, when interest rates were higher, some lenders offered tracker rates which were lower than the (then current) base lending rate. This has led in recent times to the phenomenon of some tracker rates turning to zero (or even negative) as the base rate has fallen. This in turn highlights a danger: base lending rates at the time of writing are now so low that there is little scope for any future reduction, and it is likely that that the next change to the base lending rate will be to increase it. This should be borne in mind if you are considering a tracker rate mortgage, and you should make sure you investigate how easy it will be to 'escape' from such a mortgage (that is, whether you can redeem the mortgage and replace it with another one without onerous exit penalties being applied) should you need to do so. (We would also add that as in the case of SVRs, some lenders have recently been criticised for raising the interest rates of their tracker mortgages.)[42]

---

[42] Usually citing some obscure small print in the back of their standard terms and conditions, notwithstanding that base lending rates have not themselves risen. To be blunt, apart from carefully considering whether and when you should or could switch

*Fixed rate*

As the name suggests, a fixed rate mortgage offers the mortgagor the advantage of having his or her interest rate fixed at a specified rate for a specific period of time; typically for two years though occasionally you may encounter some mortgage providers who are willing to offer fixed rate terms of longer duration, for example for three or five years. (In the United States, fixed rate mortgages can be found that last for as long as 25 years but such mortgages are effectively unknown in the UK.) The principal advantage of a fixed rate mortgage is that you know what your interest payments will be for the duration of the fixed term, and thus during this period will be unaffected should interest rates rise sharply. In times of economic uncertainty, this can be a considerable advantage. At the end of the fixed rate period, the mortgage will usually either revert to becoming a variable rate mortgage or the mortgagor may be offered the option (usually on condition of paying an arrangement fee) of fixing his or her mortgage again at whatever the prevalent fixed interest rate is on offer from their mortgage provider. A third alternative of course would be for the mortgagor to seek a new mortgage from a different provider. It is worth adding that a home owner with a fixed rate mortgage can sometimes get a shock at the end of their fixed rate period if rates have risen and the resulting increase in interest costs have not been allowed for. Conversely of course, anyone with a fixed rate mortgage will not benefit from falls in mortgage rates should any occur during the fixed rate period, though as previously noted, there is now less scope for further falls in mortgage rates than was the case a few years ago. In addition, fixed rate mortgages tend to be somewhat more expensive than comparable variable rate mortgages, not only in terms of the interest rate charged at the outset, but also in terms of fees. Early exit penalties from such mortgages can also be relatively high.

*Capped rates*

These are essentially a variation of the fixed rate model – interest rates are 'fixed' in that the mortgage provider promises they will not rise above a specified point for a fixed period (again, typically two years), but if mortgage

---

mortgage providers, there isn't a great deal that ordinary borrowers can do about this in the real world.

rates fall, at least some of the benefits of the fall will be passed on to the homeowner.

*Discounted mortgages*

In the case of a discount mortgage, the borrower is offered a discount or reduction in interest rate as compared to the mortgage provider's usual SVR (for example, 0.5% less than the SVR). The discounted mortgage rate will generally track movements in the SVR for a specified period of time. Such mortgages have been scarcer since the onset of the Credit Crunch.

## Payback time

Probably the most important thing to assess when considering whether to take out a mortgage or how much to borrow is the question of whether or not the mortgage is affordable. This is of course potentially a complex question; much depends on an individual's personal circumstances and likely future prospects, and there are various different factors which must be weighed and considered. Key issues can include:

How much will mortgage providers lend to me? Thirty or forty years ago, there was a general 'rule of thumb' answer to this question: most providers had strict rules which restricted the value of the capital sum a single borrower could borrow to three times his or her (usually gross) salary. In the case of a working couple, providers would usually lend three times the higher salary plus the other salary (or, occasionally, two and a half times combined (gross) income). Borrowers also often required would-be mortgagors to demonstrate that they could themselves contribute a fairly hefty deposit towards the purchase price of the property (either via savings or as a result of equity accumulation) before agreeing to provide a mortgage.[43] This generally sensible approach largely disappeared in the frenetic years leading up to the Credit Crunch, when providers were increasingly willing to provide borrowers with mortgage sums amounting to far more than three times salary – five, six or even seven times salary mortgages were not unknown. Coupled with this was the rise of the

---

[43] Indeed, in the 1960s and 1970s, mortgage providers effectively 'rationed' mortgages, agreeing to lend only specified amounts by way of mortgage every month, so many would-be first time buyers in those days – even if they could demonstrate that they could pay a deposit – were obliged to wait months or sometimes years before their 'turn' for a mortgage came.

'self-certified' mortgages, when would-be borrowers were simply asked to 'estimate' their likely salaries with little or no checking by the providers. For the self-employed, this did offer a degree of flexibility, and a lessening of the red tape surrounding the process of gaining a mortgage: however (probably inevitably) some borrowers were tempted to exaggerate their earnings considerably (sometimes with the encouragement of irresponsible mortgage advisers who of course stood to gain commission and/or fees from successfully concluded mortgage negotiations). The result of this was that some borrowers (not only in the UK but in many other countries too, most notably, of course, the United States) took out mortgages that they had little or no realistic chance of ever repaying, and as soon as economic difficulties arose, they began to default on their mortgage payments. In a remarkably short space of time, this led to the onset of the Credit Crunch. Today, mortgage providers are much more wary about lending excessive amounts by way of mortgage (indeed one complaint widely heard is that they may now be too cautious), and they are more likely to insist that borrowers only borrow a sensible proportion of their (verifiable) earnings (for example, three to four times). In view of the serious difficulties arising as a result of excessive borrowing, it is hard to characterise this retrenchment in attitude by borrowers as anything other than a good thing, even though it means (inevitably) that the difficulty of obtaining an affordable mortgage is yet another problem that would-be first time buyers must face.

Will I be required to provide a deposit? Coupled with the issue of what proportion of salary constitutes a sensible level of borrowing is the question of whether the mortgage provider will require the borrower to fund a deposit himself or herself; for example, to provide a lump sum equal to 10% of the purchase price of the property that the borrower wishes to buy (or putting it another way, is the mortgage provider only willing to provide on a 'loan-to-value' or 'LTV' ratio of 90% of the purchase price?). As we have previously noted, 30 or 40 years ago, a deposit would generally have been required. There have, however, been periods in the more recent past when the answer to the question of whether a deposit was mandatory would have been 'not necessarily'. At various times, most notably in the late 1980s and early 1990s, and (of course) again in the years running up to the onset of the Credit Crunch some – in fact many – mortgage providers were sometimes willing to provide '100% mortgages'; i.e. where no deposit was required, and the mortgage provider was willing to lend the entire purchase price. Indeed, on occasions some providers were willing to lend more than 100%. By no means was every borrower deemed suitable to receive such a mortgage (though many were) and inevitably, the price of such generosity was usually expensive arrangement fees (which were often simply added to the sum borrowed). Again, the onset of the Credit Crunch means that 100% mortgages are now far less common than they were and the answer today to the question of whether a deposit will be required is once again almost certainly yes. The principal reason for this, of course, is that a deposit by the borrower constitutes a 'safety net' of equity protecting the mortgage provider's interests in the event that there is a fall in house prices – if the value of the property in question falls 5% but the provider has insisted that the borrower funds 10% of the purchase price himself, the lender can still be reasonably certain of recovering its money in full should it be obliged to foreclose on the property for whatever reason. (The ability to provide a deposit - depending on how it has been accumulated of course! – may also give the mortgage provider some reassurance that the borrower is capable of saving appreciable sums of money over lengthy periods.) The amount of the borrower's deposit may affect the interest rate at which the loan can be borrowed; better rates may be available if the buyer has 25%, 35% or more of the purchase price available as a deposit. However, given current house prices, saving a sum of this size is no easy feat.

What type of interest rate mortgage should I consider? We have already described the principal types of mortgage that you may encounter. There is, however, another type of mortgage that we have yet to consider; namely 'interest-only mortgages'. In the case of an interest-only mortgage, the borrower only (initially) makes regular (usually monthly) interest payments to the lender and the capital sum that has been borrowed is not reduced by those payments. This immediately raises the question of how the capital sum is eventually to be repaid at the end of the mortgage term. There are, as we will see, a variety of possible methods of repaying the capital and the mortgage provider will need to be satisfied that that the borrower will eventually be able to repay the capital before it is willing to offer an interest-only mortgage. Interest-only mortgage are potentially dangerous in that it is all too easy for a borrower to pay too little attention to the need to repay the capital sum borrowed until it is too late to put in place a sensible plan for meeting this objective – in which case the borrower, as the end of the mortgage term approaches, may have to consider taking out yet another mortgage (if he or she can get one). It becomes harder (and potentially more expensive) to obtain a mortgage as one approaches retirement age. As an alternative, the borrower could consider selling the property and repaying the capital sum from the sale proceeds, but in this case the borrower would then have lost his or her property (which may very well be their home). Furthermore, if house prices have fallen with the result that the borrower has negative equity at the time the capital sum must be repaid, the sale proceeds alone will be insufficient to repay the capital sum in full, leaving the borrower in acute financial difficulties. On the other hand, used sensibly, interest-only mortgages can be helpful for buy-to-let investors, for example, establishing a property portfolio, since the need to fund only interest payments can help to alleviate potential cashflow difficulties in the first few years of the investment.

How is the capital sum repaid? This very much depends upon the type of mortgage you have. If the mortgage is a repayment mortgage, your monthly payments to the mortgage provider will include not only interest but also an element of capital repayment. Thus, with every month that goes by, you repay a little of the capital sum you initially borrowed. At first, almost all of your monthly payment will be interest, but as the capital sum diminishes, so too does the interest element of your monthly payment,[44] whilst the amount of capital you repay each month increases. If, however, you have an interest-only mortgage, your monthly mortgage payments will be pure interest, and you will have to find some other way of repaying the capital sum. Of course, there are various ways that this might be achieved – for example, by inheritance. However, most people who take out an interest-only mortgage also look for an associated savings vehicle which they hope to use to build sufficient savings to allow them to redeem their mortgage. One example of this (though one which has fallen into disfavour in recent years) is by means of an endowment policy.

*Endowment mortgages*

Historically, endowment mortgages were a popular means of funding property purchases. The borrower would take out an interest only mortgage, and at the same time enter into an endowment policy. An endowment policy is effectively a savings vehicle (but one which also offers some life assurance protection)

[44] This of course ignores the effects of possible rises in interest rates.

which operates for a fixed period of time (typically, but not necessarily, as long as the mortgage period). In addition to making (interest only) mortgage payments, the borrower would also pay premiums in respect of the policy, the intention being that over time, the value of the investments under the endowment policy would grow with the result that when it came time to redeem the mortgage, the proceeds of the endowment policy would be sufficient (or even more than sufficient) to meet this cost. Furthermore, if the borrower died before the mortgage term expired, the life assurance element of the endowment policy would generate a (tax free) lump sum that would be available to pay off the outstanding mortgage. At one time, endowment policies were very popular (their popularity enhanced by the fact that until the mid-1980s, a degree of tax relief was available in respect of policy premiums – this relief is no longer available). Their popularity has diminished in recent years, partly because they are less tax-advantageous than they were, and partly because it was (eventually) realised that they are in fact fairly risky investment products at least for someone who is using them to fund the purchase of their home (since they typically involve (indirect) investment in stock markets). Moreover, many were sold on the basis of projected investment returns which now (partly with the benefit of hindsight) seem extremely optimistic thanks to changing financial circumstances and especially reduced levels of inflation, and it is now apparent that many are unlikely to generate sufficient money to pay off the mortgages to which they relate. Furthermore, endowment policies generally require regular fixed premium payments, and there is usually little scope to reduce or miss premium payments for a temporary period in the event of, for example, temporary financial difficulties. Probably inevitably, some holders of endowment mortgages eventually complained that they had been sold them without a full appreciation of all the risks, and the alleged mis-selling of endowment policies became a major financial scandal a few years ago (much as the alleged mis-selling of personal pension schemes did a few years earlier). Today, few mortgage advisers would recommend endowment policies as a means of funding home mortgage payments alone. Having said that, a large number of people still have endowment mortgages, and thus potential problems if the projected returns from their endowment policies are less than their outstanding mortgages. Anyone in this position should now be giving urgent thought (if they have not already done so) to how they will meet any shortfall that may arise when their mortgage term expires, and should seek appropriate financial advice. Making matters worse, whilst endowment policies can usually be surrendered before the end of their terms, surrender values are often quite poor. Again, it is usually advisable to seek appropriate financial advice before deciding to terminate an endowment policy.

Endowment mortgages are sometimes referred to as 'investment mortgages' since you invest under an arrangement that is distinct from the interest only mortgage in order to accumulate the sum you will eventually need to pay off the mortgage capital sum itself. Another type of investment mortgage, again one which enjoyed a brief flurry of relative popularity in the early and mid-1990s but which has diminished in popularity in recent years is the pension mortgage. In the case of a pension mortgage, instead of investing via an endowment policy, the borrower contributes to a pension scheme – typically (but not necessarily) a personal pension scheme. This type of mortgage relies on the fact that pension schemes – provided they satisfy certain requirements – allow the member, when he is able to take his pension benefits (for example, upon retirement) to take part of his benefit entitlement in the form of a tax-free lump sum. Broadly speaking, a pension scheme member can take up to 25% of the capital value of his accumulated pension entitlement in tax-free lump sum. The intention of course is that the tax free lump sum will be used to pay off the mortgage.

Pension mortgages have certain advantages. In particular, they are relatively tax efficient, since (unless you earn more than £130,000[45]) you can usually claim tax relief on contributions you pay to the pension scheme with the result that you pay such contributions out of gross income rather than taxed income – an important potential saving – and if your employer also contributes, to the pension scheme you will generally not be taxed upon your employer's contributions; i.e. they will not be treated as constituting a 'benefit in kind' liable to income tax or national insurance contributions. Income and capital gains made by your pension scheme will also generally accumulate tax free. Moreover, they have the advantage of encouraging pension savings – with a pension mortgage not only are you contributing to paying off your mortgage but you are also saving for your retirement.

---

[45] Even if you earn more than £130,000, you can still usually enjoy a degree of tax relief on contributions paid to pension schemes.

However, there are also certain disadvantages. Like endowment mortgages, they are relatively inflexible; indeed in some respects, they are even more so – as a general rule, unless you are taken seriously ill, you are not permitted to access your pensions savings until age 55. Thus a pension mortgage is generally not suitable if you want to use the resulting lump sum to pay off your mortgage before you reach that age. In addition, people tend to underestimate how expensive pensions can be, and how difficult it can be to accumulate a pension entitlement that will generate anything like a sufficient income for retirement. Relying on your 'pensions pot' to also pay off your mortgage as well as providing retirement income will make that task even harder (though of course there is also the simple fact that if the tax free lump sum is not used to pay off the outstanding mortgage, that debt must be satisfied by some other means). In addition, there is no guarantee that your pension entitlement at retirement will in fact generate a sufficiently large tax free lump sum to enable you to pay off your mortgage. This is especially true in the case of 'money purchase schemes' (such as personal pension schemes) where the investment risks of the pension scheme are borne by the individual member, but it is also true in the case of 'final salary schemes' where a member's pension entitlement is calculated by reference to a 'pre-set formula' – after all, even if you are a member of a final salary scheme (sadly an increasingly unlikely probability), there is in reality no guarantee that your employer will keep that scheme in operation until your retirement, or that the benefits provided under the scheme will not be reduced in the future. (This, of course, is also true of endowment mortgages – indeed it is will be true for all investment mortgages where the borrower is relying on an arrangement which operates on the basis of investments that can rise and fall – that is, the investment returns may prove insufficient to allow for full mortgage repayment).

There is yet a third form of investment mortgage that we should briefly note: namely the so-called ISA mortgage. As you might expect, in this case, the borrower takes out an interest-only mortgage and then makes contributions to an ISA, with the intention that over time, he or she will accumulate sufficient ISA savings to allow their outstanding mortgage to be repaid. The ISA mortgage has the advantage that it is more flexible than either an endowment mortgage or a pension mortgage – for example, the borrower can increase or decrease (or even temporarily cease) contributions to the ISA depending on his or her personal circumstances (though in the case of an undisciplined saver, this may not in fact prove to be an advantage). Moreover, the ISA too enjoys certain tax advantages (though not quite as generous as those enjoyed by pension schemes)[46], and the borrower can access his or her ISA funds at any time – they are not restricted by an age limit of 55 as in the case of a pension mortgage. However, again the borrower will be running the risk that at the end of the day, the accumulated ISA savings are insufficient to pay off the mortgage in full.

Another point to bear in mind when considering mortgage affordability is that in addition to meeting your regular mortgage payments (whether interest only or otherwise), there will also be mortgage fees to pay. These (broadly speaking) are fees associated with taking out and paying off mortgages and they have risen sharply in recent years. They can take various forms (and often assume a variety of names); nevertheless it is important to take them into account when assessing the affordability of any particular mortgage offer, and when comparing one provider's offerings with another. Typical examples include:

*Arrangement/booking fees*
Lenders give this fee different names, but essentially it is the fee lenders charge for arranging to provide you with a mortgage. Typically such fees can range from around £600 - £800, but fees in excess of £1,000 are not unknown.

*Early repayment/exit fees*
The value of these fees can vary quite dramatically from provider to provider, and from mortgage deal to mortgage deal, and thus it is wise to obtain a clear understanding of the likely charges you may face in the event that you wish to pay off your mortgage early before you take it out.

*Valuation fees*
Lenders will want to assess what they think the property you wish to borrow against is worth, and will usually instruct a surveyor to conduct a valuation of the property, passing the costs of this exercise to the borrower. Again the likely size of this charge varies between providers, but is often calculated by reference to the value of the property in question.

---

[46] For a more detailed description of how ISAs, pension schemes and endowment policies operate, please see our sister volume: *Money and Work: An Essential Guide*.

*Higher lending charge fees*

These are fees imposed by some lenders on people who wish to borrow more than 75% of the value of the property in question. Others only impose it if the proposed mortgage has a 'loan to value' or 'LTV' of more than 90% (that is where the borrower is providing a deposit that is less than 10% of the purchase price). The fee will usually be calculated by reference to the amount of the mortgage, and can amount to several thousand pounds. Again, if this fee applies in your case, you should make sure you fully understand how it is to be calculated before entering into the mortgage.

At the end of the day, it is the responsibility of each borrower, having regard to his or her own set of circumstances, to decide which form of mortgage and how large a mortgage is most appropriate for them. In case of doubt, there is much to be said for seeking independent financial advice before entering into a mortgage. The web offers various sites which can provide you with the names of independent mortgage advisers (see for example www.unbiased.co.uk ) as well as sites that allow you to compare current mortgage products on offer by various providers[47] and these are often well worth visiting. As previously noted, interest-only mortgages can in certain circumstances play a useful role, particularly where cash flow in the period immediately following the purchase is of crucial importance; however, if an interest-only mortgage is chosen, it is critically important that the borrower has a realistic plan as to how he or she will eventually repay the mortgage sum borrowed. Given the difficulties in saving a large sum 'outside' the confines of the mortgage arrangements (and recognising the investment risks which accompany this exercise), many borrowers in fact elect to utilise a repayment mortgage. And there is nothing wrong with that.

There is one more point which we should consider before turning our attention to matters of tax, namely the simple question: if I can afford to pay off my mortgage early, should I do so? On the face of it, this seems a simple question, and yet opinion is sometimes divided on the topic. Anyone who hates the concept of being in debt would no doubt immediately answer yes, provided certain basic criteria (which we discuss below) are satisfied. However, not every commentator agrees with this. In particular, some financial advisers in

---

[47] See for example www.moneysupermarket.com/mortgages/ and www.fool.co.uk/

the past (and even today, sometimes, in the United States) argue that in fact there are still some advantages in borrowing as large a sum as possible. They essentially do (or did) this for two reasons. Firstly, in the past, tax relief was available in respect of interest payments on domestic mortgages (such relief was created in 1969 but abolished in the United Kingdom in 2000; in the United States, such relief is still available). Tax relief inevitably had the effect of making mortgages more affordable, thus allowing people (at least in principle) to buy larger and potentially more valuable homes than they might otherwise have been able to do. And secondly, purchasing a home is a long term project. In the past, when general inflation was high, whilst inflation brought many disadvantages, it did have one advantage from the perspective of mortgage borrowers – namely the 'size' of their mortgages seemed to diminish in size as prices (and to an extent, pay) rose. Thus over time, what might have seemed a large mortgage in the first year or two diminished in relative terms compared to income growth and price inflation (including of course the value of the property itself). Thus the argument went that you should take out as large a mortgage as you could, but then keep it on the basis that inflation would over sufficient time make its (eventual) repayment a relatively easy task. True, the absence of high inflation over recent years has somewhat weakened the latter argument, but it is by no means impossible that high inflation could yet return – indeed many economic commentators think that it is quite likely.

Be that as it may, there are nevertheless some very good reasons why repaying your mortgage early is a good idea – subject, that is, to the satisfaction of certain points. To begin with, owning your home mortgage-free provides a useful degree of security – both for yourself and for your family. It also means that the full value of your house is freely available should you want to access it for whatever reason – for example, should you decide to tap some of your house equity by borrowing against it in order to assist in the purchase of a second property in due course. It is also worth adding that paying off your mortgage early is a significant personal achievement and one that is not achieved by many people under the age of 50.

Having said all this, the principal advantage of paying your mortgage off early is the saving you will make in interest payments – the earlier you can redeem the mortgage the greater those savings will be – and various financial websites provide useful (and sometimes strangely beguiling) calculators which allow you to investigate the various savings you can make by increasing your regular mortgage payments (assuming you have a repayment mortgage) and thus accelerating the rate at which you are repaying the borrowed capital sum. The potential savings can be dramatic. However, it is important to stress that generally speaking, mortgage interest is generally cheap interest – mortgage interest rates are usually lower than those for unsecured loans, and much lower than the interest rates typically charged by credit card companies. If a borrower has large (non-mortgage) interest debts in respect of which the interest rates are higher than his or her mortgage rates, then as a general rule,[48] it would be better to pay off the more expensive non-mortgage debt first, ideally starting with those debts with interest payments at the highest rate(s). But in the absence of such factors, if you can afford to pay your mortgage off early it would usually be worth considering doing so.

## Tax

Property issues frequently require a consideration of tax and tax-related issues. In this section, we outline some of the tax issues which may be encountered when buying, selling or renting out property in the UK. Inevitably, this is a potentially complex area, and we are able to provide only a broad overview of some of the tax-related issues that you may encounter. Where appropriate, you should consider seeking specialised advice.[49]

This section deals with tax as at 30 June 2010, i.e. post-General Election and 'emergency Budget'. Further changes are likely later in 2010.

### Stamp duty

The buyer of a property is liable to HM Revenue & Customs ('HMRC') for stamp duty (strictly speaking 'stamp duty land tax' or SDLT) on completion of the purchase of the property, assuming the price exceeds the SDLT threshold which is currently £125,000 for residential property. For non-residential property (which can include commercial property such as shops and offices,

---

[48] And here we would add the usual warning that this book does not purport to provide investment advice and independent financial advice should always be sought where appropriate. Nevertheless, we are right.

[49] Given the complexities and the wide scope for the interactions of differing tax regimes, we have not attempted to summarise the tax treatments that you may encounter when buying, selling or letting abroad.

agricultural land, forests and any other land which is not used as a dwelling) or 'mixed use property' (that is, property that incorporates both residential and non-residential elements), the threshold is £150,000. SDLT rates for residential property as at March 2010 are as follows:

| **Purchase Price** | **SDLT Rate**[50] |
|---|---|
| Up to £125,000 | 0% |
| Over £125,000 up to £250,000 | 1% |
| Over £250,000 up to £500,000 | 3% |
| Over £500,000 | 4% |

It is worth noting that if six or more residential properties are purchased as part of a single transaction, they will be deemed to be non-residential property for the purposes of determining any SDLT liability. However, if you ever find yourself in the interesting position of buying six houses or flats simultaneously, you should note the points we make below about SDLT and 'linked transactions'.

The rate at which SDLT is charged generally depends upon the purchase price of the property, but is applied to the whole of the price, so as the property price increases, there are sudden 'jumps' in the SDLT that is payable. For example, the purchase of a residential property for £250,000 would attract an SDLT levy of £2,500 (i.e. 1% of £250,000), but the purchase of a property for £251,000 would attract an SDLT levy of £7,530 (i.e. 3% of £251,000).[51]

Having said this, in certain circumstances, special SDLT rates can apply. This can be a complex area, but your solicitor should be able to advise you if any non-standard SDLT rules will apply to you. Examples of where this could occur include:

---

[50] Between 3 September 2008 and 31 December 2009, the SDLT threshold for residential property was temporarily raised to £175,000 in an attempt to mitigate the impact of the Credit Crunch: however, this temporary easing of SDLT rates ended on 1 January 2010. Following the Budget in 2010 first time buyers can claim relief from SDLT on residential transactions up to £250,000 between 25 March 2010 and 25 March 2012. Also, Alistair Darling announced that the SDLT rate for residential properties worth more than £1 million would increase to 5% in 2011. It remains to be seen whether the Coalition Government will change this.

[51] At this point HMRC might take a close interest in the amount of the purchase price attributed to fixtures and fittings (see page 75).

1. If the residential property in question is located in an area deemed by the Government to be disadvantaged. In this case, the SDLT threshold is £150,000 rather than £125,000.

2. If there is a series of 'linked transactions': for example, if a buyer purchases three properties simultaneously from a property developer. If this occurs, HMRC could deem them to constitute one transaction even though strictly speaking there are three separate purchases. In this case, SDLT would be chargeable on the aggregate value of the properties, rather than individually in respect of each transaction, possibly resulting (depending upon the actual purchase prices of the individual properties) in a higher SDLT liability than would otherwise have been the case.

3. If the house in question is a zero-carbon home. Since October 2007, any house qualifying as a zero-carbon home will be exempt from SDLT when purchased provided the purchase price is less than £500,000. For zero-carbon homes bought for £500,000 or more, the SDLT levy is reduced by £15,000. To qualify as a zero-carbon home, the building must be connected to mains electricity and gas but itself generate (by means of renewable energy sources such as solar power) sufficient energy to meet the household's average energy consumption over the year. In practice, very few houses have qualified as zero-carbon homes since this relief was introduced (indeed, in January 2009, the Labour Government admitted that the total amount of relief granted in respect of zero-carbon homes was approximately £70,000); nevertheless, more houses may qualify as zero-carbon homes as renewable energy and home insulation technologies improve over the next few years.[52]

SDLT is payable to HMRC within 30 days after the completion of a property purchase. In practice, your solicitor will usually arrange for the payment to be made on your behalf and you will need to ensure that you provide him with sufficient sums in order to allow him to do so.

---

[52] Further details can be found on HMRC's website at: www.hmrc.gov.uk/sdlt/rates-thresholds.htm

## Income tax

Income tax considerations will arise whenever you use your property to generate an income, for example if you rent it out to tenants under an assured shorthold tenancy, or a holiday let. Broadly speaking, you will be taxed on any income you may generate at your marginal rate subject to the usual income tax rules. Again, however, special rules apply in certain circumstances.

*Rent a room scheme*

For example, if you rent out furnished accommodation in your only (or principal) home to a lodger and your total income from this source (for example, rent plus any other income from meals, laundry service etc) – but excluding expenses – is £4,250 or less, this income is treated as being tax free under the 'Rent a Room Scheme'. However, if the income so generated exceeds £4,250, you can choose between either paying tax on your actual profits (i.e. total gross income less expenses and capital allowances (which we discuss below)) or simply on the gross income in excess of £4,250 but without the benefit of any deductions.

*Rental income*

If you rent out UK property (other than as part of the Rent a Room Scheme), various expenses and allowances can be deducted from your rental income when determining your taxable profit (or loss). Essentially, HMRC consider a property rental to be a business for tax purposes and treat it accordingly. Depending upon your personal circumstances, you may wish or need to seek appropriate specialised tax advice when considering such matters; however in broad terms, allowable expenses include:

- Letting agent's fees
- Accountant's fees (and in certain limited circumstances, legal fees)
- Buildings and contents insurance
- Rent and service charges
- Interest payments on property loans (which need not be secured on the rental property provided they have been entered into as a consequence of your 'rental business' for example where you borrow against your home to fund a 'buy-to-let' property – you may need to demonstrate this to HMRC). However, you cannot claim for any element of capital repayment in connection with such loans.
- Utility bills

- Council tax
- Maintenance and repairs

You cannot claim for any 'personal' expenses; i.e. expenses that are not connected with establishing or operating your 'rental business'. Furthermore, if any otherwise allowable expense is only partly connected with your rental business, or if you on occasions use the property yourself, you may only be able to claim part of the expenses that would otherwise have been allowable. Expenses must be allocated to the year to which they apply for tax reporting purposes, regardless of when they are actually paid.

If the annual income (before the deduction of allowable expenses) from your rental property is less than £15,000, then you can simply report the total expenses on your tax return. If, however, your total rental income exceeds £15,000, HMRC will require you to provide a breakdown of your expenses. Thus as a landlord, it is vitally important to ensure that all your paperwork is in order and that you keep copies of all relevant receipts.

In addition to expenses, there are various 'allowances' that you may be able to claim in order to reduce your taxable income from your rental property. Again, this is a complex area. As an example of the allowances that might be available, if you rent out furnished accommodation, you can usually claim a 'wear and tear' allowance for furniture and equipment, the allowance being 10% of the net rent (i.e. rent less allowable expenses). Alternatively, you may be able to claim a 'renewals allowance' (but as a general rule you can't claim both a renewals allowance and a wear and tear allowance simultaneously, and having made an election for one or another in one year, you cannot change your mind and select the other until the following year). The renewals allowance is intended to cover the cost of replacing items used in your rental business, such as kitchen equipment or furniture. Broadly speaking, it is calculated by taking the cost of the replacement item and deducting from it:

- any payment you may have received when disposing of the original item; and
- if the replacement item is a 'better model' than the item it is replacing, any element of the purchase price of the new item that is attributable to that improvement.

In addition, you can usually also claim a capital allowance on the cost of items which are needed in the operation of your rental business, such as cleaning and gardening equipment. The amount of allowance you can claim depends on the item in question – for some items deemed environmentally friendly, you may be able to claim 100% of your expenditure. Usually however you can claim 50% of the purchase price of the relevant item when it is bought, and each year after that, a specified percentage of what is left, such as 25%, though you should note that HMRC varies the permitted percentage figure from time to time. Again, if you sometimes use the relevant item for personal purposes, the extent to which you can claim an allowance will be reduced by HMRC.

Lastly, if your rental business is operating at a loss, you can usually 'carry forward' such loss for tax reporting purposes and offset it against profits which you enjoy from your residential property business (but not against any other income you may enjoy) in a later year.

Given the complexity of the UK tax system generally, and particularly in relation to property matters, it is unsurprising that many landlords require the assistance of financial advisers when completing their tax returns.

*UK furnished holiday lets*

We ought to pause briefly here and mention the tax treatment of UK holiday lets. Provided they satisfy certain criteria, holiday lets enjoy a more generous tax regime than ordinary 'residential lets'; for example, losses can be offset against all of the landlord's income, not just that deriving from the holiday let itself. This more favourable regime is commonly known as the Furnished Holiday Lettings Rules or FHL Rules. In the 2009 Budget, it was announced that the FHL Rules might not be compliant with European law (since the more favourable treatment only applied to landlords operating furnished holiday businesses in the UK and not elsewhere in the European Economic Area, or EEA), and consequently the Labour Government decided to abolish the FHL Rules with effect from April 2010. This change did not become law as it was lost in the pre-Election 'wash-up'. In the 'emergency Budget', George Osborne said the FHL Rules would be left as they are.

## Capital gains

A capital gain is essentially the profit that can be made by purchasing an asset at one price and subsequently selling it at another (higher) price, or otherwise disposing of it. Similarly, a capital loss is the financial loss incurred when an asset is sold for a price that is lower than the original purchase price. As a general rule, subject to certain exemptions (for example, property transfers between spouses or civil partners are not subject to capital gains tax ('CGT')), individuals are liable to CGT on any capital gains they make (above a CGT annual exempt amount which is set each year), after allowing for any capital losses they may have incurred in any particular tax year. Following the 'emergency Budget', the CGT rate is 18% for basic rate taxpayers and 28% for higher rate taxpayers, and the annual exempt amount is £10,100 (for individuals, personal representatives and trustees for disabled people).

CGT issues can arise in respect of property disposals. However, if you are selling your principal residence (that is, your main home) you will not be liable to CGT on the proceeds of the sale provided you qualify for full private residence relief. In order to qualify for this relief, the property being sold must be your only or main home, and used only for residential purposes. However, this relief may not be available (or not available in full) if your garden or other land associated with the property and the house itself exceeds 5,000 square metres, or if any part of the home has been used exclusively for business purposes[53] or if you have let out part or all of the property. (Having said this, if you have been renting out part or all of your property, you may be entitled to another form of relief known as 'letting relief.')[54]

Even if you are no longer living at the property when the time comes for you to sell it, you may still be able to qualify for private residence relief provided not more than three years have passed since you moved out (or it otherwise ceased to be your principal residence), if the property was your main home from when

---

[53] If you are self-employed and work from home, you can still qualify for private residence relief when your home is sold (assuming of course that it would otherwise qualify for the relief in any event) provided you still use the entire property for residential purposes. If, however, you use part of the property solely for business purposes (for example, an outbuilding that has been converted into an office used in your business, or for storing business goods) then CGT may be chargeable on at least part of any gain you may make upon the sale.

[54] A short description of how this relief operates may be found on HMRC's website at www.hmrc.gov.uk/cgt/property/sell-own-home.htm

you first bought it and you would otherwise have qualified for private residence relief had you not ceased to live there.

If you have been absent from the property because you have been working abroad for some or all of that three year period, you will be treated as if you had continued to live in your UK-based property and thus still be entitled to private residence relief provided that before and after you moved abroad you lived in the property and you have no other property that qualifies for private residence relief.

A question that often arises is how CGT is calculated when a person owns (and lives in) more than one property. Such a person can contact his or her Tax Office and nominate one of the properties as their principal residence for CGT purposes, regardless of whether or not they are actually living in the property chosen at the time of the nomination. The nomination must be made within two years of changing the number of properties in which you live (regardless of whether you are increasing or decreasing the number of properties). If you fail to make a nomination, HMRC will effectively decide which property should be treated as your principal residence on the basis of the facts. For a couple who are married or in a civil partnership who own two or more properties between them, any nomination must be made jointly and in writing. Private residence relief will only be available on one home per couple at any one time.

As we have previously noted, property transfers between spouses or civil partners will generally not be chargeable to CGT. Transfers to children or grandchildren (even if intended as a gift) will not generally be exempt and thus can attract CGT charges. If you are contemplating making such a gift, we would recommend that you seek appropriate financial advice before doing so.

What if you purchased the property (in your name) for the use of another person (for example, an elderly relative) to live in and do not live in it yourself? In this case, as a general rule, you will not be eligible for private residence relief, and CGT will be chargeable on any gain you may make on the sale. However, just to complicate matters, if you bought the property before 5 April 1988 for the (rent-free) use of an infirm relative who is unable to live independently, or a mother or mother-in-law,[55] and subject to the satisfaction of other criteria beyond the scope of this book[56] private residence relief may still be available to you. This loophole does not apply in respect of property purchases made after 5 April 1988.

There is no exemption from CGT on the sale (at a profit) of a property which you have rented out, if you have never lived in that property as a main residence.

### Income from commercial property

For an individual, income and capital gains received from direct commercial property letting are taxed like any other income (although the system of allowances may need specialist advice). Income from shares in certain publicly quoted property companies known as Real Estate investment Trusts or REITS is treated differently from income from shares in other companies, because REITS have certain tax benefits - see page 271 for an explanation.

## Property and pensions

Lastly (at least in this chapter) we want to say a few words about the interaction of property and pension schemes, if only because for most people, the two largest financial assets they are likely to acquire during their lives are their home and their pension scheme.

Some people of course have chosen to avoid 'traditional pension schemes' as a means of saving for their retirement, and instead have chosen to invest in buy-to-let property or other property-related investments, as a means of ultimately funding their retirement income. They do so typically for a variety of reasons: some because they prefer to retain (personal) control of their assets, and dislike the fact that investing in pension schemes restricts their ability to freely access their investments whenever they wish[57], whilst others cite the ever-increasing complexity of the UK's private pensions system. Still others point to charges

---

[55] It has to be a mother or a mother-in-law we are afraid (whether or not she is infirm). Apparently, fathers and fathers-in-law do not count for these purposes unless infirm.

[56]But see www.hmrc.gov.uk/helpsheets/hs283.pdf for further information.

[57] As a general rule, a member of a registered pension scheme (that is one that enjoys the usual tax advantages that pension schemes typically enjoy) cannot enjoy the benefit of his or her accrued pension rights under that scheme until the age of 55, save in the case of serious ill-health.

levied by pension scheme providers and advisers for the services they provide. These are perfectly sensible reasons for avoiding traditional pension schemes, but it should be pointed out that there are some drawbacks in saving for retirement (solely) by means of personal property investments.

In particular, even today, registered pension schemes such as occupational or personal pension schemes enjoy substantial and valuable tax breaks (albeit that at the time of writing, the Labour Government has started to whittle away at those advantages, particularly for high earners). For example, as a general rule, income and capital gains enjoyed by a pension scheme on its investments are largely exempt from taxation, and members of such schemes also enjoy tax reliefs (subject to certain limits) on contributions paid not only by them but also by their employer. Furthermore, upon retirement, members are usually offered the opportunity of taking 25% of their 'accrued pension entitlement' in the form of a tax-free lump sum – which is generally considered a valuable benefit indeed.

As previously noted, whilst it is true that there are various tax exemptions that can apply in respect of property investments, these are not as all-encompassing as those that apply in respect of registered pension schemes. Consequently, avoiding pension scheme saving entirely means that these potential advantages are lost. In addition, the 'flexibility' argument which is sometimes cited as a reason for relying solely on property investment as a means of retirement saving is open to challenge in at least two respects. First, whilst it is true that there are no age restrictions that prevent a person from realising profits from property (and furthermore, there is no requirement that the proceeds of the sale must ultimately effectively be used to purchase an annuity, which is one of the bugbears of the UK's private pensions system), property is not a completely liquid investment and there may be various reasons why a property owner cannot realise his investment immediately should he or she need to do so. Secondly, the fact that pensions savings cannot be 'raided' prematurely (and must be used for retirement benefit purposes only) can be regarded as a plus point – once the money is in a pension scheme, it cannot be applied for other purposes, possibly jeopardising the member's retirement income in the process (there may of course be other reasons why a member's pensions savings ultimately prove unequal to the costs of retirement but that is beside the point). Ultimately, whether a pure 'pensions savings' regime or a pure 'property-savings' regime is the best approach to adopt for retirement savings purposes will depend on a variety of factors, including the temperament and financial resources of the relevant individual and his or her long term goals and wishes. For many, it may be that a combination of the two approaches may prove the best approach to adopt. In any event, it will always be wise to regularly review the approach taken with (where appropriate) the benefit of specialist advice.

As regards those who have joined or otherwise 'taken out' a pension scheme, a typical question that often arises is whether an individual can use his or her pension scheme to invest in residential property. Here, we are usually considering pension schemes which allow the individual member (or members) of the scheme the opportunity to dictate (or at least influence) the scheme's investment policies. Most schemes (for example, employer-sponsored occupational pension schemes typically comprising many members of a workforce) do not offer members this opportunity, and investment decisions are either taken by the trustees or managers of the relevant scheme or (as in the case of 'typical' personal pension schemes) members are offered the opportunity to invest in a narrow selection of pre-approved investment funds selected by the personal pension scheme provider. However, there are some schemes that do allow members the opportunity to select or otherwise influence scheme investment decisions, the typical (and most commonly encountered) example being self-invested personal pensions, or 'SIPPs'.

Historically, before 6 April 2006 (known to the pensions world as 'A Day'), SIPPs offered members a relatively wide range of investment choices; however, that choice was limited to a specific list of permitted investments, and residential property was not on that list.[58] On A Day, the current registered pension scheme regime was introduced, and as part of that process, there was a considerable relaxation of the rules governing pension scheme investment. Indeed, the view was generally taken that (barring a few limited exceptions such as the ability of pension schemes to invest on an unrestricted basis in the assets of any sponsoring employer), all investment restrictions were to be swept away. In the months leading up to A Day, the pensions industry and pension scheme investors alike anticipated (partly as a result of Government announcements) that following A Day, SIPPs would be able to invest in

---

[58] Pension schemes could, and can, invest in commercial property however.

residential property (including for example, holiday homes), and there was considerable anger when the Government suddenly (and somewhat late in the day) announced that SIPPs would not in fact be permitted to invest in residential property without losing their tax advantages (so in practice there would be little point in investing in residential property via a SIPP), and this despite the Treasury having given the impression that that such investments were to be permitted.[59] There were widespread complaints and, eventually, it was decided that in certain carefully limited circumstances, SIPPs would be permitted to invest (indirectly) in residential property portfolios after all (for example, via specialised commercially available investment funds) without losing their tax advantages. However, the fact remains that from the point of view of the private investor, it is not possible to use a SIPP to invest directly in residential property without jeopardising the tax advantages of that pension scheme.

[59] It wasn't and isn't just residential property that is deemed to be an inadmissible investment for SIPPs – chattels such as fine wines and classic cars are similarly restricted. To be fair there are in fact good reasons for preventing SIPPs from investing in such assets – in the case of residential property, there were concerns that the tax reliefs enjoyed by SIPPs would lead to a massive surge in property prices, disadvantaging those who could not purchase via a SIPP. In addition, there is a (good) rule that scheme members should not gain personal enjoyment from the assets of their pension schemes which, after all, are intended to fund long term retirement savings and benefit from tax reliefs as a result. It would be difficult (if not impossible) to enforce this rule if SIPPs were permitted to invest in residential property with impunity.

# CHAPTER 6 LOOKING AHEAD

## Introduction

The purpose of this rather euphemistically titled chapter is to identify the most obvious and common difficulties which can befall you as a property owner, and identify what protective measures you can take in advance to prepare for them, and what practicalities are required if they do occur.

The impact in most cases is as to your 'money' rather than 'property', but because for most people most of their money is in their property, a misfortune or an unexpected event in relation to their property has a major impact on their money, and vice versa.

For convenience, we have grouped these 'events' alphabetically rather than consecutively, namely:

## Death, debt, defects, dementia, disputes, divorce

These guidelines for preparation and protection are gathered here to avoid overloading the earlier chapters with negatives. Primarily, we are addressing these issues in the context of the purchase of a property as a home rather than an investment, although where the principles or practicalities differ for investments, including buy-to-let, we have identified those differences. We have not attempted to cover the position outside the UK and you will need to seek advice locally, at the time you buy. For example, the inheritance laws differ substantially in most countries, particularly as they apply to land and buildings, and you should not assume that a UK will, or a local will based on UK principles, will have the consequences you expect.

### Death

It is beyond the scope of this book to protect you against death, but it is within your power to ensure that your property affairs are in as good an order as they can be when your turn comes.

There are two good reasons to do so: first, the (arguably) selfish motivation of ensuring that your assets including your property (that is, your 'estate') pass to the person(s) you want them to, and secondly the unselfish motivation of ensuring that your family and friends can deal with the estate you leave as easily and cheaply as possible.

The most important step is to make a will. Buying your first property should be a prompt to you to make a will. If you have already done so, then buying a property should prompt you to re-read it and make sure that it reflects your new circumstances, and if necessary, to make a new one.

If you die without leaving a will (or if your will is deemed to be invalid for whatever reason), you are said to have died 'intestate' and your estate will be subject to the rules of intestacy. We discuss these rules in detail below. The problem with relying on the rules of intestacy is that you may find that your estate, or at least part of it, is left to people who you may not wish to benefit from your death; conversely, you may find that someone who you wanted to benefit (for example, your spouse) may not do so, or at least not to the extent that you had hoped. And if you have an unmarried partner, you may find they are in fact not entitled to any share in your estate at all! For these reasons alone, we have no hesitation in saying firmly: you should have a will!

Assuming that you are making your first will, you will initially need to consider:

Do you want to make any specific gifts (for example, of jewellery or a sum of money) to any particular person or people?

On what basis is your property owned? If it is in joint names with your partner or spouse, is it as 'joint tenants' or 'tenants in common' (see page 103 for an explanation of these terms)? If it is owned as a joint tenancy it will pass automatically to the other joint tenant on your death without needing to be mentioned in your will (and in fact it is better not to mention it) but if you and your spouse or partner own the property as tenants in common, then your share of the property will be treated as part of your estate and you will need to specify in your will who you wish to inherit it. Do you need to make care or maintenance arrangements for any children? This may include use of the property as well as providing funds.

Who do you want to receive the benefit of the 'residue' (that is, whatever is left of your estate after the specific gifts, maintenance arrangements and tax)?

Who will you select to carry out your wishes: that is, to act as executors and, in the case of children, guardians? (Usually two executors, and one or two guardians.)

What happens if your other half dies first?

Of course, home owners' personal circumstances vary enormously. An unattached first time buyer is in a very different position from an older person, who perhaps has elderly parents, a wife, a former wife and children and step-children from the current and previous marriages, some but not all of whom are living as part of the family. It is for you to consider carefully who should get what, but bear in mind:

1. The other half of an unmarried couple has no automatic right to inherit (subject to the 'joint tenants' rule if the property is in joint names).
2. Children under 18 cannot own property or other substantial assets, so these will have to be held in trust until the youngest reaches that age.
3. A marriage automatically cancels all previous wills. Divorce or judicial separation, or dissolution of a civil partnership, or the death of the other half of a couple does not.
4. Couples should normally make wills at the same time so as to ensure they are complementary.
5. Inheritance tax (IHT) applies to any estate worth more than £325,000 (the 2009/2010 tax year figure) at a rate of 40% on the amount in excess of £325,000, although the threshold is affected by any lifetime gifts. Inheritance tax is covered in Chapter 5. This did not change in the 'emergency Budget'.
6. You should not forget the running costs of the property after your death, both during the period while probate is obtained and once it has been passed on through your will. For your heirs, inheriting the property with no cash or income, unless they have sufficient income of their own, will give them problems.
7. Where you are holding property for pure investment purposes, rather than as a home, you need to plan in a similar way – who will inherit, the tax consequences, and the need for cash to cover running costs both in the short term during the period of probate and in the longer term. This applies particularly to buy-to-let. If investments or investment properties are held through a trust or company, special care needs to be taken and you

will need legal and tax advice specific to you and your family's circumstances.

Going beyond the need for a will and for what it can or should contain or allow for, you need to think about making things easy for your executors and those who will inherit.

For example, you could gather together the following property-related information and ensure that your executor knows where it is, or has a copy:

- A copy of the title deeds (including a copy of the lease if the property is leasehold)
- The name and account or roll number of the mortgage lender
- The name of the insurer and the policy number for buildings and contents insurance
- The name of the insurer and the policy number of any 'mortgage protection' or other life insurance policy tied to the mortgage
- The name and account number of the local authority for council tax purposes
- The name and account number of the water/sewage authority for water and sewage rates
- The name and account number of the utility providers, that is gas, electricity, telephone and internet
- The names and addresses of the landlord and managing agent if the property is leasehold
- Copies of any relevant guarantees such as woodworm, dry rot, roof insulation (for flat roof) or NHBC
- If you have one, the energy performance certificate for the property.

All of these will be required by your executor(s) to manage the property during the probate period and to pass on the right information at the time of passing the property on to your heirs or selling it.

If the property is mortgaged, the key documents will be with the mortgage company. If not, you need to make sure that your executor knows where the originals are.

Gathering and sharing this information, and the contents of the will itself, will make the task of the executor(s) and the people inheriting your property much easier.

A will is an important legal document that needs to be prepared and signed in a particularly formal way, and is invalid if it is not. It is possible to get a 'do it yourself' will kit either through stationers or from the internet, but in view of the consequences of getting it wrong, this may be a false economy and we would usually always recommend using the services of a solicitor.

It is possible to give informal instructions to the family, for example about funeral arrangements or the destination of particular personal items, but this is not effective for land and buildings.

*Intestacy: what happens if you don't make a will?*

If you don't make a will, or the will is invalid, your assets will pass to the Public Trustee who will be responsible for the administration of your estate. Usually, members of the family will step in and take responsibility as 'administrators' of the estate by obtaining the equivalent of probate, called 'Letters of Administration'. If not, the Public Trustee will carry on.

After allowing for any funeral and other expense and debts and inheritance tax, and the costs of administering the estate, whatever is left is to be distributed to any family beneficiaries according to the intestacy rules dating back to the Administration of Estates Act 1925.

If there is a surviving husband or wife or civil partner they have priority and will receive the personal effects of the person who died, and the first £125,000 or £200,000 of the estate (£125,000 if there are children or grandchildren, £200,000 if not), but if the deceased has children or brothers or sisters or parents still alive, part of the estate after the first £125,000 or £200,000 will be reserved for them.

For the reasons already discussed, in relation to the home, it is important to establish whether the property was owned in joint names, and if so whether it was owned as joint tenants or as tenants in common since, if it is owned in joint names and as joint tenants, the property will pass automatically to the other owner (irrespective of the lack of a will or the Intestacy Rules).

However, if it is owned in joint names and as tenants in common, the part share owned by the person who died will fall to be part of the estate and allocated according to the intestacy rules.

If it is owned in the sole name of the person who died then subject to any claim for a share of the property by the 'other half' (because of any contribution to the purchase or upkeep of it) the whole will fall to be part of the estate of the person who died and allocated according to the intestacy rules.

The last two circumstances can be overridden by the 'other half's' right to buy the deceased's interest in the property, within 12 months of the death, setting off against the value of the property the value of his or her entitlement under the estate (section 5 of the Intestates Estates Act 1952 if you're interested).

If there are more complicated family circumstances, matters can get very complex.

For example, if there is no surviving husband or wife or civil partner, the intestacy rules set out an order of priority for inheritance - children, grandchildren, siblings, parents, grandparents (unlikely, but you never know), aunts and uncles and if none of those exist the value of the estate, including the property, will pass to the Crown as 'bona vacantia'!

Specialist legal advice will be required if any of these circumstances may apply, hence our strong recommendation to make a will (and regularly review it) if you buy a property.

*Post-death changes*

Surprisingly, a will is not necessarily the last word on the subject of who gets what.

There are two ways in which the outcome may be changed after the death of the person who made it. The first is under a deed of family arrangement where (usually for tax reasons, or because circumstances have changed since the will was made) the beneficiaries of the will can, with the agreement of the executors, effectively re-write it after the event. If made within two years, this should have the result that the will is read as if it was originally written that way. This might be useful, for example, if a husband's will passes all the assets to his wife but the wife dies before him and he does not make a fresh will passing his assets to the children. Or, if she is still alive, it may be more tax efficient to pass some assets direct to the children or to pass down assets from his parents direct to his children rather than everything going to his widow, so that the inheritance tax that will eventually be payable on her death is reduced. (Of course, this is only relevant where the value of the combined estates would be over the IHT threshold, and the widow has sufficient assets to support herself – for many families, this is unlikely to be the case.)

Secondly, if the person who died has been maintaining someone else (perhaps a previous wife or children from a previous family) for whom provision is not made in the will, then those who were being maintained can apply to be given a share of the assets of the deceased's estate, under the Inheritance (Provision for Family and Dependants) Act 1975. This rarely happens, and usually occurs in unhappy circumstances when there is animosity between different parts of the family, but the procedure exists to ensure that the person making a will makes proper provision for those for whom he or she is responsible. The court process is a deterrent against failing to do so.

*Recommendation*
MAKE A WILL!

## Debt

We certainly do not want to tell you how to run your life, but if you do get into debt it is important to ensure, insofar as you can, that your property assets are protected as best they can be, or at least you remain in control of them during any sale process. Debt is inherently linked with property: what after all is a mortgage but a form of debt? (Amazingly, far too many people fail to realise this, even today.) True, it is long term debt and secured against substantial assets, but in principle it is no different from the debt you enter into by borrowing a tenner from a friend so you can buy a round of drinks.

The concern in this section is how to deal with circumstances when a person finds that they cannot pay the mortgage payments due on their house.

If a person finds himself or herself in this predicament, it is likely that they also have other debts – credit cards, overdrafts, even court judgments – piling up. The stress is even greater if the person's property is in negative equity, that is, worth less than they borrowed in order to buy it, so that even selling it will not pay off the debt owed on the mortgage.

Whether the situation is triggered by a change in a borrower's circumstances (illness or redundancy) or a change in external circumstances – the sudden rise in mortgage interest rates to 15% in the late 1980s springs to mind, or the expiry of a reduced interest rate period on the mortgage - the worst thing that anyone can do is to bury their head in the sand and hope it all goes away. Missing a regular mortgage payment is a serious alarm bell for lenders, and should be one for the borrower too. If the owner of a property on which there is a mortgage fails to make their mortgage payments the lender will (eventually) be entitled to evict the owner and family, and sell the house (a process popularly known as 'possession' or 'repossession') in order to recover its money, leaving the homeowner and family homeless as a result. (From the mortgage lender's perspective, this will usually be very much of a last resort, as we discuss further below). Despite what you may read in the newspapers or see on the television, responsible lenders are usually reluctant to seek possession of a borrower's home for a variety of reasons, and would much rather see if they can reach some sort of sensible deal with the borrower. However, if this isn't possible, then ultimately lenders can and will seek to repossess the property via the courts. Lenders are less reluctant to enforce loans against properties which are not the borrower's home, such as buy-to-let properties, but are unlikely to do so while it is tenanted and producing income (as long as the loan was intended for buy-to-let, rather than a home loan where the property has been let without their permission).

The resulting court judgment will also be a black mark against the homeowner's credit record and will therefore affect that person's ability to borrow or even to rent in the future. Unfortunately, that is not the end of the bad news. If the proceeds of selling the house are not enough to pay off the mortgage and the related interest and costs (including the costs of any court proceedings and the cost of sale incurred by the lender) the homeowner will still be liable for the difference, which is likely to lead to bankruptcy. However, if the proceeds of selling the house are more than the mortgage, interest and costs, then any remaining balance will come to the homeowner.

Repossessions were predicted by the Council of Mortgage Lenders to increase from 40,000 in 2008 to 75,000 in 2009, later revised down to 65,000, and, the final figure for the year was 'only' 46,000, which was the highest since 1996 (although these figures include buy-to-let mortgages). The CML predict 53,000 repossessions in 2010.

However, if you have no choice but to miss a single regular mortgage payment, all is not necessarily lost. Advice and support are available, and the principal mortgage lenders have committed themselves to act reasonably, according to principles that give borrowers the best practicable chance of recovering their financial position without losing their homes.

For advice, the Citizens Advice Bureaux (CAB)[60] is an excellent starting point, as is Shelter[61], particularly if you are renting. The CAB gave advice on debt problems to over half a million people in 2006/7 and that figure is likely to have been higher in subsequent years. The Government has also set up a national debt helpline[62] which has a wide range of helpful factsheets.

Specifically in relation to mortgages, the Financial Services Authority has published guidance called 'What to do if you Can't Pay Your Mortgage'[63] and the National Homelessness Advice Scheme[64] (a partnership between Citizens Advice and Shelter) also has a useful leaflet called 'Are you Worried About Your Mortgage?'.

CAB gives simple four-stage debt advice, which we cannot improve on. This covers all debts, not just property-related mortgages, but if you want to take control of your financial position you need to follow these guidelines.

Step 1 – make a list of your debts.

Step 2 – work out your budget.

Step 3 – sort out your priority debts.

Step 4 – sort out your non-priority debts.

The first two steps force you to make a realistic assessment of what you owe and what you can pay.

Priority debts include mortgage (or rent) payments and home-related expenses such as food, fuel bills and council tax, as well as court orders, transport and income tax or VAT arrears. These are priority debts because you may lose your

---

60 www.citizensadvice.org.uk

61 www.shelter.org.uk

62 0808 808 4000 or www.nationaldebtline.co.uk

63 www.moneymadeclear.fsa.gov.uk

64 www.nhas.org.uk

home or have the fuel supply cut off if you do not pay them, or because failure to pay will lead to bailiffs being instructed to seize goods, with the ultimate penalty being prison for non-payment.

Non-priority debts include credit debt such as overdrafts and credit card accounts, student loans, benefit overpayments and money borrowed from friends and family.

So, assuming you have taken steps 1 and 2, how should you deal with your lender as to the mortgage payments?

First, check whether your lender is a member of the Council of Mortgage Lenders (CML)[65]. Most of the household name banks and building societies are. If so, it has signed up to a 'pre-action protocol' which sets out clearly the time the lender should allow for payment and the steps the lender should take before starting any court proceedings against you for non-payment of the mortgage payments due (this agreed protocol applied from 19 November 2008).

The purpose of the protocol is to encourage the lender and borrower to communicate and to resolve disputes over arrears and mortgage payments without the need to go to court, for example by the lender setting out clearly the amount which is owed in writing.

So, assuming the lender is a CML member, you should have clear information about how much you owe (both capital and interest).

Major lenders (but not all CML members) also agreed with the Government in late 2008 to allow three or six months before beginning possession proceedings against home owners who are in arrears with mortgage payments (but note this does not apply to buy-to-let mortgages). This gives both you and the lender time to comply with the protocol, and allows you time to take advice. It also allows you time to claim on any mortgage payment protection policy you may have.

Mortgage payment protection policies are designed to protect you if you become unemployed, have an accident or are too sick to work. This type of insurance would usually have been taken out at the same time as your

---

[65] www.cml.org.uk

mortgage and, if you have a valid claim, will cover your mortgage payments for 12 months or more.

The protocol encourages borrowers to offer a payment plan which may involve deferring payments for a limited period, reducing the regular payments, moving a repayment mortgage onto an 'interest-only' basis to reduce the size of your regular payments, or extending the period of the loan, and encourages lenders to respond quickly and, where practical, positively to a borrower's proposals. It does not force lenders to accept the borrower's proposal, or to write off any part of the loan, or to reduce the interest rate or any penalty charges or costs.

The earlier you make contact with the lender, the more options are available to find at least a short-term solution.

The protocol also encourages lenders to allow the borrower a reasonable period to market the property for sale him/herself – although the lender is entitled to ask for proof that the borrower is actively doing so, including providing the identity of the selling agent and solicitor or conveyancer, a copy of the agent's sales particulars, the home information pack and any purchase offers.

The protocol is both carrot – for the lender and borrower to communicate and resolve the arrears – and stick. If the lender and borrower do not reach agreement and the lender takes court proceedings for possession, the court will be entitled to take account of whether each of them complied with the protocol. If the court considers the lender did not – for example if the court concludes they should have accepted the borrower's proposal, or that they acted too quickly – it can write off part of the interest and costs (but not of the original loan itself). If the court considers that the borrower did not follow the protocol – for example by not making serious efforts to sell – it can apply a higher rate of interest to the debt.

The court rules have also been amended as from 1 October 2009 to back up the CML protocol, by changes to the Civil Procedures Rules Part 55 which govern possession proceedings, so that the lender must:

1. send written notice addressed to the tenant or occupier of the property within five days of being notified of the possession hearing date, giving the details necessary for the recipient to appeal. This is to ensure that the

borrower is aware, but that also any other tenant or occupier of the property is made aware the lender is seeking possession

2. notify the local housing authority of the possession proceedings, so that they can anticipate the need to re-house the occupiers, in particular by assisting those who could benefit from the Mortgage Rescue Scheme or other support services.

This applies to all lenders, not just CML members.

The introduction of the protocol coincided with the outcry arising from a legal case known as *Horsham Properties v Clark* which was reported in the press in November 2008. In that case the borrowers lost their right to possession of the property when the lender (a member of the CML) exercised its power of sale within the mortgage conditions and sold the property at auction. The lender did not need a court order to exercise its power of sale. The effect was that the borrowers took the property without the opportunity to contest a court application by the lender.[66] The buyer who acquired the property at auction was therefore able to get possession without the borrowers having an opportunity to agree a repayment schedule. This had the consequence that the borrowers lost the ability to repay the mortgage. This was found not to be in breach of the Human Rights Act 1998.

In an attempt to address the discrepancy between the position where a lender is seeking possession by means of a court order, and where it is seeking to exercise a power of sale, a private member's Bill (The Home Repossession (Protection) Bill 2009 was introduced in Parliament to ensure that in future lenders must apply to court for permission before exercising any powers of sale they may have in relation to a dwelling house, but this did not proceed (although a similar bill in Scotland did). A more limited bill protecting tenants did pass into law in England and Wales in April 2010, The Mortgage Repossession (Protection of Tenants) Act 2010, which is not yet in force but is likely to come into force in autumn 2010. This will give tenants – even those who are unlawful because the owner did not get the lender's consent to let the

---

[66] In this case, the loan appears to have been a buy-to-let mortgage where the borrowers went into occupation of the property upon which the loan was secured, in breach of the terms of the mortgage, but the principles remain the same as if the mortgage were a normal 'home mortgage'.

property – the right to be notified and to appear at court if a mortgagee seeks possession. The tenant will be given the right to suspend a possession order made against the owner for two months, and to delay the enforcement of vacating. However, the Act does not directly address the *Horsham Properties v Clark* situation.

The protocol does not prevent the lenders from pursuing other legal actions which do not directly seek possession of the home against borrowers who fail to pay. However, if the lender seeks possession as a money claim at the same time, it does apply. For example, lenders can sue the borrower for payment of unpaid amounts simply as a debt, or seek to make them bankrupt, or appoint a receiver in respect of the property if it is tenanted and so producing an income, so that they take over the running of the property and receive the benefit of the income. However, in most cases the sums owed by way of unpaid mortgage can only be recovered by selling the property.

As we mention above, it is important to remember that selling the property does not cancel the mortgage debt: if the sale proceeds are not enough to pay off the mortgage the balance is still due.

A borrower may take out more than one mortgage at a time. The position for second (and later) mortgages is more complicated than if there is only a single mortgage on the property.

If there are two mortgages outstanding, the second mortgagee (that is, the second mortgage lender) is usually the one with the higher risk, and who is likely to be more aggressive than the first lender about pursuing mortgage arrears, because they are in a weaker position legally than the first lender when it comes to forcing the borrower into a sale, or to recovering possession of the property – or indeed recovering the amount they have lent if they do so.[67]

The second mortgagee can force a sale or seek possession through the courts, but if the first mortgagee also enforces its security in the same way, the first mortgagee will be in control of the possession process and their debt will be

---

[67] And if there are three mortgages – rare but not totally unheard of in relation to domestic property – the third mortgagee's position is likely to be weaker than that of the second.

paid off first out of the sale proceeds with the second mortgagee recovering only what they can get out of any amount left over.

Second mortgagees are therefore more likely to pursue other routes such as suing the borrower personally for the arrears as a debt, or threatening to make the borrower bankrupt. Not all second mortgagees are members of the CML. The court protocol does apply to second mortgages as well as first mortgages, whether or not the lender is a CML member, but we still strongly recommend you take advice if you have missed any second mortgage payments and before any second mortgagee takes action.

It should be remembered that no lender is entitled to take possession of the property without a court order if it is occupied, and it is a criminal offence to do so under The Protection from Eviction Act 1977. This does not prevent a lender from taking physical possession of a property that is vacant, and it can usually do so under the terms of the mortgage without prior warning if the mortgage payments are in arrears.

The Government has also gone further than the CML protocol to put in place what it calls a safety net, through its Income Support For Mortgage Interest (ISMI) Scheme (which was originally announced in the Queen's Speech in December 2008 and enhanced when announced more fully in January 2009) and its Homeowners Mortgage Support Scheme and Mortgage Rescue Scheme. These schemes are for homeowners, not buy-to-let landlords. When first announced, these schemes were greeted by the property industry with some scepticism, but they may prove very helpful for some. In principle, they are intended to help home owners who are at risk of repossession to stay in their homes, either by deferring interest payments, or by receiving a loan from a housing association to help reduce their mortgage costs, or by selling the property to a housing association who will then rent the property back to the (former) home owner.

Local authorities have also been given funding for providing small loans to homeowners to help prevent repossession or eviction.

The ISMI Scheme is intended to help homeowners on benefits with their mortgage payments. It is available to people claiming income support, income-based job-seekers' allowance, income-related employment allowance or pension credit.

The Homeowners Mortgage Support scheme (available only through certain lenders[68]) allows a deferral of mortgage interest payments for up to two years, if the borrower suffers a 'significant and temporary' loss of income such as redundancy. This approach does not reduce the amount payable overall, but may help to stave off financial difficulties during a period of a temporary loss of income. The effect is to defer interest payments on the mortgage for up to two years; the mortgage loan will still be owed, as will the interest, and repayments to the mortgage lender will restart once the 'payment holiday' period is finished. The lender has the security of a Government guarantee if the borrower defaults.

To qualify for the Mortgage Rescue Scheme, the borrower must have an income of less than £60,000 per annum, have dependent children or someone in the household who is pregnant, elderly or disabled and the mortgage must be no more than £200,000.

Application for the scheme is to be made to the housing department of the local authority, who will direct eligible borrowers to a housing association that operates locally.

Part of the property industry scepticism that greeted the Mortgage Rescue Scheme (and still persists in some quarters) derives from the fact that no new funds are being made available by the Government to housing associations in order to enable them to operate this scheme. The contrast between the figure of 75,000 repossessions originally estimated for 2009 by the CML, and the figure of 3,000 families that the Government said it hoped would benefit from the scheme when it was announced also gave grounds for doubt, particularly in light of the subsequent disclosure by the Treasury Select Committee in August 2009 that only six families had actually benefited from the Mortgage Rescue Scheme.

It has been reported in the press that some lenders (specifically Halifax and NatWest – part, of course, of the rescued Bank of Scotland and RBS) will in practice, if asked, agree to renew mortgages when fixed rate mortgages expire, despite the borrower being in negative equity – thus avoiding some

---

[68] See www.directgov.uk and search for Homeowners Mortgage Support.

repossessions – or will allow negative equity to be rolled over from a house being sold to one being purchased.

The above approaches should not be confused with a superficially similar arrangement proposed by some private companies, usually called 'sale and rent-back' (SRB) or 'sell to let' or 'mortgage rescue' or something similar. In simple terms, these companies offer to buy the property from the home owner at a discounted price, and give the home owner a tenancy agreement in return, so that the home owner can stay in occupation, paying rent instead of mortgage payments. However, the form of tenancy will be an assured shorthold tenancy, not the more protected form of assured tenancy that a housing association will offer (we discussed these types of tenancies in Chapter 2). Therefore, if the buying company gives the occupier notice to quit, say, six or 12 months later, that notice would usually be effective (which would not be the case if the tenancy were an assured tenancy). Moreover, this threat of possible eviction could be used as a lever to increase rents. Following an Office of Fair Trading report in 2008, the Government has now recognised the dangers in this practice and since 1 July 2009 the Financial Services Authority has regulated SRB operations under an interim regime, with a full regulatory system to be implemented on 30 June 2010. The FSA requires proof of who owns the SRB provider, and their financial worth. About 80 firms have applied for interim authorisation.[69] The Office of Fair Trading has also challenged advertising claims by a number of firms, and 12 firms have agreed to change their websites or close them down altogether. Typical claims include that residents are able to live in properties for life after they have sold them, and benefit from low rents or the right to buy back their houses at any point - which may not in practice turn out to be the case. Under the full FSA regulations it is likely that 'cold calling' and 'doorstepping' will be banned, and that SRB providers will be obliged to check that the customer can afford the deal, and that the customer will get security of tenure. You can check whether a sale/rent-back firm is authorised by the Financial Services Authority at www.fsa.gov.uk.

So if you sign up for one of these sale/rent-back schemes, the evil day of losing both the value of the property and a place to live may only be postponed, not

---

[69] It is estimated that at the height of the property boom there were up to 2,000 SRB providers.

avoided. As a consequence, we would not usually recommend that you enter into one of these sale/rent-back schemes, but if you are considering it, we would urge you to take appropriate specialist advice first so you understand clearly the risks you are taking.

But what if you have already entered into a sale/rent-back arrangement? Well, the outlook is not entirely bleak. Shelter has won an important case (*Redstone Mortgages Plc v Welch, Jackson and Jackson*) for a vulnerable family who sold their home under threat of repossession, in return for a tenancy agreement which was to last 'indefinitely' but then found two years later that they were again under threat of eviction because the new owner of the home defaulted on her mortgage.

Mr and Mrs Jackson were, until October 2005, the owners of a house in Shrewsbury. The property was mortgaged to Cheltenham & Gloucester Building Society and Welcome Finance. The Jacksons fell into arrears in 2005 when Mr Jackson lost his job. They saw an advert in their local paper for 'Repossessions Stopped' who offered to buy properties from owners in arrears, pay off the mortgages and grant tenancies to the former owners.

Repossessions Stopped offered to buy the property for £63,000 (in circumstances where Mr & Mrs Jackson believed the property was worth £85,000 and it was actually worth £100,000) and told them they could stay for the rest of their lives so long as they observed the conditions of the tenancy. They would also be entitled to buy the property back in the future at a price 10% less than market price and, to top it all off, their 18-year-old daughter could be a joint tenant and inherit the tenancy.

In due course a tenancy agreement described as a 'Short Tenancy Agreement' was signed and the property was sold to a Ms Welch who was a partner in 'Repossessions Stopped'. The C&G and Welcome Finance mortgages were discharged with the benefit of a further advance from Beacon Homeloans Ltd. Redstone later took over the Beacon mortgage.

Repossessions Stopped/Ms Welch then stopped paying the mortgage payments to Redstone. Repossessions Stopped later went into liquidation. Redstone enforced its mortgage. The question was the extent to which the agreements made by Repossessions Stopped could bind Redstone.

The judge found that Mr and Mrs Jackson had an Assured (so protected) Tenancy to which their daughter could succeed rather than an assured shorthold tenancy, and the option to buy the property back and that they had (as against Ms Welch) a right to set aside the sale to her for fraud. Those rights took priority over the rights of Beacon (and Redstone). So the judge held that the Jacksons should be able to continue with the tenancy on the original terms (including succession to the daughter) or repurchase the property at a discount. Alternatively, they could set aside the sale to Repossessions Stopped/Ms Welch on terms relating to the financial compensation of Redstone (essentially, paying mortgage payments to Redstone instead of rent, the amount to be agreed).

The judge was perhaps influenced by the fact that the Jacksons were made promises that were not delivered and by Ms Welch's clear attempt to create an insecure tenancy instead of a protected one (despite her promises to the Jacksons) by the way it was drafted.

By way of balance however, the Court of Appeal did validate a sale/rent-back, and dismiss various spurious attempts by the seller/tenant to claim an additional payment, in *UK Housing Alliance (North West) Ltd v Francis.*

The *Jackson* and the *Horsham* cases both demonstrate an important practical point: the lender or SRB provider does not necessary keep the property itself; it is running a business which means it will probably sell on the property or the loan once you have signed up. So even if you 'trust' the person you deal with, they may not be there to help you in future.

As a last resort, local authorities have legal responsibility to house those who are homeless, but not everyone is entitled to emergency housing. Shelter is the best starting point. Their website has a useful emergency housing rights checker, and they have a network of advisers to advise individuals on their particular circumstances.

*Recommendation*

If you are in arrears with mortgage payments, *be realistic,* get advice, and communicate with your lender as soon as possible.

## Defects

What happens if your building has a structural defect of some sort? How should you approach this problem and will you have a potential claim against anyone? These are important questions that we tackle in this section.

It is beyond the scope of this book to advise on building techniques, but we can give you some clues as to how to handle a problem with a property if it arises, and particularly whether you have rights to claims against anyone else. As a starting point, the owner of the property is responsible for it and any defects are primarily for the owner to deal with. Having said this, there are a number of circumstances where there may be claims against others that could be pursued, as we discuss below.

Defects can cover a wide range of problems – no building method is perfect and/or everlasting – but we cover the following:

- insurable problems;
- problems with new buildings;
- problems with 'pre-owned' properties; and
- asbestos.

You may be able to claim against another person either if you have a contract with them, and they are in breach of their obligations under that contract, or if they commit a 'tort' against you (a legal wrong such as trespass, nuisance (in the legal sense) or negligence if the other person owes you a duty of care), or if liability is imposed by statute.

Insurance is a form of contract where you pay the insurance company a premium and they agree to pay out to you if certain (bad) things happen. A typical buildings insurance policy covers damage to a building by certain specified risks – most obviously, fire but also (usually) flooding, subsidence and heave.[70] In areas where subsidence is common, insurance for that risk is expensive or difficult to get; in areas prone to flooding, cover for that risk may also be expensive or difficult. In both cases, there are likely to be higher excesses than for other risks.

---

[70] Which means the upward movement of the ground usually caused in clay by removing weight – demolishing a building – or by reducing water absorption – by a tree dying or being removed – so that the ground moves back up to its natural level).

A wise property owner will carry sufficient insurance to cover the cost of completely re-building the property if it is completely destroyed (known as reinstatement value) plus the cost of clearing the site. If you have a mortgage, your lender will insist on this, as a protection for their money. As mentioned earlier, remember the amount you need to insure is the cost of rebuilding, not the market value, and the two are seldom the same.

In the case of flats, the buildings insurance is usually by the block owner who is responsible for the structure, so any claim will be on the block policy. If you are a leaseholder or tenant of a house, responsibility for building insurance will be spelt out in the lease. Under a long lease the leaseholder may insure (unless the property is part of a large estate); under an AST, insurance will be by the landlord.

Anyway, assuming you have buildings insurance, and your property suffers damage from one of the insured risks then you should be able to make an insurance claim to cover your loss.

It is worth remembering that insurance covers damage, not the cause of the damage. So, if a pipe bursts causing water damage to decorations or carpets, the insurance should cover the cost of the redecoration and new carpets but not the cost of the plumber to repair the leak.

*Problems with new buildings*

If you buy from a reputable developer, it should have a procedure for dealing with 'snagging items'. You will need to carefully document the things you inevitably find once you move in – missed painting, sockets that don't work, loo handles that fall off – put a list of them in writing to the developer and check off the items as they are done. Usually, the developer will agree to be responsible for these items for a fixed period of, say, six months after completion, as long as you notify them of the problem. You may have to be persistent. The HomeBuilder Consumer Code (mentioned on page 78) introduced in April 2010 should strengthen your case if the builder is evasive.

Bigger problems with a new building should (even if the developer has gone bust) be covered by the NHBC (National House-Building Council) certificate, known as 'Buildmark' which will be provided by the builder at completion. This is a warranty from the NHBC to cover any failure to the main structural elements of the building for a period of 10 years from completion. It does not cover minor items, and does not cover services such as electricity or gas, central heating or plumbing, but is a valuable protection against catastrophe. Since the NHBC have independent monitors who inspect and 'sign off' buildings before the Buildmark certificate is issued, they also act as a discipline for builders. NHBC cover is not (usually) available for conversions, only for new construction. The NHBC guarantee is not a substitute for a builder doing the work properly, and if building defects become apparent the buyer should be able to claim against the builder for poor design or workmanship up to 6 years from the date of completion.

More than 80% of the new homes in the UK are covered by the NHBC; there are insurance-backed alternatives such as Zurich's New Build Guarantee (although Zurich stopped offering new cover from 1 October 2009. Previously issued policies are still valid).

In extreme cases – illustrated by a case called *Bole v Huntsbuild and Money*, where the builder failed to construct adequate foundations for a new house, and their structural engineer failed to design them, so that the house was structurally unsound so required major underpinning works[71] – a building may be so badly built that it is 'unfit for human habitation' under the Defective Premises Act 1972. It followed that Mr Bole was entitled to the full cost of repairs, and damages for distress and inconvenience.

The Act requires those designing or constructing a dwelling to work in a professional or workmanlike manner, to use proper materials, and to see that the completed house or flat is fit for human habitation.

*Building Regulations*

As we explain in Chapter 9, building works (both for new buildings and for alterations to existing buildings) are subject to quality standards, approval and (to a limited extent) supervision by the local building control officer or an appointed specialist under the Building Regulations. This undoubtedly forces most builders to operate to higher standards (although the Regulations are so

---

[71] An example of 'heave' since it was the removal of trees that caused the ground to move upwards, de-stabilising the house, after it was built. The real claimant was Mr Bole's buildings insurers.

complex and detailed, and change so often, that it is difficult for them to keep up).

A reputable builder should be a member of the NHBC and should accept in a contract an obligation to build in accordance with Building Regulations (membership of the NHBC implies this anyway) and therefore to be liable for breach of contract if it doesn't. If it turns out later that works have been done (or designed) which were not in accordance with Building Regulations, you may be able to recover the cost of making them comply from the builder (or designer).

You might think you can sue the building control officer for approving plans they shouldn't have approved, or failing to supervise the works properly. It appeared from the House of Lords case of *Anns v Merton Borough Council* that you could because the Council owed the building owner a duty of care to act in a way which is not negligent – although in that case the owners finally lost because of the time elapsed between the problem arising and the issue of court proceedings. To the relief of local Councils' insurers', the later House of Lords case of *Murphy v Brentwood District Council* came to a different conclusion, limiting the scope of the claim to injury to individuals or their health, not financial loss. Your primary right is still against the builder (or designer) who did (or designed) the work.

A particular issue on building regulations is mentioned in Chapter 9 – on page 299 – where the seller had previously done work on his home which required building regulations approval, applied but was refused, didn't tell the buyer that, and the buyer's solicitors were found liable in negligence for the consequences because they didn't check the facts with the local building control officer. The buyer may also have had a claim against the seller for misrepresentation.

This illustrates the other possible right you may have if there is a building defect in an existing, rather than new, building namely against the seller for failure to disclose a problem. Another example (illustrated in *Howd v Console-Verman*) would be the seller answering a question as to whether a (riverside) property had ever suffered from flooding by saying 'not during their ownership'. It appears that the garden had previously flooded, but not the house, and the sellers thought the question related only to the house – which was called 'Tide's End'.[72] The case settled, but the claim was for the full £1.9m price of the property plus damages.

The underlying principle is still 'buyer beware' or 'caveat emptor', but where a question is asked though lawyers, and answered, there are legal consequences if that answer is (deliberately or otherwise) inaccurate.

Separately, if defects in the property come to light after completion, and you had a survey carried out before exchange, you may have a right of claim against the surveyor based on you demonstrating that the surveyor failed to use the standard of expertise a properly qualified and experienced surveyor should have used in carrying out the survey. The expectation level will be higher for a full structural survey than for a HomeBuyer Report, because a survey is intended to be more detailed and to dig deeper (metaphorically) than a Report. In practice, the surveyor will normally put into their written report some material limitations – for example, excluding liability for things they cannot see, or do not test, such as drains. However, if they do miss something significant, and you suffer loss, you will have a claim. They will have professional indemnity insurance cover, for their own protection, to back up such a claim. If you relied only on a valuation – normally commissioned by your lender rather than by you, and which is NOT a survey – you do not have a contract with the valuer so would have to argue that the valuer owed you a duty of care (which he or she probably does – *Smith v Eric S Bush*), and that he or she was negligent, and that you suffered as a consequence. Unless the defect was sufficiently obvious at the time of the valuation and sufficiently significant to affect the value - subsidence is an obvious example – your claim against the valuer is unlikely to succeed. That is why we recommend you have a survey, or at least a HomeBuyer Report.

In a leasehold situation, the liability for defects is likely to be different, and will be governed by the terms of the lease (which is itself a form of contract).

Generally speaking, in the case of a leasehold house held on a long lease, the landlord will pass on all responsibility for repairs and making good defects to the tenant so (unless the landlord built the property from new so has contractual liability for it, and/or there is an NHBC certificate or a

[72] Which some might think should have been a clue.

misrepresentation in replies to enquiries), the responsibility falls on you as tenant/buyer (although you may have a claim against your surveyor if he or she got it wrong).

In a short lease such as an AST, the landlord is normally responsible for repairs and therefore for defects. This allocation of responsibility is reinforced by Section 11 of the Landlord and Tenant Act 1985 which provides that under a lease granted for less than 7 years the landlord has an implied obligation to:

"(a) keep in repair the structure and exterior of the dwelling (including drains, gutters and external pipes); and

(b) keep in repair and proper working order the installations in the dwelling for the supply of water, gas and electricity and for sanitation, and for space and water heating."

This does not necessarily cover all defects (in a local authority property, condensation was so bad that it was uninhabitable but this section did not make the authority liable – *Quick v Taff-Ely Borough Council*) but it is a good starting point.

Inevitably, the story is more complicated in a block of flats, because repair responsibility is shared between the leaseholders, who will usually be responsible for the inside of their own flats including, for example, central heating pipes and water and electricity supplies inside the front door, but the block owner will usually be responsible for the physical structure of the building, and communal services and facilities such as gutters, lifts, and communal boilers. In practice, if there is a defect, it is probably in the latter so if it affects your use of your flat you will need to pursue the block owner to rectify it. Some issues will arise between flat owners – the classic example is the pipes or bath in the flat upstairs leaking through your ceiling – where in practice you need to persuade your upstairs neighbour to fix the pipe and make good the damage, but legally you may need to claim against your landlord who in turn would claim against your neighbour (and/or the block insurance policy).

*Asbestos*

We mention asbestos separately because it illustrates some of the difficulties property owners face in dealing with defects.

Asbestos is of course now known to be a major health hazard. Inhalation of asbestos fibres can cause malignant lung cancer, mesothelioma and asbestosis. Since 1 January 2005 all processing and use of asbestos has been banned through the EU. However, asbestos was widely used in buildings, particularly in the 1950s and 1960s, because of its fire-resistant and insulating properties, so it is often found as lagging around boilers and pipes, as fire-proofing inside doors and walls and in lofts, and as part of a cement mixture.

Thee are different types of asbestos, some of which are more dangerous to health than others; generally asbestos is not dangerous if left alone but disturbing it - by removing the lagging, or replacing the boiler pipes - can be dangerous because that activity releases the fibres which cause illness. So clearing asbestos (and disposing of it) is a specialised and expensive business. So, if you have bought a property with asbestos in it, without knowing it, and later find there is asbestos, perhaps when you want to carry out alterations, can you sue anyone for the cost of removal?

If it is a building bought from new it is highly unlikely that there is asbestos, but certainly the designer should not have specified it, the builder should not have built it and the local authority inspector and the NHBC inspector should not have approved it. Your primary claim would be against the developer you bought it from. If you had a survey done, you may have a claim there too.

If it is a re-sale, but the building is less than 6 or 10 years old, you may have a claim against the developer or the NHBC, under the contract or the NHBC guarantee. It is also likely that the developer is in breach of the Defective Premises Act.

If it is a re-sale of an older building, you may have a claim against your surveyor if you had a survey or HomeBuyer Report, if the surveyor could reasonably be expected to have noticed the asbestos (which may be well-hidden). If your solicitors asked the standard set of pre-contract enquiries, that includes a question relating to asbestos (amongst other so-called 'deleterious materials'). If the answer given by the seller's solicitors was 'there are none', then you may have a claim against the seller. If the answer given was 'not so far as the seller is aware', you probably won't have unless the existence of the asbestos was known or obvious to the seller, which is unlikely. If the answer given was 'please rely on your survey', tough luck on you.

This illustrates three further challenges of any litigation: firstly you cannot claim indefinitely; it is likely that if you bought the property more than 6 years earlier your claim would be out of time (unless the seller withheld information deliberately). Secondly, your claim is only worthwhile if the person you are suing has money (or insurance) to cover it (hence Mr Cottingham sued his own solicitors rather than the seller). Thirdly, the measure of damages you would be entitled to recover will be the difference between the price you paid, and the price you would have paid for the property if you had known the asbestos existed. Often, but not always, this is the same as the cost of removing the asbestos. However, if the removal is required as a result (for example) of you carrying out an extension to the property which the seller could not know about, the courts may take the view that the cost arises from your decision to build the extension, not the seller's non-disclosure.

## Dementia

The housing needs of elderly or ailing members of the family can pose particular and serious difficulties, especially if and when it becomes necessary for a person to move into accommodation where care services are available. It is beyond the scope of this book to advise on medical conditions, but we do focus on the options for housing elderly or ailing members of the family, and make some suggestions as to how to deal with their affairs.

As the UK population ages and life expectancy increases, caring for the elderly is an increasing challenge.[73] According to the Office for National Statistics, by 2033 (when David and Ruth will be the same age their parents are now) there will be 3.2 million people in the UK aged over 85 compared to 1.3 million in 2008. At least 700,000 now have dementia to a greater or lesser extent and, according to the Alzheimers' Society, that figure is likely to rise to one million by 2025. This has huge implications for the pensions industry and the UK economy generally, and for the way we use and perceive property.

Moving from the general to the specific, many of us know from our own family experience that the transition out of living in one's own home can be one of the most difficult changes in life – no one finds it easy to admit that they are not as

[73] In 2010, for the first time the number of people aged over 60 in the UK population will exceed the number under 16.

capable as they were and ceasing to be a home owner is as significant a marker in one's life progress as is becoming one for the first time. For some, the change is sudden as a result of illness or choice, but for many the need for change grows gradually and the point of no return may be difficult to recognise. Of course, family circumstances and the availability of care facilities differ very widely, and the options we explore in this section do not include the traditional (and under-reported) option of bringing the affected relative into the home of his or her family. That is not available or practical for all.

A useful starting point, both for information and for a discussion with the affected relative, is either the Age Concern booklet 'Housing Choices in Retirement', which is available from Age Concern[74] or 'Planning for your needs in later life', available from BUPA[75].

As Age Concern say, 'As you get older you may think about moving house. Your current home may be bigger than you need or too expensive to run, or your needs may change because of disability or for other reasons.'

Possible options to consider are:

1. Adapting your existing house (for example changing a bath to a shower, or installing a stair lift). Grants may be available from local authorities, particularly to improve facilities for someone who is disabled. In Wales, there is an additional programme for those who are either physically disabled or aged 60 and over, under the 'Rapid Response Adaptations Programme' which can be applied for via a health professional (probably the GP). The Rapid Response Adaptations Programme is run by Care and Repair Cymru[76].

   There are also home improvement agencies, which are not-for-profit organisations run by housing associations, local authorities and charities which may be able to help those who own their own homes, or who live in privately rented accommodation. They can arrange for repairs, or for funding of repairs and deal with the fitting of small equipment and alterations to help you or your relative live independently in your or their

[74] www.ageconcern.org.uk

[75] www.bupacarehomes.co.uk

[76] www.careandrepair.org.uk

own home, and also with security measures. These agencies tend to be locally based and may or may not be available locally to you or your relative but are worth investigating. The contact point in England is Foundations[77] or in Wales is Care and Repair Cymru.[78]

2. Moving house:

- to a smaller home through the conventional market – for example downsizing from a large family home to a smaller house or flat;
- into a 'granny annexe' or other part of another family house. Although bear in mind this can have tax consequences for the house owner as it may lead to re-assessment of Council Tax as two separate dwellings if they are physically separate; the 'annexe' may not fall inside the 'principal private residence' exemption from Capital Gains Tax when sold, and there could be IHT implications;
- to retirement housing, often known as sheltered housing or 'assisted living'. This is housing in individual units, usually apartments, intended specifically for older people, and usually purpose built. There may be a minimum age requirement, usually 50 or 55. There is usually an alarm system and an on-site warden but not regular home or nursing care. Some schemes have shared on-site facilities such as a lounge, laundry and/or communal gardens. This kind of housing is often bought rather than rented.

  Some housing associations offer sheltered accommodation so if you are in housing association accommodation now, you could consider a transfer to a more suitable property in due course when this becomes necessary. If you are in housing association accommodation (or are considering moving into it) you may wish to check whether your housing association offers such an opportunity or has connections with another housing association that can do so.
- 'Extra Care' or 'Assisted Living' sheltered housing offers the same individual apartment set-up, with a higher level of communal facilities: in particular, meals and some kind of ongoing care is provided, but not full time medical care. 'Extra Care' is usually provided in the public sector by

---

[77] www.foundations.uk.com

[78] www.careandrepair.org.uk

housing associations or local authorities; 'assisted living' is the private sector equivalent. Such accommodation is usually rented rather than bought.

Special types of 'extra care' sheltered housing are offered by almshouses, which are usually run by charitable trusts in a particular area, or for retired workers from a particular industry; and by the Abbeyfield Society which owns and manages around 200 houses (with another 250 affiliated houses) across the UK. The accommodation offered by Abbeyfield mostly consists of unfurnished bedsitting rooms in houses of six to 12 units, with a resident house manager. Two main meals a day are also generally offered. Abbeyfield also operates a number of care homes.

- Care or nursing homes provide a higher level of personal care as well as accommodation, and some provide nursing care. Care homes are intended to provide accommodation for those who can no longer live independently, and inevitably, because of the staffing level required, they are expensive. To meet the costs of a care home you may need or be entitled to support from the social services department of your local authority. Some care homes offer accommodation specifically designed and managed to cope with those with Alzheimer's or dementia.[79]

The availability of these different types of accommodation, the pricing and the ability or willingness of the local authority's social services department to fund care varies considerably from area to area, and you will need to research what is available, at what cost and with what support in your local area.

The local authority's financial support is (usually) means tested so that those with assets or savings of £23,000 or more (including a property which the elderly person can no longer cope with living in, or the sale proceeds of it) will not get financial support.

The Labour Government acknowledged that the availability and cost of care and support for the elderly or otherwise vulnerable is unfair and inadequate and badly publicised. It issued a Green Paper in July 2009 called 'Shaping the Future of Care Together' setting out options for the future, ranging from a compulsory payment towards future care costs, to private or government

[79] An example is Barchester's unfortunately named 'Memory Lane Community'.

insurance-backed schemes. Neither their proposals published in February 2010, nor the Conservative Opposition's reaction were convincing. It is clear that the demographic change we have mentioned presents a really difficult challenge for future Governments (and future taxpayers).

Increasingly, with US experience as an example, 'retirement villages' or 'care villages' are being developed which include on the same site different facilities providing increasing levels of care and so creating the potential for progression from sheltered housing, to extra care, to residential home to full nursing care. There has been something of a bandwagon effect as conventional 'housing for sale' developers have realised not only the extent of the current demand for retirement housing, but also that such demand is increasing rapidly. Should you consider moving to such a site, we recommend that you ask about the experience of the manager in providing services, as well as the range of facilities on offer.

As with any other change in property status, careful consideration of your and/or your relatives' needs and financial position, and then thorough research before making any commitment in relation to any type of sheltered or care accommodation, are vital. To this end, with or without care support, the following check list may be helpful:

- Location: do you know the area and have friends/relatives nearby? Access to shops, post office, doctor's surgery, social facilities such as clubs, places of worship.
- Accessibility: are there steps or a slope, or other obstacles to getting in or out of the property, or inside? If it is on an upper floor, is there a lift?
- Size: is it big enough to be self-contained, small enough to be manageable? Do you need a spare bedroom for sleepovers? Do you really need all that furniture?
- Garden: yes or no? Communal or your own?
- Parking: for visitors as well as yourself.
- Public transport: can you get where you need to go by public transport? (You may drive a car now but not for ever.)
- Look ahead: will the accommodation suit you in one, three or five years' time?
- If you are moving as a couple, what if one of you dies or becomes less able?

- Rent or buy: if you buy, you are buying for the long term but think about re-sale. And if you rent, is the landlord aware of your circumstances? Under the Disability Discrimination Act landlords and letting agents are subject to the UK's anti-discrimination legislation. It is illegal to advertise for or choose tenants on the basis of race, gender, religion, sexual orientation or age. The disability discrimination legislation goes further, by providing that the landlord may also have a duty to provide facilities for the disabled. This includes not only those who are physically disabled but also those with mental disabilities.
- A disabled person can require a landlord to make 'reasonable adjustments' to the property he/she occupies, or allow the disabled person to do so, or to the common parts. For an example of a claim about a stair lift - which did not succeed in that particular case, but could in a different building - see page 40.

BUPA produces guides called 'Choosing a care home' and 'Paying for a care home' which are helpful (although not independent since BUPA operates its own care homes).

Two other aspects of growing older need to be covered here:

- equity release
- powers of attorney.

*Equity release*

Equity release is a way for an older person to stay in their own home but release cash from it, either in a lump sum or in instalments.

Many of those who have done well through the property boom since the 1960s have reached retirement age and have found themselves with a family property worth more than they ever expected, but with a pension that is smaller than they ever expected. Converting some of the capital value tied up in the property into expenditure for living - rather than selling the property and downsizing – is at least to some an attractive proposition and likely to become increasingly popular. It is not, however, without its disadvantages.

There are two main types of equity release: the 'lifetime mortgage' and the 'home reversion plan'. Of the two, lifetime mortgages have to date proved to be the more popular: according to the Council of Mortgage Lenders' figures, there were 105,000 lifetime mortgages in existence in 2005, compared with

12,685 home reversion plans held by SHIP members (who represent 84% of the regulated equity release market, in terms of volume.

The leading specialist independent adviser is Key Retirement Solutions[80] and their booklet 'Finding Freedom in Retirement – a guide to equity release' is a useful summary of the options available.

*Lifetime mortgages*

Essentially, a lifetime mortgage is a loan, backed by the property value, which is not repayable until the borrower dies or goes into long term care, following the sale of the property.

Key aspects of a typical lifetime mortgage scheme are as follows:

The mortgage is available to home owners over 55, whether or not still working.

The cash can be taken as a lump sum or in instalments. The instalment arrangement is sometimes called a drawdown lifetime mortgage. The owner may borrow up to a specified maximum percentage of the value of the property – 15% at age 55, rising to 35% at age 84. There is no restriction on how it is spent or reinvested.

The home owner continues to live in the home.

The value of the property is, in effect, reduced by the amount of the loan (and interest) for inheritance tax purposes. The amount received may affect means-related benefits.

The minimum value of the property must be at least £100,000. Any previous mortgages will have already been paid off or be very small.

The loan becomes repayable upon the death of the owner, or the owner going into long term care, although if the property and mortgage are in joint names, the survivor can continue to live in the property.

There are no monthly instalments to pay. Interest is payable (at a fixed rate), but is rolled up and added to the amount to be repaid.

---

[80] www.keyrs.co.uk

The home owner and family keep ownership of the house (and so responsibility for it, including repairs) and in particular keep control of any sale. If, for example, they choose to sell before the loan is repayable, they can do so and repay the loan. There may be early payment charges for doing so.

The mortgage can be transferred to another property, as long as the mortgage conditions are satisfied.

Some providers of lifetime mortgages offer a 'no negative equity guarantee' so that if the sale value of the property drops below the loan value, only the sale value has to be paid.

*Home reversion plans*

By contrast, a home reversion plan (or HRP) is a property arrangement under which a home owner of retirement age sells the property to the HRP provider and then becomes a tenant, normally at nil rent. The tenancy comes to an end only when the tenant (or the last tenant to survive, if there is more than one owner) dies or no longer uses the property as his or her principal home, so the tenancy is usually called a life tenancy.

HRPs can be full (that is, 100% of the property value is sold) or partial, so that only a proportion is sold, for example 50%, with the (former) home owner retaining an entitlement to, say, 50% of the value of the property (but does not jointly own the property with the HRP provider). The value paid will reflect the fact that the home owner will continue to live there.

The cash so released can be paid either as a lump sum, or in instalments (usually by the HRP provider buying an annuity for the home owner/tenant's benefit).

Again, the value of the home owner's estate is, for inheritance tax purposes, reduced accordingly and the money received from the HRP sale may affect means-related benefits.

Many of the typical features of HRPs are similar to lifetime mortgages - the ability to stay for life, the ability to transfer to another property. A significant difference is that HRPs are usually available only to those between 65 and 80 at the time of application. Furthermore, in the case of a HRP (but not a lifetime mortgage), a landlord/tenant relationship is created. This is so even though there is usually no rent, and, at least in theory, the HRP provider could terminate the tenancy, to the disadvantage of the former home owner, if he or she did not comply with their obligations under the tenancy agreement. And when it comes to sale, the HRP provider is in control of the sale process. Whilst the HRP provider will usually be financially motivated (and arguably legally obliged) to achieve the best possible price for the property, there is scope for argument as to value or timing, particularly where the former home owner has retained a partial interest in the value of the property.

There has been some concern about the 'hard sell' techniques and subsequent behaviour of some HRP providers. In particular, there were press reports several years ago that some HRP providers underpaid for the properties they bought and so achieved windfall profits. When they were first introduced in the 1960s, there was no regulatory control of HRPs, but in 1991, the main providers set up 'Safe Home Income Plans' (www.shipltd.co.uk) as a trade organisation to regulate themselves. SHIP members' plans require no monthly rent, and give the customer the right to live in their homes for life. Despite this, the increase in the popularity of such plans, and the general trend to greater regulation of financial markets led the Government and the Financial Services Authority to conclude that consumers were not sufficiently protected by self-regulation alone and so, since 6 April 2007, HRPs have been regulated by the Financial Services Authority. Lifetime mortgages have always been so regulated.

Before agreeing to enter into a lifetime mortgage or a HRP, it is always advisable to seek independent financial and legal advice. You will need independent legal advice to implement the lifetime mortgage or HRP and you should also reconsider your will at the same time.

*Powers of attorney*

Powers of attorney can play an important role in preparing for, and coping with, the challenges of old age. The principle of a power of attorney is for an individual to authorise a trusted friend, relative or advisor to act as their 'attorney'; that is, to act on their behalf in their business and legal affairs. The power of attorney itself is the formal paper giving the attorney the legal authority he or she needs in order to act, and which the attorney can use to prove to others that they have the necessary authority. Before the Powers of Attorney Act 1971 the scope and form of powers of attorney were varied and there were risks of confusion and legal uncertainty. That Act spelt out that powers of attorney could only be given by those aged 18 and over (in other words, by those who have attained the age of legal majority), and only by those who are 'mentally competent'. Moreover, the donor of a power of attorney permitted under the 1971 Act also has to be competent at the time the power is used. The power can be general or limited. Under a general power, the attorney can do almost anything the donor could do, such as buying and selling assets belonging to the donor, including property, but with a few notable exceptions, such as executing a will or entering into a marriage. In the case of a limited power, the attorney's power to act is limited to a particular purpose (for example, signing a specific document) and/or a particular period of time. To prevent abuse, the power of attorney is subject to verification with the donor if more than 12 months has passed since the date on which it was given and the date on which it is exercised. The forms of power, at least for the general power of attorney, have become standardised.

The requirement that the donor of a power under the 1971 Act must be mentally competent not only at the time of the power being given, but also at the time of it being used, means that the powers allowed by the 1971 Act are not usually suitable for the common situation where an elderly or infirm person becomes incapable of managing their own affairs.

Until a few years ago the only available legal mechanism to deal with this problem was for the intended attorney to apply to the Court of Protection in order for him or her to be appointed by the court as administrator of the affairs of the person in need of protection (known as a 'receiver'). This was a painful and bureaucratic (and needlessly costly) process. In an attempt to tackle this problem, the law was extended further in 1985 to provide for enduring powers of attorney – powers which would be effective after the donor was no longer 'mentally competent', and in practice such powers were only intended to be used after that time. The purpose of the enduring power of attorney was to authorise a family member or trusted advisor to administer the donor's affairs (for example, to operate a bank account, collect their pension and pay their bills) once the donor was no longer capable of carrying out these tasks themselves and once the power was requested with the Court of Protection. It did not (and was not intended to) give the attorney the power to make decisions about the donor's medical care. One of the beneficial consequences of such a power was to reassure the donor (and members of the donor's family and friends) that their affairs would be looked after.

Whilst in most cases enduring powers of attorney have worked as intended there were some reported instances of abuse where enduring powers of attorney were given to a doctor, or a nursing home manager, a lodger (or the donor's accountant in at least one reported instance), against the wishes of donor's family, or to one member of a donor's family without the knowledge of the others, and then misused. It was thought that 15% of powers were abused (mostly by family members). The Law Commission considered the position, prompted in part by a campaign led by 'Action on Elder Abuse'[81]. It was also apparent that many of the institutions to whom these enduring powers of attorney had to be produced (banks, building societies, company registrars) did not understand how they were intended to be created and used, and how to protect themselves against claims of abuse of the power of attorney. For example, the banks would not know whether the power had been registered with the relevant Court of Protection. So, the Law Commission recommended a greater level of control and publication in the giving and use of this very wide-ranging power. They also recommended that the power of attorney did not take effect until after it was registered and knowledge of its existence was notified to the family and publicly available. So under the Mental Capacity Act 2005, and with effect from 1 October 2007, the enduring power of attorney was superseded by the lasting power of attorney. Enduring powers of attorney signed before 1 October 2007 are still valid, whether or not the donor has become 'mentally incompetent' or the power has been used but new enduring powers of attorney cannot now be validly made. Furthermore, existing enduring powers of attorney are required to be registered with the Office of the Public Guardian at the time when the donor becomes or is in the process of becoming 'mentally incompetent' although the power can be used before registration takes effect. The registration fee is £120 (2009 figure). It has also now been made clear that abuse of a power of attorney by the attorney is a criminal offence.

The lasting power of attorney comes in two versions, one for handling the donor's financial affairs – such as his or her bank accounts etc – and known as a

---

[81] www.elderabuse.org

'property and affairs power', and the other for medical issues, known as a 'personal welfare power'. This does have the benefit of enabling the donor to choose different people for these very different roles, but the result is that there are two versions of the lasting power of attorney form which are similar and could be confused, so it is important to ensure that the right form (or forms if both are required) is used. It is not necessary to create both versions of the lasting power of attorney, or to create both at the same time. It is possible, indeed it is often a good idea, to appoint two or more people as attorney, for example, two attorneys each with the property and affairs powers. This can be done in one of two ways – either each attorney can act independently (although this does raise the possibility of each attorney issuing instructions which conflict with the other's) or they must act jointly together (for example, both need to sign cheques or documents).

If the donor has granted an enduring power of attorney, that will not cover issues relating to personal welfare so he or she could in addition (if still mentally competent) grant a lasting power of attorney to deal with such matters without invalidating or contradicting the enduring power of attorney relating to their financial affairs.

The process of granting a lasting power of attorney is now more formal, and the power will not be effective until it has been registered with the office of the Public Guardian[82] which is responsible for the administration of such powers, and maintains a public register of all enduring and lasting powers of attorney.

Unfortunately, the laudable intention behind the legislation intended to protect both the donor and the donor's family against abuse was translated into a process which was over-complex for its intended purpose. Originally, each form of lasting power of attorney was 26 pages long (as opposed to the four pages of the enduring power of attorney) and the guidance notes for completing the lasting power of attorney form ran to 12 pages for each type of power. The combined guidance booklet was a further 60 pages. The absurdity of this was (finally) recognised by the Government, and simpler forms became available to be used from 1 October 2009 so the new forms are now 11 or 12 pages long each (plus guidance notes). They are now no more complex than

---

[82] www.publicguardian.gov.uk

completing a passport application form. [83] Nevertheless, because the effect of the power of attorney is so significant for both the giver and the receiver it would still be unwise to complete the forms without taking legal advice from a solicitor who has previous experience of completing them. Solicitors specialising in such matters often belong to a national association of lawyers, 'Solicitors for the Elderly'[84].

The forms can only be completed and signed by the donor while he or she is mentally competent to give the lasting power of attorney. It is necessary, as part of the form, to obtain a certificate from an independent person – often the donor's GP – to this effect. For obvious reasons, this certificate cannot be provided by a member of the donor's family or by the intended attorney or his or her family, or by the operator of the care home in which the donor may be living. It can be given by the solicitor who prepares the forms. It is also necessary to nominate the people to be notified when an application is made to register it and for the donor to sign the lasting power of attorney in the presence of a witness (usually the certificate provider).

Once signed, the lasting power of attorney is not immediately effective (unlike an enduring power of attorney). There are two further formal steps that must first be followed:

- notice must be given to family members
- the power of attorney must be registered with the Office of the Public Guardian.

The purpose of the notice requirement is to prevent the attorney from being appointed or acting without the knowledge of family members, or other relevant people chosen by the donor (for example, a social worker). The notice rules, which form part of the guidance notes, are not easy to follow but in essence the requirement is to notify the two or three or more (subject to a maximum of five) nearest family members in writing that the power has been given and that an application is being made to register it. The notices should be given by the person applying to register the LPA, that is, either the donor of the

---

[83] It seems inappropriate, bearing in mind the circumstances where they are likely to be used, for the principal publication of the power of attorney forms to be on-line.
[84] www.solicitorsfortheelderly.com

lasting power of attorney, or the prospective attorney. Proof that these notices have been given is necessary to achieve the second step, registration.

Registration is with the Court of Protection, part of the High Court in Birmingham, via the Office of the Public Guardian, and a fee is payable (£120 per power in 2009). Unfortunately the Office of the Public Guardian has a significant backlog. This is partly caused by the fact that a high proportion of forms submitted have to be returned as they have not been properly signed or completed (no doubt due to their complexity) which can cause a problem because it may be too late to get the donor to re-sign or otherwise complete the form creating the power because by then he or she is no longer mentally competent. The registration process includes a compulsory 42-day notice period, to give time for objections. The Office of the Public Guardian has also received many more forms than initially expected - some 10,000 enduring or lasting powers of attorney registration applications are now being made each year.

What if there is no enduring or lasting power of attorney?

In such circumstances, there is no alternative but to apply to the Court of Protection for a decision (if all that is needed is a one-off decision – such as selling a house or switching off a life support machine) or more commonly for a suitable person - usually a family member or trusted advisor - to be appointed as administrator of the person's affairs (now known as a deputy). This is still a slow and bureaucratic court process and, even after the appointment of the deputy, the Office of the Public Guardian has an on-going supervisory role, and so there are significant initial and future costs involved.

*Recommendation*

(1) Following retirement, considering carefully what housing options you may want to consider, and research availability in your preferred area.

(2) If managing your own affairs is becoming difficult, or burdensome, consider appointing an attorney through a lasting power of attorney.

## Disputes

This is a book about buying, selling and investing in property, not about disputes and how to avoid or resolve them, but as property matters generate a large proportion of the cases that go to court, and probably an even larger proportion of disputes which do not reach the courts but nevertheless affect people's lives significantly, some guidelines may be helpful in case you find yourself involved in a dispute.

We cannot cover every eventuality because property-related disputes can arise in as many ways as human beings can devise, but amongst the most common are:

- disputes with neighbours: here, flash points tend to be boundaries, shared driveways or other facilities, noise and parking, or extensions/developments. One rare but difficult kind of dispute, often with neighbours, is 'adverse possession' claims – see page 112.
- disputes with tenants/landlords: flash points tend to be rent payments, releases of deposits, damage to furnishings and noise or other nuisances. We discuss typical landlord/tenant disputes in Chapter 7.
- disputes with mortgage providers: these are almost invariably about money – see the section in this chapter on debt. Borrowers can also get into disputes with lenders if they let or share their property without the lender's permission.
- disputes between sellers and buyers – such disputes tend to arise in relation to issues such as whether contents should have been left or taken, or whether other disputes (for example, with neighbours) have or have not been disclosed.
- disputes within blocks of flats - flash points tend to be the high cost of service charges, and the standard of repairs and maintenance (often simultaneously).
- disputes with surveyors – for failure to identify physical problems such as subsidence or asbestos when pre-purchase surveys are done.
- disputes with building contractors – typically in respect of matters such as poor workmanship, missed deadlines or overcharging.
- disputes arising from divorce or separation – these are covered later in this chapter.

Of course, a great many disputes are resolved without the need for any court or other formal intervention – the moment passes, or one or other party compromises, or a third person steps in and finds a solution.

And that is our first and strongest recommendation: wherever possible achieve an agreement you can live with, without going to court. Pursuing or defending even the simplest of claims through the courts is an expensive and frustrating experience which rarely achieves a satisfactory result for any party. In particular, disputes between neighbours are notorious within the court system for getting out of proportion, to the point where one neighbour may seek to bankrupt the other, but risk bankrupting themselves.

What can the court do? Except in relation to mortgage or rent payments, the dispute is not usually capable of being solved by payment of a specific sum of money, but instead involves a decision by the court as to whether to award damages, and if so how to quantify them. In extreme cases, in order to prevent a repeat of the behaviour causing the dispute (for example, in cases involving allegations of a legal nuisance such as excessive noise) a special court order known as an injunction may be made. It is very rare for the court to issue an injunction specifically ordering someone to do something (apart from paying money for damages): injunctions when issued usually take the form of orders requiring recipients to refrain from specific courses of action or behaviour.

In this section we focus on neighbour disputes as those are both most likely to occur and most difficult to resolve through court action. It is also where the layman is most likely to assume that he or she has 'rights'.

*Boundaries*

If there is a disagreement between neighbours as to where the boundary line between two properties properly lies, the starting point for the 'right answer' is the title deeds. By comparing the title deeds with the physical configuration on the ground, particularly the position of buildings or roads and trees or fences, the answer is often obvious. However, there are flaws to this approach.

- Firstly, the title deeds of adjoining properties do not always match with each other - there may be a gap in between, or the plans may be at different scales or of different ages so that they show different detail of buildings or trees or fences. Furthermore, plans obtained from the Land Registry are not intended to be definitive: they are usually prepared on such a scale that the red line boundary markings on the plans would if reproduced in the real world 'translate' into lines that are several feet wide so precision is impossible. Making matters worse, the Land Registry plan itself may be based on an out of date Ordnance Survey edition (particularly where there has been recent redevelopment). Adding still further to the potential confusion, Land Registry plans do not usually include measurements from fixed points, although they are to scale.

- The Land Registry plans may be wrong simply because the plans on which they were based were wrong – for example, one of the authors nearly bought a house whose garage was wrongly shown on the Land Registry plans as belonging to a neighbour, because that is what the original transfer showed.
- The plan's position may have been overtaken by events. For example, if the neighbours have fenced and used part of 'your' land for long enough without objection, they may have acquired ownership of it by 'adverse possession'.
- The ownership of some land is unknown - for example, this is common in relation to the alleyways built behind Victorian and Edwardian terraces of houses.

The Land Registry has at least standardised the scale on the format of plans – some of those used on older pre-Land Registry title documents were simply a coloured square with no scale or definition points or even roads shown, so disputes were almost inevitable. Having said this, older plans on title deeds pre-dating registration may have measurements plotted on them so it is still worth tracing those old deeds for clues if you can.

If, once the disputing neighbours have considered their respective title deeds, there is still doubt about where the boundary should legally be, then it is possible for them to agree where it should be on the ground and employ a surveyor to produce plans confirming that - with measurements from fixed points. The two neighbours can then jointly submit those plans to the Land Registry as the definitive boundary plans, to avoid uncertainty or disputes in the future. It is usual for the surveyor to mark the line on the ground with white stakes, consistent with the plan, so that the line is physically obvious on site as well as on the title deeds.

If the practicalities of the position require – for example, if a garage or outbuilding or fence serving one property extends beyond the 'official' boundary – then this can be resolved, or rectified, by the 'owner' transferring the relevant land on which it stands to the 'user', for which a payment may be negotiated. The land in question is unlikely to be extensive and probably will be of little value to the 'owner' but moving the garage or outbuilding or fence would have a nuisance value to the 'user', which an experienced surveyor can quantify.

If the dispute cannot be resolved by agreement in this way and goes to court, the judge will seek to identify the definitive boundary of the disputed property, based on historical evidence as to where the boundary is rather than where it 'should be' – in other words the judge, even if he is Solomon, cannot unilaterally impose a change of boundaries to suit the practicalities. This is yet another reason why it is usually preferable for neighbours who are in dispute as to the position of a boundary line to seek to reach agreement between themselves rather than bringing a claim before the courts. If, however, agreement cannot be reached, the dispute may well reach the courts by one means or another. If you find yourself in this position, you will need to seek legal advice as to your rights in the particular circumstances of your case. Having conceded that there are some dispute situations where you may need to seek specialised legal advice, it is probably worth us spelling out certain other aspects of the legal position between neighbours.

*Maintenance of boundary walls, fences and hedges*

Generally, the legal position here is that there is no legal obligation on a property owner to maintain walls or fences or hedges that form the boundary dividing his or her property from others. There are three exceptions.

- When the boundary is next to a road or pavement to which the public have access (this would include a private road or footpath or bridleway): if the wall or fence is in a poor state of repair and somebody is injured as a result, that person may potentially have a claim against the property owner for compensation. (Given the increasingly litigious nature of our society this unfortunately may become more and more of a problem as time goes by.)
- Where the boundary is next to a public road or pavement, footpath or bridleway, the local highway authority (usually but not always the local council) may also use their powers under the Highways Act to force the property owner to make the wall or fence safe.
- Where the title deeds impose an obligation to repair - this is usually apparent from the text or the plans forming the title deeds to the property.

Conventionally, the boundary in question is shown on the title plan with an inward facing T-mark. Sometimes this is shown on the original conveyance plan rather than on the Land Registry plan, but if so it will be referred to in the text of the Land Registry entries.

- Where there is something risky on the property that should not be allowed to escape – either non-domestic animals such as cows, or dangerous substances such as stored petrol or chemicals.

Two other boundary-related issues that often give rise to disputes are party walls and high hedges.

*Party walls*

A party wall is a wall which itself forms the boundary and may therefore be jointly owned by each of the neighbours. These are subject to special rules, and before any works of repair or alteration are carried out to or close to party walls, or a new party wall is built, the person who intends to carry it out must follow the procedure laid down under the Party Wall Act 1996. The purpose of this is to safeguard the neighbour by ensuring that suitable protections are included in the works, so that his or her land and buildings are not undermined or otherwise damaged, or left insecure during the work. A similar procedure applies if you want to carry out any works involving excavation within three to six metres of any building or structure belonging to an adjoining owner. Under the Act, at least two months' notice must be given by the property owner wishing to carry out the works to the property owner affected before any works of repair or alteration can commence. Party wall agreements, called Awards, are usually dealt with by specialist surveyors rather than property solicitors. A list of those surveyors can be obtained from The Royal Institution of Chartered Surveyors' website (www.rics.org.uk).

*Party walls and planning permission*

Generally, boundary walls and fences and hedges do not require planning permission if they are no more than one metre high, next to a public street, or not more than two metres high elsewhere. However, special rules apply to boundaries around listed buildings (because the listing will include the setting and surroundings of the building as well as the building itself) and in some cases in conservation areas where the continuity of, for example, holly hedges is an important feature of the conservation area and so specifically protected (as is so, by way of example, in Merton Park). Bear in mind also that if the boundary includes trees, they may be subject to tree preservation orders and in a conservation area trees are usually automatically protected.

Occasionally, specific obligations about the type of boundary treatment may be imposed in the title deeds - the usual 'T-mark' covenant may specify the kind of boundary as well as responsibility for repair of it - or (rarely but if you encounter it, take it very seriously!) by a formal collective agreement between all the house owners as in Hampstead Garden Suburb. As to blocking of light – typically (but not always) caused by the dreaded 'leylandii' or by the building of an extension – see below.

*Access to neighbour's land*

Generally, you do not have a right of access to your neighbour's land (or vice versa) unless you get his or her express (or implied) permission.

However, there are a number of exceptions:

*Party walls* - the 'award' which will be the outcome of the party wall process mentioned above can include access rights, for example to lay new foundations for the new wall, or to apply weather protection to the outside of it during repair.

*Access to Neighbouring Land Act 1992* - this gives you a right to obtain access over your neighbour's property to repair your own property, if you do not otherwise have an express right to do this and there is no alternative. Most neighbours are usually willing to agree to give each other access rights for the purpose of repairing and maintaining their properties, but if a property owner proves particularly difficult in this regard, the Act gives his or her neighbour a right to apply to court for an 'access order' which the property owner must accept. This right is only available for repairs and general maintenance, not to carry out new developments such as a new building or extension.

*Express rights* - your title deeds may themselves give you a right to access your neighbour's land, or vice versa, although the right is usually for specific purposes, for example to repair or clear a drain which passes across a neighbour's property, or to clear gutters which are inaccessible except from that side. Usually such rights are subject to reasonable prior notice, and to you making good any damage caused.

*Overhanging hedges or trees*

Generally, if there is a tree in your neighbour's garden which has branches extending over your garden, you are entitled to cut them back (provided you return the cut wood and any fruit to the neighbour). It would be neighbourly to first ask the neighbour to either do this themselves or to permit you to do so. However, bearing in mind that the tree may be subject to a tree preservation order or protected by being in a conservation area, any cutting back of the tree may require local authority consent. If this is the case, you and your neighbour may need to make a joint application to your local authority for consent. However, if the tree or hedge is wholly in your neighbour's garden and overshadows your garden you are not entitled to cut it back. If the tree or hedge is adversely affecting your enjoyment of your property, it is possible to apply to your local authority for an order under the Anti-Social Behaviour Act 2003 requiring your neighbour to cut back the hedge although the decision whether to enforce this is for the local authority to make. If an order is granted, failure to comply with an order can lead to a fine.

*Balls etc*

If your children kick their footballs or hit their tennis balls or crash their kites into your neighbour's garden, you are entitled to ask for them back as they belong to your family (although you do not have an automatic legal right to go onto your neighbour's land to get them). However, you or your children are liable to make good any broken windows or other damage they may cause to your neighbour's property.

*Shared facilities*

This section focuses on houses rather than flats.

Many houses, particularly in newer developments, share some facilities, some of which may be highly visible – shared driveways in the classic 'Y' shape, for example – and others which are less so, for example, shared drainage, or cable TV connections or the electricity supplied to the gates for those shared driveways. In upmarket developments, spas or health club facilities may be managed and paid for communally. It is logical to suppose, although not yet obvious, that as green opportunities and techniques develop, collective use of, for example, solar panels or facilities for recharging electric cars will be much more efficient if shared than if provided and used individually.

However, the more that is shared, the more opportunities there are for disagreement. Shared driveways seem to be a particular issue, perhaps because they represent space which is ambiguous - in some ways public (because others use it) and in other ways private (so you can do what you feel like on it, including storing a caravan or boat there, or a couple of broken down cars you are working on, and the kids' bikes and that pile of sand you are intending to move into the back garden next week if it doesn't rain).

The legal position will be governed primarily by the title deeds – that is, which parts are yours and which are not, which parts you or your neighbours are entitled to drive over or park on, and what obligations you or they signed up to, agreeing not to do certain things. Inevitably, some neighbours do not observe these limitations.

This is another situation where diplomacy will almost always be more appropriate and effective than litigation. If you are the aggrieved neighbour, you should bear in mind you will have to live with the consequences of escalating your complaints, so only do so if you really cannot persuade the neighbours to behave more reasonably.

Before embarking on court action, consider whether other neighbours or a residents' association, if there is one, can be more persuasive; if the activity amounts to running a business (taxi repairs is an example we have come across) the local planning officer may be able and willing to step in if your neighbour does not have planning permission to operate that business from his or her home.

*Parking*

Generally you have a right to park as you choose on your own property and (again in some new developments in particular) you may have the right to park either in a designated space or a general parking area. You do not have 'rights' to park on any particular part of the public street, or to prevent others doing so outside your home, unless they are causing a danger to traffic or an obstruction, for example, blocking your driveway. So you cannot 'claim' the public street outside your home as yours.

If you do have a driveway that is actually blocked, the traffic police may be able to assist.

Parking is, of course, an increasingly contentious issue. In certain London boroughs and other cities, residential parking permits are a prime conversation stopper at dinner parties. Some perceive that local councils make parking rules deliberately obscure in order to maximise their income. Similarly, the practice of some private landowners of hiring firms to clamp cars parked on privately owned land and charging large – many people would say extortionate – fees for their release is rapidly becoming a contentious and political issue.

*Noise*

Noise is a particular and increasing problem. It is not helped by poor quality building standards in some properties (particularly those of recent construction), by the increasing number of people living in flats, and by the easy availability of noisy equipment such as sound systems or electric musical instruments. Neighbours vary enormously in their willingness to put up with each others' noise, and in their views as to whether the noise they themselves produce is reasonable or not. If you are troubled by noisy neighbours (and if you are, you have our profound sympathy), again the most effective approach in most situations is a conciliatory one, such as asking the neighbour to keep the noise below a certain level, or to stop at a certain time, or to close certain windows.

If this does not work, and you cannot tolerate the situation, it is worth keeping a diary of the disturbance you are suffering.

Where the neighbour is a tenant, it may be worth contacting the managing agent or landlord, since it is likely that the tenancy agreement contains restrictions on the volume and timing of noise, which they may be able to enforce.

If you cannot resolve matters yourself, contact the local authority's Environmental Health Officer. The local authority has considerable powers under the Control of Pollution Act 1974 to monitor and control noise nuisance, and the necessary technical equipment to do so. They will gather information from you and other neighbours and from their monitoring, and attempt to reach a satisfactory outcome with the neighbour by discussion, failing which the EHO can serve an informal notice on the noisy neighbour. If that doesn't work, the Council can take enforcement action through the Courts, and even confiscate the noise- making equipment. The local authority has other powers if the neighbour problems extend beyond noise; under the Anti-Social Behaviour Act 2003 and in relation to licensed premises (pubs, restaurants, nightclubs, etc) under the Licensing Act 2003.

All this takes time (and may require some chasing of the EHO, and possibly chasing of the noisy neighbour by the EHO) and is likely to be stressful but ultimately should achieve the peace and quiet you seek, at least for some of the time.[85]

*Extensions and developments*

Some of the bitterest disputes arise from a neighbour's desire to extend or build on his or her land, and the other neighbours' desire to stop that happening.

The general position is that with some constraints, each of us has the right to do what we like on our own property, whether others like it or not.

There are two principal constraints applicable to building work: the town planning system, and the legal rights others may have, particularly rights to light.

The planning system is explained in more detail in Chapter 9 from the viewpoint of the intending developer. From your point of view as the owner seeking to prevent his or her neighbour extending or building, you should bear in mind the following: significant building works need planning permission, for which the neighbour must apply to the local planning authority (usually, but not always, the local council). As part of that process, the local planning authority will publicise the fact that an application has been made, with a notice in a public place near the site of the development, letters to those they think may be affected such as neighbours, and an advertisement in a local newspaper. You have the right to object to the planning application in writing, and possibly at the planning committee meeting which considers the application, but the local planning authority will make the final decision as regards the application, not you.

The strength of opposition – the number of objectors, and the logic of their case – may be persuasive but does not force the local planning authority to refuse

---

[85] In an extreme case, the resident of a flat above a noisy bar took her case to the European Court of Human Rights – *Oluic v Croatia*.

the application. Proper reasons for refusal are 'planning' reasons – the proposal may be contrary to established council planning policies, for example proposing business use of a particular property in a residential area, or an inappropriate design, or interference with a protected tree, or overloading the highway system. The decision will not be made simply on subjective grounds, such as whether you like the proposal or not.

Bear in mind that the applicant can appeal any refusal – or any conditions that are imposed on the grant of a consent – to a planning inspector. The council, particularly planning officers, will be well aware of this.

Unsurprisingly, obtaining consent is more difficult, and the application needs to be in more detail, if the property to be developed is in a conservation area, or listed.

Bear in mind also that lesser alterations do not always require consent, including some extensions. The rules on this are complex and have recently changed so many builders and local planning officers are uncertain as to what can be built without consent and what cannot (see the summary in Chapter 9). So if your neighbour starts building without planning consent, and you object, establish what is to be built and consult with the local planning officer, as it is possible consent is required and should have been obtained before any building work started.

Unlike applicants, objectors do not have an automatic right of appeal if the local planning authority grants planning permission to an applicant unless (and this is both rare and extremely expensive) they go to court and successfully demonstrate (by means of a process known as 'judicial review') that the decision made by the local planning authority was beyond the bounds of reasonableness: that is, it was the decision which no reasonable authority would have made. These claims are usually based on some procedural defect in the way the council dealt with the application - for example, not notifying neighbours of the application - rather than the merits of the proposal itself. Some high profile developments have been frustrated by claims of this kind – the redevelopment of Crystal Palace as a commercial leisure centre, and the complete redevelopment of Fulham Football Ground for housing – but these instances are rare.

The grant of planning permission does not mean that the neighbour can interfere with your land or your rights so he or she cannot build on or over your boundary (subject to the party wall legislation mentioned above) or come onto your land to build unless there is an express right to do so on your title deeds. As previously mentioned, the Access to Neighbouring Land Act 1992 does not apply to development.

This means your neighbour cannot interfere with any right of access you may have – either temporarily during the works, by using your entrance for storage of materials, or permanently by building across it – and he or she cannot stop or alter any services from which you benefit which cross his or her land, unless the title deeds say that they may (which is not uncommon). Importantly, he or she cannot interfere with your rights of light.

Rights of light are a complex area of law and practice on which specialist advice will be needed, but in outline it is likely that if the windows on your property have existed for more than 20 years, you have the benefit of rights of light through those windows. These older windows are sometimes known as 'ancient lights' (because the right to light comes from the fact that it has been used for a long time, rather than because the right was ever expressly granted in writing) although experts tend to sneer at this phrase. If the neighbour's proposed development would reduce the amount of light received through those windows below an acceptable level (sometimes defined, rather archaically, as the light received at a hypothetical desk six feet back from the window at 3.00pm on a winter's day), then you are entitled to protect those rights by obtaining an injunction to stop that interference. The claim arises because an 'adequate' level of light becomes an 'inadequate' level of light so the crucial test is the amount of light lost. If the effect would not be severe enough to justify an injunction, you may be entitled to compensation to recompense you for the loss of that amenity. If you think your light could be affected by a neighbour's proposals approach a specialist rights of light surveyor for advice. They can be contacted via the RICS website. The right you can protect is of the passage of light in through the window to your house, and to an extent, the intensity of that light: it is not a right to protect the view out of the window, or to privacy. It can cover the passage of light to greenhouses and possibly (although this has not yet been tested in the courts), the intensity of light falling upon solar panels. This right is separate from any planning permission process.

Loss of daylight and sunlight is a factor the local planning authority should take into account in deciding whether to grant planning permission, but the criteria they will use are different, and, in some circumstances, you can pursue a claim for interference with your rights of light even if planning permission has been granted.

## Divorce

It is beyond the scope of this book to offer you relationship advice but, unsurprisingly, divorce or separation can have serious ramifications so far as your property is concerned. In this section, we will briefly cover both unmarried and married couples, including same-sex couples and civil partnerships.

For married couples and those in civil partnerships the court can, and usually will, give instructions as to how to deal with the assets of the couple, including their home, alongside the order bringing the marriage or civil partnership to an end (this is known as an order for ancillary relief). That order overrides the legal ownership of the property and any previous agreements about it. The order will usually take account of the need to provide a home for any children of the relationship (including any from other relationships who have been treated as part of the family). It may include imposing responsibility on one party (for example, the husband) to pay the mortgage payments or rent for the property in which the other (for example, wife and children) live, and the court order will override the rights of a lender or landlord to object to the change.

For unmarried couples and same sex-couples who have not gone through a civil partnership ceremony, however long the relationship has lasted and however 'committed' it was, the question of ownership of the property is crucial. The way in which it was bought and has been funded, and any previous agreements about ownership of the property, will determine who retains ownership of it. Crucially, that outcome will not be determined or otherwise affected by the existence of any children or the future responsibility for them, unless specific arrangements dealing with such matters are agreed between the separating couple.

So, for an unmarried couple, the starting point is who owns the property: that is, whose name is on the title deeds. If the property is in the name of only one of the couple, that person has the legal ownership of the property and therefore, subject to the next point, can decide whether it is to be retained or sold, and who will live there in the future.

The law has recognised the inherent unfairness of this where a relationship has been long term and financial responsibilities have been shared. Where there has been more than a temporary relationship, and the party who is not the legal owner has contributed financially to the property – either directly by paying part of the purchase price or related purchase expenses, or by paying the mortgage or other running costs, or indirectly by enabling the legal owner to earn enough to pay for the purchase or running costs of the property – then the court may consider that the legal owner holds the property in part on trust for the other party. That does not mean the other party (or anyone else in the family) can necessarily continue to live there; it means that the other party has a financial share in it so that when it is sold a fair proportion of the sale proceeds representing that share (which will usually be determined by the court if the couple themselves cannot reach agreement as to the size of their relative shares) is owed to the other party.

The same logic applies equally to a same-sex couple who are not in a civil partnership.

Proving this entitlement can in itself be a painful and difficult process involving a detailed investigation as to who earned what and who paid for what throughout the period of the relationship, and the intentions of each party when they started the relationship, or when they moved in together.

If the couple are not married (or in a civil partnership) but the property is in joint names, then the imbalance of power between the couple which we have just noted does not arise. Either can force a sale (although if they do not both agree to sell it is necessary to get a court order under the Trusts of Land and Appointment of Trustees Act 1996 to make that happen). In this situation after payment of any mortgage and the sale costs the proceeds of sale would be split, usually on a 50/50 basis unless the parties have agreed otherwise under a formal and binding co-ownership agreement (which we discuss in greater detail below). In such circumstances, that agreement will usually dictate how the sale proceeds should be split. The court has a discretion to refuse to order a sale and will usually do so if the joint purpose of buying the property was to create a family home, particularly if children under 18 are still around.

The parties may have entered into an informal agreement rather than a formal co-ownership agreement. If the couple have split up it is likely that they will not agree as to what the terms of that agreement were, and proving what the couple intended without a written co-ownership agreement can be very difficult. In case of dispute, the court can be asked to intervene, but the costs of going to court, and the complexities of proving what was said perhaps years earlier, means it is almost always better for an unmarried couple who plan to co-own property to document their intentions as regards the eventual disposal of the sale proceeds in a formal co-ownership agreement rather than under some informal and possibly unenforceable arrangement.

One problem with the breakdown of such a relationship, and dealing with the property and other assets from it, is that either party can re-open the argument about what they originally agreed informally, what they agreed at the time of break up, or (if the property was in one name only) what the 'fair share' should be, at any time later so uncertainty can continue for many years.

In contrast, where a couple have been married or in a civil partnership, there is a well-established procedure for bringing that relationship to an end, making suitable financial provision for each partner and any children, and embodying that outcome in a court order which is enforceable through the courts if one party does not comply. Usually (albeit sometimes controversially) the terms of the order cannot be re-opened even if there is a change in circumstances, such as remarriage of one of the parties.

Even if the couple are married or in a civil partnership, it is still important to check who owns the property. If it is in one name only, the legal owner could sell it before the court process is concluded without the other knowing, so the non-owning party can and should protect their interest once the decision to split is made by registering a 'right of occupation' at the Land Registry, or if the property is not registered at the Land Registry, the Land Charges Registry.

Usually the terms of any financial order are negotiated between solicitors for each party, but the court can and will impose its own decision if the parties cannot agree. That order can require the transfer of the property from one party to another (even if the recipient is not one of the legal owners) or from joint names to one party, and allocate responsibility for future mortgage payments; and can include a requirement for the property to be sold either immediately or at a future date (for example when the youngest child leaves home), as well as allocating the sale proceeds.

It is worth making three points to dispel misconceptions:

1. The UK divorce courts have not usually recognised any pre-nuptial agreement (unlike some of the US states) so any such agreement or co-ownership agreement which attempts to determine who gets what on divorce may not work, assuming the divorce proceedings are in the UK. The Law Commission did suggest a change in the law as long ago as 1998 but no new law has yet been passed. For more complex international cases different outcomes may apply, but that is a matter for specialist legal advice. However, in July 2009 the Court of Appeal recognised a pre-nuptial agreement between a wealthy German woman and a less wealthy French man living in the UK (*Radmacher v Granatino*). The Court of Appeal's decision relied heavily on the specific circumstances of the case, where both husband and wife grew up in cultures where such agreements were 'normal' and they entered into the agreement freely and with the opportunity to take separate legal advice, so that the court decided that it would be 'unfair' not to treat the contract as valid. Whilst this decision was influenced by the background of husband and wife, this decision is likely to change future expectations and practice.

2. For most people, the value of one shared home will not cover the cost of buying and running two separate homes, and it is likely that either one or both parties will have to downgrade their living accommodation.

3. The position is no different for those who prefer legal separation to divorce, which some do, usually for religious reasons, or for same-sex couples who have been through a civil partnership ceremony but are now seeking to bring that partnership to an end. The court will make a financial order, taking account of the needs of each member of the family, particularly children, alongside the order formally terminating the relationship, although that order will be called a judicial separation order or a civil partnership dissolution order rather than a 'decree nisi' or 'decree absolute'.

All of the above commentary assumes that the couple, or one of them, owns a valuable freehold or long leasehold property rather than being a tenant. Where the couple are divorcing or separating, or terminating a civil partnership, as part of the order for ancillary relief the court can and will make orders about rights under any tenancy - either private or public sector - and broadly speaking the same principles will guide the court as in the case of freehold land or a long lease. Where the couple are not married, but one wants to stay in the property which they previously lived in together, and that property is held on a tenancy, the landlord's permission will usually be needed to transfer the tenancy into the name of the one remaining, and this can cause a problem where the one remaining cannot prove (particularly where rent arrears have accumulated during the split) income sufficient to cover the rents. As a generalisation, public sector landlords - councils or RSLs - are likely to be more sympathetic than private sector landlords.

*Recommendations:*

1 If you are an unmarried couple living together, a co-ownership agreement is wise to avoid disputes if you split; and

2 Divorce is bad for your wealth!

# CHAPTER 7 BUY-TO-LET

## The big picture

'Buy-to-let', like a number of other catchphrases in the property world, was invented for marketing purposes. It is a new name for an old habit, and over the years has acquired overtones, which we will attempt to demystify in this chapter. There are inevitably a number of generalisations; if you are planning a 'buy-to-let' investment, keep reading and you will find the later part of this chapter more relevant to you.

This chapter will cover only England and Wales, but many of the same comments apply to 'buy-to-let' elsewhere. Chapter 10 looks more specifically at buying property abroad, including for holiday letting.

The principle of 'buy-to-let' is very simple, and is in the name. You buy a property, but instead of living in it yourself, you let it to somebody else who pays you rent. You therefore create an investment which, at least in theory, gives you both an income from the rent you receive from the tenant, and a capital profit from the increase in value between the price you pay for the property, and the price you sell it for in the future.

This model is very similar to the beginnings of the property system in England and Wales, as described in Chapter 1, and to the mode of operation of the property companies, described in Chapter 8. Buy-to-let differs from the first in that you go and choose your property rather than taking it as one of the spoils of invasion or inheriting it, and from the second in that in the case of buy-to-let, you are usually dealing with a residential property, whereas the property companies (mostly) deal in commercial property only, with businesses rather than people as tenants. There is also a major difference in scale and experience; a buy-to-let investor is typically an amateur dealing occasionally or for the first time in a long term rental property investment, involving usually at most only a handful of residential properties without any previous training; major landowners and property companies are professionals, with knowledge and access to specialist advice, and are regularly dealing in multi-million pound transactions. The typical buy-to-let investor also faces the complication that the residential market is not simply an investment market, as the commercial property market is, because they are competing with those buying and selling their own homes.

## Why 'buy-to-let'?

So, why has 'buy-to-let' become so popular over the last 15 years? And can you outsmart the professionals?

'Buy-to-let', as any other part of the property market, can indeed be a lucrative investment, but success depends on three main factors - availability of funds, availability of tenants and most of all on timing. Patience too is vital – it can take years to realise a respectable return from a residential property investment.

The rise in popularity of 'buy-to-let' has been driven by two main long term pressures: the lack of available cheap housing, particularly for those in the first years after leaving home, and the availability of cheap funds from lenders during the last few years.

It is significant that 'buy-to-let', as a phrase, became a term in common use once it was adopted by the Association of Residential Letting Agents in 1995 as a label in order to encourage the development of mortgage products aimed specifically at this market. Before that time, the building societies and other mortgage lenders of the day aimed their products at the home buying market, making relatively few exceptions for those who wished to purchase residential property with the intention of subsequently renting it out. Once this market was 'labelled', new products from existing lenders swiftly followed – from Halifax, Cheltenham & Gloucester, Northern Rock and others - followed by specialist lenders: Paragon Finance, Mortgage Express (Bradford and Bingley) and BM Solutions (Birmingham Midshires, part of Bank of Scotland), etc – so that, according to the Council of Mortgage Lenders, the volume of 'buy-to-let' lending rose from £3 billion out of total mortgage lending of £115 billion in 1999 to £45 billion out of £365 billion in 2007 - in other words from under 3% of total lending to over 12% (although in 2009 it dropped to 6% - £9.5 billion out of £144 billion). Putting it another way, there were under 75,000 'buy-to-let' mortgages in existence at the end of 1999, compared to over a million at the end of 2009.

Why did the lenders go into this so enthusiastically and on such a scale? The answer is easy: because they could charge a little more interest than on conventional loans to home buyers, so they would make a bigger 'turn' on the money they in turn 'bought' from wholesale money markets, or a bigger margin over the rate of interest they paid to savers.[86]

## Ups and downs

As increasing numbers of amateur landlords saw the attractions of 'buy-to-let' (particularly in the late 1990s, as disenchantment with traditional pension schemes set in), developers and agents saw the bandwagon rolling, jumped on and the market heated up. The emphasis increasingly shifted to profit from capital growth, rather than income for the investor – in other words, the message became accepted that if the rental income paid the interest on the loan, the investors' upside would be the 'inevitable' increase in value of the property.

Articles, seminars and 'training courses' were sold to answer the question: 'How could you give up work and be a property millionaire instead?' More and more city centre flats were built to feed the demand for 'buy-to-let' investments rather than to address the primary need of providing affordable homes for people in locations where they actually wanted to live, and the bubble inevitably expanded.

As the wider housing market reached its peak in mid-2007 and price growth stopped and started to go into reverse, banks began to worry about value of the investments they had made in the form of buy-to-let mortgages, and it became harder for amateur landlords to finance their property purchases, and the 'buy-to-let' market started to look very risky. Headlines in newspaper property supplements changed from 'How to make a fortune in property' to 'Storm clouds gather on horizon' and finally to 'Buy-to-let, how a good idea went terribly wrong.'[87]

---

[86] Or we could just say 'so they made more money'.

[87] As an extreme example of how far things can go wrong, consider a criminal case reported in April 2009 when four men were convicted of fraud in a £365 million 'buy to let' scam based in the North East of England. Prosecutors in the case claimed that between 2001 and 2003 the four convicted men defrauded more than 1,000 investors, telling them that in return for investing £25,000 each they would own a house in an up-and-coming area of the North East of England which would be refurbished and rented out. The investors paid their money eagerly to the fraudsters, who to be fair, did indeed purchase some properties as they had promised to do. However, many of the properties were found to be in undesirable areas, of a lower value in quality than claimed, and left

The overall market for lettings has worsened since mid-2007 as three trends have developed:

- the appearance of an increasing number of 'accidental' or 'reluctant' landlords: that is, home owners who have not been able to sell their homes at an acceptable price and have instead chosen to rent them out;
- an increasing number of potential tenants (particularly younger people) are choosing to stay at home rather than take on the financial commitment of moving into rented accommodation;
- a marked reluctance on the part of lenders to provide funds to the buy-to-let market, so that both funds to purchase new 'buy-to-let' properties and funds to refinance existing 'buy-to-let' mortgages have largely dried up (it is reported that there are only 8-10 active lenders compared to over 100 in 2007).

So, at the time of writing in spring 2010, if you believe the press reports, investing in 'buy-to-let' looks like a terrible idea.

But is it?

## 2010 onwards

The first point to make is that buying a 'buy-to-let' property as an investment is a decision requiring the exercise of discretion. Unless you are an accidental landlord you do not have to do it. It also needs cash. The days of 100% 'buy-to-let' mortgages have (quite rightly) gone[88] so if you are considering making a buy-to-let investment you must have a (substantial) lump sum ready to invest. You also need to consider the investment risks specific to property – what will happen if you need money in a hurry? It is important to remember that selling property is much slower and more difficult than selling quoted shares or simply taking money out of a deposit account. And is it wise to commit your life savings to property when your other main asset, your home, is also a

---

unrenovated, untenanted and uninsured. One row of terraced houses acquired during the scam was said to be known by locals as 'the Gaza Strip'. And inevitably, the fraudsters had not hesitated to use their investors' money for themselves. The Serious Fraud Office said that the use of company funds for personal gain by some of the fraudsters was 'simply staggering' – including buying a fleet of luxury cars, racehorses, art and clothes, and a villa in Spain.

[88] Hopefully, never to return.

residential property so that if the property market crashes you are likely to suffer twice over? Are there other forms of investment that might be more suitable for you?

But if you have read this far, you are probably interested enough to want to know more about 'buy-to-let' in order to assess whether it is a 'better' investment than any alternatives available to you.

Even in difficult times, if you buy the right property at the right price and manage the property and the letting carefully, investing in residential property can generate a useful income, a profit over cost and in the longer term all signs now point to capital growth in the residential property market.

So do you want to try?

For the purposes of this chapter we are assuming that this is your first 'buy-to-let' (so apologies to those who have already learnt the ropes) and we concentrate on the simplest 'buy-to-let' model: that is, a single property (flat or house) to be let to a single tenant, or a couple or a family. Investing in student accommodation or other shared lettings or holiday lettings adds a layer of complication because they need much more 'hands on' management – but that is not to say that you may not wish to consider making such an investment in due course. But for the time being, let's keep things as simple as we can.

## The golden rules

The 'golden rules' of the successful 'buy-to-let' are:

1. Buy where people will want to rent.
2. Buy the kind of property people will want to occupy.
3. Pay the right price for the property bearing in mind you will be renting it out rather than buying it as your home.
4. Do all your sums before you buy. (And then double-check those sums.)
5. Don't forget that management of a property is a hassle (and more than that, you are potentially legally liable if it goes badly wrong).
6. Decide whether you are willing to let to tenants supported by Local Housing Allowance (generally known as housing benefit). If so, what capping applies to the maximum rent you can get?

Looking at the golden rules in turn:

## Where?

Many of the suggestions made in Chapter 2 about how to analyse where and what you want to buy for yourself apply just as strongly for 'buy-to-let', except that you need to look at the available property through the eyes of a potential tenant rather than your own. So, first, you need to think about what kind of tenant you are looking for, whether it be an individual, a professional couple or a family.

## What property?

If an individual or working couple, the key factors for them, and then therefore the best way to maximise the number of potential tenants for you, are:

- Location - close to public transport, shops and entertainment.
- Availability of car parking.
- Security.
- Facilities
  - one or two bedrooms? Or more?
  - good quality kitchen and bathroom fittings.
- Furnished or unfurnished?
- Simplistically, a couple without children may prefer a flat to a house and to rent furnished rather than unfurnished accommodation.

If you intend to rent your buy-to-let property to a family their priorities are likely to be:

- Location – again, close to public transport (but not in the centre of town).
- Availability of car parking.
- Availability of schools and parks.
- Security.
- Facilities
  - at least three bedrooms.
  - a larger kitchen.
  - good quality kitchen and bathroom fittings.
- Garden.
- Furnished or unfurnished.

A family is likely to prefer a house to a flat and is more likely to prefer unfurnished.

Clearly, in most parts of England and Wales, houses are generally more expensive than flats but will usually provide a higher rent, so you need to do your sums; with the cash you have plus mortgage finance what will you be able to afford to buy (and get ready for letting) and what income will you be able to generate? Remember if you are going to offer furnished accommodation that tenants increasingly expect the furnishing to be of a good standard, and you should factor the cost of this into your calculations.

You need to consider locations and properties where there are likely to be a pool of potential tenants. For example, cities (and London in particular) have large numbers of people who are not ready or yet willing to commit to buy property of their own; university towns have a steady stream of visiting academics and researchers and post-graduates, as well as undergraduates; hospitals also attract visiting staff; major employers (particularly major multi-nationals) have a constant turnover of short term (typically one to three years) international employees who need (generally high quality) rented accommodation.

Think also about schools – is there a specific international or American or Dutch or Norwegian school near to which you could buy so as to attract families who want to be close to those schools?

We cannot overstress the importance of researching the market, and of getting a clear idea of buying prices in your chosen area, and the likely rental levels you may be able to charge – read the local paper, see who is advertising lettings and check the property websites listed on page 361.

Research the scale and number of other rental properties in the area – there tend to be clusters in suitable areas – by talking to local letting agents as well as local estate agents, and establishing from them what kinds of property they deal with, and the locations where they think you will have the greatest chances of success both in achieving lettings and in maximising the rent (you can play one off against another – but remember the agent will be on the side of the prospective sellers, not yours, so treat the answers you get with a degree of scepticism). Ask the agents about the letting profile over the year (November and February are usually bad times to market lettings: families often want to move in school holidays and be ready for new schools in September). If possible, talk to buy-to-let landlords who have already invested in your target area.

And, don't forget, you will need to be able to visit the property yourself without too much difficulty – to make sure there is not a problem, or to deal with any that arise – so if you live in Brighton, it's generally not a good idea to buy in Newcastle or vice versa.

If you can, talk to the accommodation officers for nearby universities or hospitals or major employers to establish the nature of demand, both the kind of property, and the annual cycle, if there is one, and whether you can get yourself on their lists.

Be aware of the change in planning rules in April 2010 which means that planning permission is needed to change a house or flat from 'family' use to 'multiple' use – which for planning purposes means three rather than five people. So buying a family house and putting three individual tenants in it needs planning permission. This change was aimed at limiting 'student ghettoes' in cities like Leeds, Sheffield and Nottingham but applies throughout England and Wales.

Check what new developments are underway or envisaged in the area which could compete with what you will be letting, or possibly enhance the desirability of rental property in that area.

Check whether there is greater demand for furnished or unfurnished lettings and what tenants' expectations may be as to the quality of fittings and furniture.

Although 'buy-to-let' is linked in the public mind to new developments and it has suited developers for the general public to think so, there is no logical reason why it should be, so consider whether there is better value in buying a five- or 10-year old house or flat (or even older) rather than buying new, or 'off plan' before construction is finished. Do not be too persuaded by developers' 'rental guarantees'. If you are buying within a development, try to establish how many other flats in the development will be finished at the same time, how many are being sold as buy-to-let investments, and therefore how much competition you will have for tenants at the time when you are looking for them.

Also, research the mortgage market – as we have already noted, 'buy-to-let' mortgages are by no means as freely available as they were pre-Credit Crunch, and you will have to find a hefty amount of your own money (say 25-40% of the purchase price). Don't forget also to factor in the other costs associated with property purchases, for example, stamp duty, legal fees and so on. You will need to consider whether you will be funding the buy-to-let purchase by means of a mortgage on the buy-to-let property (a 'genuine' buy-to-let mortgage), or by means of a mortgage on your existing home (assuming you have the equity in your home to support such a mortgage). We talk about this in greater detail in Chapter 5; however, as a general rule, if you apply for a 'buy-to-let' mortgage you will be asked much more detailed questions about the property you are buying, the predictions for letting and your own financial position than you may expect. Also, the lenders' valuers' rules have been tightened to make sure they know all the incentives you are getting from the developer, not just the headline price. The lender's fees, as well as the interest rate, are significant costs for which you must budget, and the mortgage approval process will take longer than you expect. As with any other mortgage, we suggest you use the internet and comparison websites to identify the 'going rate' and then speak to three providers in more detail to establish their pricing, timing and enthusiasm.

A useful starting point may be www.arlamortgages.co.uk, which is a price comparison site launched by the Association of Residential Letting Agents, specifically for buy-to-let landlords.

## Buy at the right price for renting

Because you are competing with potential owner-occupiers to buy your property, and in most situations they are in the majority, the pricing the seller hopes to achieve will be driven by the price at which other owner-occupiers have bought similar houses in the area in the recent past, and that will form the basis of the selling agents' advice to the seller. If you are buying as an investment, you need to think about it differently, and work backwards from considering the gross rent you realistically expect to achieve, to calculate the gross yield relative to the price you are being asked to pay. You can then recalculate after deducting the costs you are likely to bear both at the time of purchase and during letting, to give you a 'net yield'.

An example of how to do this is set out below:

**What is yield - gross and net?**

| | | |
|---|---|---|
| *Gross yield* | | |
| Price paid | | £225,000 |
| Add: | purchase and mortgage set-up costs | £5,000 |
| | decoration and furnishing costs | £10,000 |
| Total purchase cost | | £240,000 |
| Rental | £1,000 per month = £12,000 per year | |
| Gross yield: £240,000 ÷ £12,000 = 5% | | |
| *Net yield* | | |
| Price paid | | £225,000 |
| Add: | purchase and mortgage set-up costs | £5,000 |
| | decoration and furnishing costs | £10,000 |
| Total purchase cost | | £240,000 |
| Rental | £1,000 per month = £12,000 per annum | |
| Less: | agent's fees for letting at 10% + VAT[89] | £1,410 |
| | agent's fees for rent collection at 4% + VAT | £564 |
| | agent's 'full service' management fee at 4% + VAT | £564 |
| | (including HIP and gas/electricity certification) | |
| | building contents insurance | £400 |
| | ground rent and service charge | £400 |
| | allowance for minor repairs during the tenancy | £700 |
| | allowance for one month void period | £1,200 |
| | mortgage interest | £750 |
| | (assuming £180,000 interest-only mortgage at 5%) | |
| | Total | £5,988 (say £6,000) |
| So net income (pre-tax) is £6,000 | | |
| Net yield: £240,000 ÷ £6,000 = 2.5% | | |

[89] We are using 17.5% as the VAT rate. It will rise to 20% on 4 January 2011.

The purpose of carrying out this calculation is to enable you to see the real rate of return that you would receive from buying and letting, compared to leaving your money in the bank, or investing in a different way – whether that be stocks and shares or anything else. This also gives you a means of comparing one potential property purchase to another so you can see which creates better value. It does not however allow for any capital gains you may ultimately enjoy if you sell the property at some time in the future.

Rental yields of private rented property have varied dramatically over the period 2005 to 2009 and there is no right or wrong answer as to whether, say, a 7% gross yield and 3% net yield is a 'good investment' or not; it is likely that if the net yield is less than 3% it is not. The calculation also gives you a means of comparing your projected income and return against your actual income and return for each year after you have bought the property so you can see if you do better (if rents rose and interest rates fell and expenses stayed under control) or not (if interest rates rose or management costs rose or you did not re-let, creating a void).

## Budgeting

You will need to carefully complete and consider the following, before committing yourself.

INITIAL OUTLAY

Purchase price

Purchase costs - SDLT (stamp duty)

Land Registry fees

Legal fees (plus VAT)

Mortgage set-up costs (initial fee, surveyor's costs, draw-down fee, legal fees for the lender if relevant)

Any decoration/repair/improvement required before letting

Furniture/furnishing, including carpets and curtains

Letting agent's costs - say 7.5% of annual rent (plus VAT)

Legal requirements (including EPC)

Electrical check/certification

Gas check/certification

BUY-TO-LET

Registration as landlord (if introduced)

Buildings and contents insurance

## ONGOING INCOME/OUTGOINGS

In - rental income (less lettings and management fees and VAT on them)

Out - mortgage payments

Service charges (for a flat or house with shared facilities)

Ground rent (if any)

Reserve for void costs: that is, council tax and water rates and utility connections between lettings and during any handover period.

Tax is dealt with in greater detail in Chapter 5 but, in outline, don't forget you will be liable to pay:

(a) Stamp Duty Land Tax on the purchase price (which is at the same rate as for any other property purchase – see page 160 for a table of rates) – the 'first-time buyer' exemption is not intended for buy-to-let properties.

(b) Income Tax on the rental income received in each tax year, after making allowable deductions (which include mortgage interest, agents' fees and an allowance for the renewal of furnishings). Be careful to claim only the interest part of the mortgage payments, not the capital repayment part. HMRC announced a 'concerted compliance campaign' against buy-to-let landlords in early 2008 with the target of recovering £300m of due but unpaid tax. They have obtained lists of landlord names and addresses from letting and managing agents and are now targeting landlords using 'let only' agents, so don't assume you will get away with it.

(c) Capital Gains Tax when you sell the property, on the 'profit' difference between the price you pay to buy and the price you achieve on sale, after making allowable deductions, which include purchase costs, including SDLT, improvement costs and sale costs: for example, agents' and solicitors' fees. You cannot deduct for Capital Gains Tax purposes mortgage interest or maintenance costs or any other items already charged as a deduction against income tax.

## Finding a tenant

Clearly, 'buy-to-let' requires a tenant. Unless you are fortunate enough to have a tenant standing by[90], you will need to find one. Depending on the location and type of property, you have the following options:

- The traditional route - that is, via local letting agents (who may be part of a national or international chain or association).

  Their fees are likely to be in the order of 15% of the annual rent as an initial fee.
- The cheap route – that is, via the local newspaper or boards in newsagents or word of mouth.
- The internet – there are many letting websites in which specialise in letting: for example, Gumtree or Loot or part of the larger websites such as Prime Location or FindAProperty.Com. Gumtree is mostly used by young professionals in cities, often to find a replacement sharer. Gumtree and Loot are free to landlords.
- Local employers or institutions – the accommodation officers of large companies, universities, hospitals.
- Relocation agents – to whom large employers may have delegated the search for accommodation for employees.

The direct costs to you are likely to be minimal, but you will have to comply with their requirements and the standards of accommodation and furnishing you have to provide are likely to be high. When advertising, or choosing a tenant, bear in mind that anti-discrimination legislation applies to letting, so any unfair discrimination on grounds of sex, race, sexual orientation, religion or belief, age or disability is unlawful.

## Finding an agent

Be careful to read the terms of any agency agreement you are offered: at least one agency (Foxtons) once included clauses in their standard terms giving them extra commission if the tenant renewed their lease, and a commission of 2% of the value of the property if the tenant bought it from the landlord. The landlord disputed this but lost his case; the Office of Fair Trading stepped in and the courts have now declared that such clauses may be unenforceable (at least

[90] In our experience letting to friends and relatives is a quick way to ruin that relationship.

where the landlord is an individual rather than a professional investor) because it is an unfair contract term - but you don't want to have an argument like that!

Be careful though: Foxtons' terms could have been found binding if the landlord was an experienced landlord, and could have been enforceable if properly flagged rather than hidden in small print.

## What kind of letting?

Almost all private sector lettings (apart from short term holiday lets) are on an assured shorthold tenancy, or AST, which we discussed in Chapter 2. Broadly, that means the tenant does not have court protection as to the amount of rent, so is legally liable to pay the negotiated amount, and does not have the right to stay on after the tenancy period has expired, unless you as landlord agree to extend or renew the tenancy.

How long should the tenancy be? You and the tenant can negotiate whatever length of tenancy you want. However, the usual length of tenancy for most situations, used by most letting agents, is one year with a minimum of six months. Many ASTs have included a right for the tenant to walk away earlier (usually after a minimum of six months, on two months' notice) – to allow for changes in circumstances such as a change of job location - and/or for the tenant to choose to extend for a further period of one year (usually with the same right to walk away on two months' notice during that time), and sometimes with the right to extend again for a third year. Often, if the tenant can extend, there will be a rent uplift of say 5%, or perhaps in line with the Retail Price Index.

Who is the tenant? If it is a couple, is it both of them? If a group of sharers, is it all of them?[91] If an employer, is it the employee personally or the company? If the tenant is a non-earner or low earner (for example, an undergraduate or post-graduate student or a student medic) should someone like a parent guarantee the tenancy?[92]

## Tenancy agreements

ASTs are freely negotiable but are in practice relatively standard documents. Sample forms are available from a number of sources, including law stationers

---

[91] Legally there cannot be more than four people as tenant under one tenancy agreement.
[92] In our opinion, yes.

such as www.lawpack.co.uk. A useful online resource for landlords - run by a solicitor – is www.landlordlaw.co.uk. There are different forms for houses or flats, furnished or unfurnished.

## The terms of the letting

Apart from the key points of the rent and the length of the tenancy and the identity of the tenant, important points to consider are:

(1) *The amount of the deposit, who holds it and who gets the interest*

Usually the tenant puts down a deposit equivalent to either four or six weeks' rent which is held either by the landlord or by the agent. The purpose of the deposit is to protect the landlord against the tenant failing to pay the rent, or causing damage which is not made good at the end of the tenancy. The deposit should remain the tenant's money. Logically the interest should belong to the tenant, but many landlords provide in their tenancy agreements that they get the benefit of the interest on the deposit.

Landlords and letting agents are now required to sign up to one of the three Tenancy Deposit Protection Scheme providers – see page 45 for details – and the landlord pays a fee for this. The penalties for not complying - either at the beginning of the tenancy, in taking the deposit, or at the end of the tenancy, in returning it subject to any appropriate deductions - are severe and can include repaying more than the deposit or even losing the landlord's right to recover possession of the property.

(2) *Which outgoings are paid by the landlord and which by the tenant?*

Conventionally, the tenant will pay for outgoings related to his occupation - electricity, gas, telephone and internet, water (whether it is water rates or metered) and TV licence – and the landlord will pay for outgoings relating to the property or the building of which it is part: for example, buildings insurance, ground rent and any service charges for shared facilities. One recent change to be aware of is that the water company can pursue the landlord for water rates if the tenant agrees to, but does not, pay.

(3) *Repairs and decoration*

The landlord is usually explicitly responsible for repair and maintenance to the structure of the building (roof, walls, floors, foundations) and the main installations within it – electrical, gas and bathrooms and toilets (this is imposed in any event by Section 11 of the Housing Act 1985 but is usually set out specifically). The tenant is usually responsible for minor repairs – replacing light bulbs etc – and is also required to make good any loss or damage he or she causes to the property, or to the furniture and contents. Fair wear and tear is usually excluded from the tenant's responsibility. There is plenty of scope for argument as to who caused what, and what is meant by wear and tear, which tends to come to light at the end of the tenancy, and particularly when the tenant's deposit is due to be repaid.

The tenant is not usually given the right to redecorate.

*(4) Cleaning*

You as landlord will normally be expected to pay for professional cleaning of the property before the tenant moves in. Many tenant agreements, however, impose an obligation on the tenant to pay for professional cleaning after he or she moves out.

*(5) Inventory*

Assuming the property is furnished, it is important to record what is there at the beginning of the tenancy so that you can identify when the tenancy ends whether anything has gone astray, or has been damaged, which may be the responsibility of the tenant so you can reclaim it from the tenant before they go. If you are letting through an agency, they will normally arrange for a specialist inventory clerk to make an inventory at the start and end of the tenancy, the cost of which is conventionally split 50/50 between landlord and tenant, but this is negotiable. From the landlord's point of view, the inventory at the beginning of the tenancy should include every item down to the teaspoons, and the inventory should be rigorously checked at the end of the tenancy for any losses. The purpose of the inventory is to avoid later arguments about what was in the property at the beginning.

*(6) Rent*

This is usually payable monthly in advance by standing order. Depending upon the nature of the property, some tenants may be claiming 'housing benefit'. Under the previous housing benefit system the rent was paid direct to the landlord. A change was introduced in April 2008 so that the new version of housing benefit, applicable to private sector tenants, known as Local Housing Allowance, is paid by the local authority to tenants instead, who are then responsible for paying their rents to their landlords. However, if a tenant is unable to handle their own financial affairs, or is more than eight weeks in arrears, or has a history of failing to pay rent, the local authority may pay rent direct to the landlord.

According to research by the National Landlords Association published in April 2009, this system is not working because many tenants are failing to pass on the LHA payments they receive to landlords to pay the rents, and so many landlords have had to take action to claim the rents, including in some cases repossessing the property from the tenant. 52% of NLA members surveyed said they would not want to let to LHA tenants for that reason and 43% of those who have already tried the new system say they now plan not to re-let to an LHA tenant in the future.

The substantial reduction in LHR proposed in the 'emergency Budget' will be enforced by capping the maximum rent payable for particular categories of property – for example, £400 per week for a four-bedroomed house. This will impact directly on rents.

*(7) Insurances*

Normally the landlord is responsible for insuring the building, and any fixtures, fittings and contents he or she provides; any contents introduced by the tenant – which may include valuable items such as TVs and laptops – are for the tenant to insure.

*(8) Pets*

Will you as landlord allow pets in the property? If so, will this be limited, perhaps (as we have seen) to a named dog or cat?

*(9) Smoking*

Will you prohibit or allow smoking?

The remaining provisions are mostly either general obligations on the tenant to behave him or herself so as to look after the property and not annoy the neighbours, or procedural clauses. They are worth a read at least once although do not expect Shakespearean prose. One important clause which we will refer to later is the right to terminate.

## Letting a property – legal requirements

1. 'Landlord Licence' – to cover each of the landlord and the letting agent. Voluntary licensing schemes exist; some local authorities already offer accreditation schemes; landlord representative bodies such as the Association of Residential Letting Agents already have or are producing licensing and regulation schemes on a voluntary basis. A mandatory system of licensing of landlords was proposed in 2009. The Coalition Government has indicated that they will not seek to introduce one.
2. Tenancy Deposit Protection Scheme - a compulsory scheme to protect the tenant's deposit. There are three alternatives: the Tenancy Deposit Scheme (backed by Aviva Insurance), My Deposit, a joint venture between the National Landlords Association and Hamilton Fraser Insurance, or the Deposit Protection Service. The first two are insurance-backed schemes and the third is simply a way of holding the cash representing the deposit. The landlord or agent must give details to the tenant of how the deposit is protected within 14 days after the tenancy begins. The landlord is required to release the deposit within 10 days after the end of the tenancy unless a good reason is given. If there is a dispute about the return of the deposit, the deposit scheme will hold the deposit until the dispute is resolved.[93]
3. An EPC – to be available before the letting is concluded.
4. If the property is a 'house in multiple occupation' or HMO, a Local Authority Certificate (and maybe planning permission).
5. An inspection certificate for the electrical installations.
6. An inspection certificate for the gas installations.[94]
7. An inspection certificate for air conditioning if relevant (this requirement is being introduced gradually).

---

[93] The penalties for failure to follow these procedures are severe: the landlord may have to pay a penalty of three times the deposit, and cannot take repossession proceedings, even if the tenant is in default. The landlord's agent may get away with following the procedure late (*Draycott v Hannells Lettings*) but there are appeals pending in the Court of Appeal which may reverse that decision.

[94] For a guide to a landlord's legal obligations in relation to its tenants' gas safety, see www.hse.gov.uk/gas/landlords/index.htm.

8. Fire safety compliance for upholstery, that is sofas, chairs etc.
9. Tax Return.

## Assured tenancies

We mention in passing a different kind of tenancy known as an assured tenancy, also created under the Housing Act 1988. These are used by public sector landlords such as housing associations, for a more permanent tenancy likely to last a number of years. They give the tenants greater rights of continued occupation, because the landlord can only terminate for certain specified reasons. Conversely they allow for regular rent reviews (by reference to comparisons of other similar property being let at the time) as the tenancy will last longer, so that the landlord has the right to gradually increase its income.

Two other kinds of tenancy deserve special mention.

## Holiday lettings

The idea of using a UK second home for holiday lets is an attractive one - it can be a way of getting the best of both worlds by combining investment (assuming house prices rise), income (assuming holidaymakers want to use it) and holidays for yourself. There is an obvious potential conflict between your desire to make money, and your desire to use your second home, which means some awkward decisions about what you buy, how you furnish it, and when you occupy it yourself - do you take the peak weeks, or the ones nobody else wants?

You should also not under-estimate the hassle factor of advertising, managing bookings, arranging handovers (usually weekly) including cleaning, and dealing with maintenance.

Some tips:

1. Think before you buy. Make sure that you are clear about the letting market you are aiming for. The seaside, country cottages or big city flats are all very different markets with different pricing (to buy, or as rent), different markets, and different seasons. Research the local competition.
2. Decorate to let. You will need to de-personalise the space - your taste may not suit everyone – and clear out your own clutter. It is useful to have a secure room, or cupboard, so you can tuck away your own personal things (photos of your family are for you, not guests).

3. Budget carefully. As well as comparing the price you pay with the rent you hope to get, factor in running costs - repairs and replacements, cleaning, insurances, utility bills, council tax, advertising costs.
4. Advertise wisely. Local agents may be expensive and limited in scope; holiday lettings specialists such as English Country Cottages, West Country Cottages or Welcome Cottages will usually be cheaper and focussed on your target market (although your property will be one of many on their website) and will take care of advertising and bookings for a percentage commission.[95] Some web advertisers such as www.holidaylettings.co.uk charge a fixed fee for you to use their site but leave you to manage the bookings.
5. Present the property well. Words and pictures are important. You will usually provide these yourself rather than the letting agent. Make the property look attractive, and emphasize the positive points and activities in the local area. Look at other holiday letting websites to see what attracts or repels you.
6. Simplify handovers. If you live locally and enjoy cleaning, good for you. If not, you will need to hire a local cleaner or cleaning company to do this for you. Some property management companies, particularly in traditional holiday areas, will provide this and a handover service, at a cost.
7. Remember the legals. Make sure your documentation is clear, and spells out rates, deposit arrangements and responsibility for breakages. Standard forms can be downloaded but make sure you understand them and they are appropriate. It is worth paying a solicitor to check them. Also make sure your mortgage company and insurers are aware you are letting, otherwise you will be in breach of the mortgage or insurance policy.
8. Don't forget tax. VAT is chargeable on rents for holiday lettings. If the annual turnover exceeds the level at which VAT registration is required (£70,000 in 2010), you need to register and file VAT returns. For income tax purposes, holiday lettings will usually be treated as a trade, which means different rules on deductions and allowances apply. Careful bookkeeping will be needed. There are currently beneficial tax allowances for furnished holiday lettings. These were to be removed following the 2010 Budget. This

[95] Website addresses for these are in Appendix 2

provision was lost in the pre-election scurry to pass the Finance Bill, but it would not be a surprise if this proposal was revived, maybe in a different form..

## Letting to students

Lettings by education establishments to students fall outside the scope of this book. Lettings by individuals do not. A typical example may arise when parents buy a house for their student child to live in while at university, and share with a few friends. This section is addressed to you as parents.

Before you go down this road, just think why you are contemplating it. Is it as an investment? If so, what will you do once your child has moved on? Re-let or sell? Is it fair on your child (or are they willing or mature enough) to act as 'landlord' for their mates, and take responsibility for bills, breakages and resolving disputes?

Secondly, you need to consider whether the property will be bought in the parents' names – easier to control, and raise a mortgage against, if the parents are earning, but less tax efficient – or in the child's name – which depending on circumstances, may be attractive for inheritance tax purposes. Remember income tax will be due on the rents (less annual allowances and deductions) and capital gains tax on any increase in value (less relevant costs).

The following hints are from the personal experience of one of the co-authors:

1. Remember that students are generally noisier and messier than 'professional' tenants. Allow for replacement of crockery, cutlery, furniture and bed linen more often than with other tenants, and for bigger cleaning bills at the end of the tenancy.
2. Don't be too casual. Put a proper tenancy agreement (AST) or agreements (per individual) in place to document who is paying the rent, how much, and when.
3. Students may expect a property to be fully furnished down to pillows and teaspoons, whereas 'professional' tenants may provide smaller items themselves. Make sure there is an inventory. Students will also expect broadband to be available.
4. You will need either rent deposits or parental guarantees to make sure the rent is paid. If you take deposits, you will need to comply with the Tenancy Deposit Scheme.

5. Tenancies for undergraduates will normally be on a 10 month basis – end September to end July, or mid September to mid July, depending on the university term dates. Postgraduates may need a 12 month tenancy.
6. If the number of occupiers is three or more, and the property has not been used for 'sharers' before, then planning permission may be needed to allow the use of the property as a 'House in Multiple Occupation'. This change in planning regulations was rushed through pre-Election to address concerns about 'student ghettos' but it is difficult to see how it can work in practice.
7. If the number of occupiers is five or more, depending on the layout of it, it may qualify as a 'House in Multiple Occupation' for licensing purposes so that you will need to register, and as part of that registration probably make changes to improve fire safety for the occupiers (for example by ensuring there is a fire alarm system and a secondary means of escape). If the property is in your child's name, and the child is living there, it should be outside this requirement but if it is re-let to students after he or she leaves, the HMO regulations may apply. If the proposed requirement for all landlords to be registered becomes law, the registration system will apply.
8. If you take out a mortgage on the property, you will need to ensure that the mortgage lender is aware you are letting it, otherwise you will be in breach of the mortgage.
9. You will need to disclose to the insurers of the building the fact that the property is being let and make sure the students are aware of and comply with any relevant conditions such as setting the burglar alarm when they are out. You may need to notify the insurers if the property will be empty for more than 30 days - for example, over the summer vacation.
10. It may be beneficial for the long term to link up with the university's accommodation service so that you are aware of any standard requirements they may have, and you may be able to get on their approved list of landlords for future years.

## What is an HMO?

An HMO – a house in multiple occupation – is a larger building occupied by more than one household who share at least some facilities (commonly the kitchen and bathroom). Imagine Rigsby's empire in 'Rising Damp' and you have the picture! With greater concern about the quality of accommodation and particularly fire risk in multi-tenanted buildings, a compulsory licensing system for HMOs was introduced with effect from 6 July 2006 under the provisions of the Housing Act 2004, so that the landlord (or manager) is required to be registered as responsible for a property, and to prove that he or she is a fit and proper person, and that the property itself is suitable for occupation, up to a specified maximum number of occupants.

The licence is not transferable, and can be made conditional on specified improvements being carried out. HMOs cover everything from hostels where the occupiers stay only one night, to properties occupied on year-long tenancy agreements, and may include properties with tenants who have been in place for many years.

It is the landlord's (or manager's) responsibility to apply for the HMO licence from the local authority. In principle, this requirement applies to all properties with three or more storeys that are occupied by five or more people in two or more households.

More specifically, an HMO is defined in the 2004 Act as a house in multiple occupation which:

(a) is occupied by more than one household where more than one household shares or lacks an amenity such as a bathroom, toilet or cooking facilities;

(b) comprises non-self-contained bedsit accommodation and houses occupied by sharers where there is no family relationship;

(c) is occupied by more than one household and is in a converted building - but not entirely self-contained flats, whether or not some amenities are shared or lacking; and

(d) comprises converted self-contained flats that do not meet the minimum standard requirements of the Building Regulations 1991 and where at least one third of the flats are privately rented.

Conversely, if a building is split into entirely self-contained flats, then no HMO registration is required.

Non-registration is a criminal offence carrying a fine of up to £20,000; breach of conditions is an offence carrying a fine of up to £5,000.

The Government changed the planning rules in April 2010 so that HMOs fall into a separate category for planning purposes (so that planning permission would be required to turn a house into an HMO). In particular, concern has been expressed about the concentration of large numbers of HMOs in certain areas, often 'student ghettos' in University towns. For this purpose (but not licensing) an HMO means three or more people sharing, not five or more.

## Managing your 'buy-to-let'

Many buyers of 'buy-to-let' flats, and those who find themselves as accidental landlords, assume that the property will take care of itself while it is let, and so fail to plan or budget properly for the cost of management.

That may work in the short term, but in the longer term lack of proper management creates significant risks and is likely to affect lettability – so it may increase the period between lettings, or decrease the rent - and may reduce the value of the property at the time of the sale or refinancing, and also open you up to legal claims.

'Management' falls into two parts:

- *Managing the tenancy; and*
- *Managing the property.*

### Managing the tenancy

Some first-time landlords think that all they have to do is to give the tenant their bank account details and wait for the money to roll in. Sadly, it is not that simple.

If you are letting through a reputable letting agent, they will organise the set-up of the tenancy: that is, finding the tenant (including showing the property to various potential tenants), taking up references (which should include references from the tenant's bank and employer, and from any previous landlord), producing the form of tenancy agreement, getting it signed, formalising the deposit arrangements (and holding the money), arranging the inventory, producing the relevant certificates to the tenant, reading the meters and notifying the utility providers and the local authority (for Council Tax purposes) and generally managing the keys, co-ordinating the move in, and liaising with the tenant as part of their initial service.

If you find a tenant privately you will have to do all this yourself.

Once the tenancy is up and running, the rent is normally paid monthly, by standing order (with the first month's rent being paid on or before the date the tenancy starts, in addition to the deposit). If you have let through a letting agent, they will offer to collect the rent on your behalf and then pay it over to your nominated account, after deducting their fee. A typical fee is 2% of the monthly rent (plus VAT).

If you have let privately, you can arrange for payment by the tenant direct to your bank account.

*Problems with payment*

So far, so good. But what if the tenant does not pay?

Agents tend not to be particularly proactive in chasing rents, but at least they have experience of dealing with non-paying tenants. You need to keep a close eye on receipt of payments, and make sure that the agent is forewarned to alert you if there is any delay in payments being received, so that they can take action immediately, including notifying you. You can then work with the agents to understand the reason why the tenant is not paying, or paying late, or less than the full amount, and to take the appropriate measures to ensure it does not happen again. You should only need to escalate, or need legal advice, if there is a further failure to pay. If you have let privately, and your tenant misses a payment, you are likely to need legal advice immediately. Unfortunately the cost of legal advice will probably exceed the missed rent.

So here are some principles:

1. The tenant is liable to pay the contractual rent, so that is the person you need to chase, not his employer, nor the relocation agent.
2. If there was a guarantor they should equally be liable and you should notify them of the rent shortfall in writing if the tenant does not pay after a first reminder.

If neither of these steps produces the desired results, then you should consider taking legal proceedings and consult a solicitor.

In view of the sums involved it may well be that the solicitor's advice is to pursue the matter yourself through the small claims procedure in the County Court rather than using a solicitor to issue court proceedings.

Essentially you have two ways to proceed: either to chase the rent payment or payments by suing for the money as a debt, or to seek to terminate the tenancy and claim the rent up to the date of termination only.

The small claims court route is available for money claims up to £5,000, or £1,000 if the claim relates to damage to property. Local small claims courts are attached to each County Court. You are entitled to proceed in either the court applicable to where you live, or the court applicable to where the property is, or (if the tenant has moved out and you have an address) where the tenant is. Lists of courts, court forms and guidance notes are available at www.hmcourts-service.gov.uk.

Court fees are payable for issuing proceedings, on a sliding scale according to the value of the claim – for example the court fee for a claim for £1,500 is £75. Claims can be issued online (www.moneyclaim.gov.uk). Court fees are slightly lower if issued online. Further fees may be payable at later stages of the proceedings.

Bear in mind that you will be entitled to claim interest on the unpaid rent. If the tenancy agreement provides for it (which they usually do) you can claim at that rate from the due date. If not, you can claim from the date you issue proceedings at the rate the court allows. Legal costs can be recovered in small claims cases, but only a small amount (if the tenant can pay!).

We cannot generalise about the prospects of success: that will depend on the particular circumstances of the particular case. You can improve your chances by demonstrating a paper trail of a proper tenancy agreement, a detailed written breakdown showing the payments due and the payments made and not made and proof of any attempts by you to chase the tenant, and any attempts by the tenant to pay. You will also need to demonstrate that the tenant has actually been served with the proceedings properly. If the tenant has genuine money difficulties, even if you are successful it is likely that the court will allow the tenant time to pay off the arrears in instalments. Unfortunately, there is a small minority of tenants who use the court system to their own advantage as a means of delaying payment, which can be extremely frustrating for landlords.

*Terminating the tenancy*

Whilst the landlord and tenant relationship is hardly likely to survive the landlord issuing proceedings for arrears, if the landlord issues proceedings for possession that will usually be terminal. Having said this, it is by no means necessarily a simple matter for a landlord to regain possession of his property from an erring tenant. In order to terminate the tenancy, it is necessary to look carefully at the termination provisions in the tenancy agreement (known to lawyers as the 'forfeiture clause'), before taking action. For example, most such clauses allow the tenant a seven- or 14-day period of grace for payment after the date the rent was due.

The practicalities of termination are very different depending on whether the property is still occupied.

If the tenant (or anyone else) is still in occupation, you need to be careful. The Protection From Eviction Act 1977 makes it a criminal offence to repossess the property without going to court for a possession order, so you must go through that formal process. If the tenant has allowed someone else to occupy even without your permission, that person may also be entitled to relief, provided they pay all the arrears.

If no one is in occupation, then you can terminate simply by changing the locks and telling the tenant you have done so (although the latter is difficult to do if you do not have a forwarding address). If the tenant has moved out but left some of his possessions behind, you are subject to a legal requirement to look after those goods and hold on to them until the tenant can recover them from you, although you can give notice under the Tort (Interference with Goods) Act 1977 giving the tenant a fixed period of time to collect them, after which you have the right to sell the tenant's possessions (which is usually done at auction) and put any sale proceeds against the arrears of rent. Some forms of tenancy agreement expressly include this right which avoids the obligation to serve notice first. You can hang on to those goods until the tenant has paid his arrears of rent if the Tenancy agreement says so.

This may not be the end of the matter: the tenant is entitled to seek relief against forfeiture (or in other words, ask that his tenancy agreement not be terminated) for non-payment of rent by applying to court. There is an automatic right of relief if all the amounts claimed by the landlord as rent arrears and costs are paid into court at least five days before the hearing. The court also has discretion to allow relief even if payment is made later, or only in part. If the claim goes to a hearing, the court will give the tenant four weeks to pay up before the order for possession can be enforced.

If the tenant complies with the order to pay, or gets relief, the tenant is then entitled to stay in occupation of the property.

If you do seek possession through the courts, again the County Court is the appropriate venue. This must be the County Court for the district in which the property is situated. In very exceptional circumstances, it may be appropriate for the proceedings to be transferred to the High Court. The enforcement officers for the High Court have more powers, and tend to be more effective than the County Court Bailiffs.

Again, forms and guidance notes are available from your local court or from www.hmcourts-service.gov.uk. The fee for issuing possession proceedings in the County Court is currently £150, or £100 if you use the online version at www.possessionclaim.gov.uk. This is suitable where the possession proceedings are based on non-payment of rent, rather than other breaches of the tenancy agreement.

Again, a small minority of tenants will use the court system to drag out the possession process, which will be extremely frustrating for you.

If you believe the tenant would be homeless if you get possession, it may be possible to agree with the tenant to persuade the local housing authority to provide alternative accommodation for them: however, it is likely that you will still need to obtain a court order for possession in order to justify to the local housing authority that the tenant is genuinely homeless. Legal costs can be recovered in possession proceedings – if the tenant has the money to pay them!

## Managing the property

Managing the property encompasses all the repairs and maintenance you do, or arrange, on your own home - fixing broken gates, cutting the grass and weeding the flower beds in your garden, replacing any slipped roof tiles and clearing a blocked gutter, unbunging the drains, switching off the burglar alarm where there is a false alarm, working out why the washing machine or the dishwasher flooded the kitchen floor, fixing a broken window. Unless the tenant has agreed to take on these responsibilities, which will be unusual, they are down to you. Less frequently, the inside and outside of the property will need painting, the boiler will need regular servicing, and domestic appliances or furniture such as the toaster or kitchen table will in due course need replacing. If you are not there and you are busy (and maybe you are not very good at these things anyway), what will you do? The easy but expensive option is to employ the letting agent to do all this on your behalf. Most have access to local plumbers, electricians etc and arrangements for emergency call-outs. They are likely also to be local to the property so that if the tenant has a quick problem to solve - where is the switch for the immersion heater? where is the key for the shed? the bath is leaking! – they may be able to solve it without bothering you. The downside is that they will of course charge you for this. A typical 'all in' property management service will cost around 10-12% of the annual rent; an 'enhanced' service which will make decisions for you on, for example, redecoration and replacement of furniture on re-letting and so on, will cost about 12.5-15% of the annual rent. These fees are negotiable. Some agents charge more for the one-off letting fee and less month-by-month for management. Remember that these fees are subject to VAT.

Bear in mind also that if you are not careful to put limits on the agents' ability to make decisions on your behalf you may find that they have spent significant sums on minor, or more significant, visits, repairs and replacements which will eat into your rental income.

Alternatively, you can do it yourself – which means being on call 24/7 and ensuring you have access to reliable tradesmen, including emergency call-outs – or finding a 'friend' or 'jack of all trades' local to the property who is willing to take on this responsibility.

Do not underestimate the cost of management or the time it takes, or the anxiety level created by the fact that you are permanently 'on call'.

On the other hand, if you are well-organised, have the requisite practical ability[96] and have time, and live reasonably locally, you can save a significant cost by managing your own property.

The choice, as they say, is yours.

---

[96] Which excludes the authors…

# CHAPTER 8 INVESTING IN COMMERCIAL PROPERTY

## The big picture

An increasing number of individuals have chosen to invest a portion of their savings in commercial property, as part of their overall investment strategy. Increasingly, independent financial advisors are aware of investment products based on commercial property. Why?

There are three principal components to the answer - size, performance and accessibility.

In terms of the size of the UK commercial property market, the aggregate value when last estimated (by the Investment Property Forum (IPF)) in 2008 was around £529 billion compared with the residential property market at £3,805 billion and the equities market, as measured by shares of companies quoted on the London Stock Exchange, at about £1,288 billion.

In terms of performance, looking back from 2007, the UK commercial property market produced returns greater than equities, gifts or bonds (government or large company debt) or cash deposits over the previous three, five and 10 year periods (IPF again).

In terms of accessibility, the commercial property market has historically been one for professional and institutional investors. For professional and institutional investors choosing between investing in equity, gilts or bonds or commercial property or other alternative investments, commercial property (most of the time) has the advantage that its values move at a different pace and less often than those other markets. In the long term, those investors perceive that equities represent good value, gilts and bonds represent security and commercial property has something of both. More recently, several new types of investment products aimed at individual investors and based on commercial property have been developed and promoted, so that individuals can now invest in commercial property through ISAs, unit trusts and other collective structures.

## Ups and downs

When this book was first conceived in mid-2007, commercial property was a 'hot' investment. When we started work on this book in mid-2009, commercial property looked like a disaster zone, with property values reported as having fallen by 50% on average since mid-2007, with apocalyptic predictions about the future of the sector and the leading property investment companies losing 50-90% of their own value, with the most high profile fund for private investors, New Star (remember all those ads on the Tube?), forced to sell itself to a more stable competitor to ensure withdrawals are covered. The sector was one of those most immediately affected by the 'Credit Crunch'. Those within the industry argue from past history that commercial property is likely to be one of those sectors that will recover first. Rather surprisingly, the second half of 2009 saw a bounce back for commercial property values, to the extent that some financial commentators were again warning in early 2010 of the risk of a 'bubble'and even the Financial Services Authority warned of the risk of a 'meltdown'.

In this chapter we are not giving any investment advice or recommendations; we hope only to explain the system and jargon within which commercial property investment operates.

## Investment options

The purpose of this chapter is to explain how you could invest in UK commercial property if you choose to. The decision whether to do so is yours. If you do, the principal options are as follows:

- direct investment: that is buying a commercial property yourself
- buying quoted shares in property companies (including REITs)
- some kind of collective investment, for which there are a number of different structures.

Bear in mind that the major UK pension providers generally invest 5-10% of their funds in commercial property, and have done so for many years. That means that if you have invested pension monies with them, you are likely to be invested in this market already, perhaps without realising.

The optimists say that now is the time to invest because (to reverse the usual warning) values can go up as well as down.

## Health warnings

However, let's start with the health warnings: the principal risks associated with the commercial property market are:

- Market risk
- Property risk
- Product risk
- Tax risk.

In order to understand the market and these risks, you need to understand the concept of 'yield' as a means of assessing value, and comparing one investment with another.

*Yield*

Yield is simply a property professional's way of calculating value. It is the annual rate of return on an investment, expressed as a percentage of the amount invested. So, as a simple example, if you buy an office building for £1,000,000 which has a rental income of £50,000 per year, then you are buying at a 5% yield – £50,000 is 5% of £1,000,000. It follows that the lower the yield, the higher the price – so the same property at a 4% yield is worth £1,250,000. Conversely, at a 6% yield it is worth £833,333. Professional property investors generally estimate values by assessing income, then multiplying by a yield to get to a price. Price is strongly influenced by the risk factors we mention below; when buyers are keen, average yields for high quality property may go below 5% (early 2007); when buyers are unwilling to commit so that prices are dropping, yields for property of the same quality may go up towards 10% (2008).

So yield is comparable to the rate of interest on a deposit account (not in terms of security, but in terms of the income return capable of being earned).

We have somewhat over-simplified this explanation; in practice there are various types of yield calculation which take into account other factors such as costs of purchase, costs of ownership (for example rates payable on empty parts of a building) and potential rent increases or decreases (if, for example, a lease is due to expire) but usually do not take into account the costs of borrowing.

Some old-fashioned investors or agents refer to 'years purchase' – so a £1,000,000 property at a 5% yield is equivalent to 20 'years purchase' because it would take 20 years at £50,000 per annum to accumulate enough rental income to recover the amount paid for the property.

## Market risk

Like all other markets, the property market has cycles. In 1973-1975 and 1990-1993 downturns were driven by general weakness in the economy, high interest rates and an oversupply of property. From 1995/6 to mid-2007 the market was in a strong upward phase so that average values rose by 75% between 2002 and 2007. As mentioned, the commercial property market has been severely affected by the financial troubles of the Credit Crunch, so that average values dropped by roughly 50% between mid-2007 and mid-2009. This dramatic change (more extreme, and certainly more rapid than in earlier cycles) was less a consequence of a cycle within the property market itself – there were specific instances of over-supply but not a general problem of empty properties in the market – but more a consequence of the pressures on bank funding. As seen in previous downturns, the commercial property sector is particularly vulnerable to changes in the cost and availability of bank funding.

As well as the risks to the commercial property market as a whole from the economy generally, there may be sector-specific risks, for example if the retail sector of the economy is particularly affected by a downturn then the retail property sector is likely to be adversely affected more than other commercial property sectors.

## Property risk

Any individual investment property has the potential either to outperform the general investment property market or underperform against it. The key factors in assessing value usually are:

- location;
- physical characteristics – age and convenience (a new property should not require maintenance and conversely an older property will be likely to need more spending on it);
- the financial stability and quality of the tenant(s). If the credit rating of the tenant decreases materially, or if the tenant leaves and transfers the lease to a weaker company, the investment value will be affected. In extremis, insolvency of the tenant will affect investment value severely; and

- lease length – for many, a great attraction of the investment property market is that it offers predictable long term income because leases run for a number of years (traditionally 25 years although that has reduced in recent years to, in most cases, a maximum of 15 years, and an average of below 10 years) without the tenant having the right to break. If the lease is for a long period the value will be higher than if the lease is for a shorter period or contains the right for the tenant to break.

## Rental risk

The value of the property at the time of purchase may assume a certain level of future rent increase at rent review. If circumstances change so that the rent uplift is (or is anticipated to be) less than anticipated, that will affect value. Likewise, values may be affected by the fact that an occupier's lease may soon expire, so that the tenant may leave, or if not the rent may change, and the current tenant does leave, the rent and the nature of the tenant may change, for better or worse.

Investors can minimise these risks by buying only the best properties with long leases to good quality tenants, but of course those are the most attractive properties to all investors, and priced accordingly. In practice, the best properties are inevitably owned by large scale professional or institutional investors. Private investors can endeavour to minimise property-specific and sector-specific risks by investing in a good fund or company with a broad spread of good quality assets.

## Product risk

Buying commercial property direct may sound like the simplest and most risk-free way of investing, but doing so magnifies the impact of the property-specific risks – if the tenant of your only property becomes insolvent, you will be much more severely affected than if you have a small percentage of a portfolio of hundreds of properties and one tenant at one building becomes insolvent. Even if stable, direct property investments are expensive to buy and difficult to turn into cash, compared to equities or gilts. Even in normal market conditions, the sale of a commercial property may take months and cost a significant amount to achieve. If the general market is unfavourable, a sale may not be achievable at all, or only on disadvantageous terms.

If you invest in shares in a publicly-quoted vehicle – a property company, including a REIT, listed on the London Stock Exchange – you can access daily published price data about your holding of shares, and a relatively simple and predictable cost-free means of sale through the stock market. On the other hand, the value of the shares will be influenced by general trends in the stock market as well as those specific to the commercial property investment market, and the company in question, and the value of shares will be much more volatile than the value of the property itself. The timing and scale of the ups and downs may differ from that of the property market. For example, City of London property prices fell by 40-50% through 2008/9, but the share price of Minerva plc, whose principal properties were two large City office developments, fell by 95% in a few months. Even the largest and most respectable of the UK property companies, Land Securities plc, dropped from £23.40 per share in January 2007, to £9.49 per share at the end of 2008, to £3.44 per share in March 2009.

Shares in an unlisted property company, or the collective investment vehicles mentioned in this chapter, are not easily sellable, particularly at times of general market stress. Those investment vehicles which allow investors to 'cash in' or redeem their holding of shares or units offer a more predictable exit route but at times of either general market stress or pressure on that particular fund the fund manager may protect the interest of the fund as a whole by preventing or deferring redemption so that the requests for redemptions do not turn into a flood that the fund cannot satisfy without being forced to sell properties under unacceptable pressure, which will damage the fund and its other investors.

## Tax risk

As well as the liquidity risk (that is the risk that you will not be able to recover your cash immediately or when you need to), there are tax risks inherent in some of the more complex vehicles. Several have used off-shore or artificial structures to buy properties with no, or a reduced rate of, SDLT. They may have been set up in a way that was appropriate and tax-efficient at the time, but subsequent changes in tax legislation may create challenges for the fund in selling its assets without incurring adverse tax consequences. It is difficult to identify or quantify this risk, as the future intentions of Government and HMRC are not clear, beyond their general determination to crack down on 'tax avoidance'.

## Characteristics of the UK commercial property market

Size – at 2008, the estimated total value of UK commercial property owned as an investment was £529 billion.

Shape – traditionally the three main sectors into which the market is divided are:

- offices
- retail
- industrial (that is, both factories and industrial estates, and storage and distribution warehouses).

More recently, new property investment sectors have developed, such as hotels, pubs and restaurants, student accommodation and nursing homes. Unlike many other countries, residential property does not form part of the UK property investment market, although it is rumoured that (with Government encouragement) 'private rented sector' funds may be promoted during 2010 by Aviva and others.

Unlike the residential market, the majority of the value of commercial property is created by income (rent) rather than directly by increases in the capital value of the building itself. Capital values are usually calculated on a yield basis; that is, by calculating a multiple of the rental income, then applying various adjustments.

## Leases

Lease lengths – unlike the residential market, leases are usually for a period of five years and often longer. Traditionally the institutional form of lease was for 25 years but this is no longer common practice.

Management – unlike the residential market, the tenant is generally responsible for carrying out repairs, and paying for outgoings for the space it occupies (including the cost of insurances and provision of services where that applies) leaving the landlord with the rent as clear income.

VAT – unlike the residential market, VAT applies to many rents (the landlord has a choice whether or not to elect to charge VAT on rents, and on a sale of the investment interest in the property, and in most cases has elected to do so).

## Methods of commercial property investment

### Direct investment

By which we mean simply buying a property, rather than shares in a company or units in a fund.

As the bigger investors, the pension funds and overseas investors and property companies, have concentrated on larger properties, some smaller properties have come to market so that your local high street shop or bank or a nearby industrial estate may be within your reach.

The advantages of a direct purchase, as with a buy-to-let residential property, are direct control and the sense of ownership that comes from investing in something you can go and see and touch.

The principal disadvantages relate to the percentage of risk you take if you have all, or many, of your eggs in one basket, and to the cost and hassle of managing the tenancy; you also need to factor in the heavy costs of purchase and sale, and the liquidity risk.

### Shares

(a) Public company shares – by which we mean buying shares in one of the property companies listed on the London Stock Exchange, or the Alternative Investment Market (AIM). See page 276 for thumbnail sketches of the 10 largest public property companies.

The advantages are simplicity of purchase and sale, through the usual share dealing services such as those offered to individuals by Barclays or Halifax, or traditional stockbrokers like Brewin Dolphin or Hargeaves Lansdown, or web-based brokers like Interactive Investor or TD Waterhouse.

The principal disadvantage is the volatility of share prices. Most of the property companies listed on the LSE are now REITs[97], but there is a disadvantage for those which had not converted to REITs due to the double tax effect (explained on page 271). Companies listed on a recognised Stock Exchange (but not AIM) can qualify as a REIT. Companies listed elsewhere,

[97] For an up to date list of companies that have converted see www.reita.org.

for example, Dublin, Luxembourg or Guernsey, can qualify as REITs provided they are tax resident in the UK.

(b) Private company shares – these are not for the novice investor. Such a company is likely to be controlled by a small number of major shareholders who you will not be able to influence, and the shares are likely to be difficult to sell.

(c) Investment trusts – a UK investment trust is a particular kind of investment company with specific tax benefits, and listed on the London Stock Exchange. These have the tax advantage that they do not pay tax on capital gains. Basic rate tax payers pay no further tax on dividends, and higher rate tax payers pay an effective rate of 25%.

As with any other UK company, the sale of shares attracts stamp duty at 0.5% (payable by the buyer).

These investment trusts are limited as to their source of income and their income must be derived from either 'securities' (that is, shares or bonds in other companies) or residential property.

Examples of investment trusts with a focus on property are:

- TR Property Investment Trust
- Invesco Property Income Trust
- F&C Commercial Property Trust
- ISIS Property Trust.

## Collective investments

(a) UK Authorised Property Unit Trusts (APUTs) – 'authorised' means authorised by the Financial Services Authority for sale of units to individuals in the UK.

The unit trust will invest in UK land and buildings or (up to 20% of its funds) in indirect investments such as limited partnerships.

The unit trust is free from capital gains tax on capital gains but pays only 20% corporation tax on income profits.

The trust assets will be held by a trustee (normally a bank or subsidiary of a bank) but effectively the trust is run by a promoter. The investor is subject to income tax on distributions from the unit trust in the usual way; basic rate tax is deducted at 10% from distributions (in the same way as in company dividends) and higher-rate taxpayers will be liable to additional tax. The investor is subject to capital gains tax on the sale of the units.

On sale, the units may attract a stamp duty cost of up to 0.5% of the value of the units (payable by the buyer).

APUTs are regulated by the UK Financial Services Authority.

Examples of APUTs are:

- Scottish Widows Investment Partnership Property Trust
- M&G Property Portfolio
- Blackrock UK Property Fund
- Aviva Investors Property Trust.

Legal & General, Threadneedle and others offer similar funds.

(b) Unauthorised property unit trusts – these are described as 'unauthorised' because the Financial Services Authority has not authorised the promoter to sell units to individuals in the UK, only to institutional investors.

Some are set up in the UK and are available to tax-exempt investors such as charities and pension funds. Others are set up outside the UK, usually in Jersey or Guernsey (and therefore referred to as JPUTs or GPUTs) and are designed for non-UK based investors (both individuals and companies or institutional investors). They are regulated by the financial regulator in the jurisdiction in which they are set up.

A number of JPUTs or GPUTs have been created since 2004 with SDLT saving in mind.

If the unit trust is UK-based, it pays 22% tax on gross income, and tax on capital gains, subject to exemptions. If the unit trust is non-UK, it pays 22% on net rental income but is exempt from UK tax on capital gains.

Unit holders will pay income tax on distributions and capital gains tax on disposals of units.

Sales of the units in a UK unit trust are likely to attract stamp duty at 0.5%. Sales of units in an off- shore unit trust should not attract stamp duty.

Examples are:

- on-shore – Hermes Property Unit Trust and Schroders Exempt Property Unit Trust

- off-shore – The Mall and The Junction Funds, Hercules Property Unit Trust and West End of London Property Unit Trust.

(c) A unit linked life or pension fund - there are a number of commercial property sector specific funds offered to individual investors by the major life and pension companies. Most of these companies offer a number of alternative sector-based funds. Unit linked pension funds will be targeted at company or personal pension plans. Unit linked life assurance policies are for individuals to invest in either by regular savings or lump sums. The latter are usually called life bonds or investment bonds.

Unit linked pension funds are promoted by many pensions providers.

Unit linked life assurance policies are promoted by many life assurance providers.

(d) UK limited partnerships – institutional investors have used limited partnerships (a structure deriving from the Limited Partnerships Act 1907) for investing in commercial property, particularly when combining with developers or other non-institutional investors. For them, this structure has two advantages, firstly of separating ownership and management - the limited partners own most of the value of the fund but do not take an active role in management, and so are not exposed to legal liabilities relating to the property – and secondly being tax transparent so that the tax status of the investor governs what tax the investor pays, rather than the status of the limited partnership itself. So, if a tax-exempt investor such as a pension fund wants to combine forces with a developer, who would pay UK tax, then a limited partnership structure enables each to pay according to their own tax status.

Until 2004, these structures were also efficient from an SDLT point of view, as the transfer of interests in the limited partnership was free of SDLT. However, this was changed in the Finance Act 2004 so that SDLT is payable on transfers and limited partnerships have been used less for property investment since then.

Limited partnerships are not regulated by the Financial Services Authority and therefore cannot be marketed to individuals, other than investment professionals and high net worth individuals. It is unlikely that a private investor would directly invest in a limited partnership, but some of the investment vehicles available to private investors have investments in limited partnerships.

The partnership agreement will determine a partner's entitlement to income and capital gains. Each individual partner is taxed as though having a direct investment in their share of the partnership assets.

The partnership itself is tax-transparent so there should be no tax levied on the vehicle itself.

Stamp duty land tax at up to 4% applies to the acquisition of a partnership interest. The amount due is based on the value of an investor's share of the underlying property assets(s).

The VAT treatment of a transfer of an interest in a partnership is not straightforward and will depend on the circumstances.

(e) Off-shore UK listed property companies – some smaller property companies, particularly those investing in property outside the UK, have chosen to establish themselves outside the UK, usually in Jersey, Guernsey or Luxembourg, but are listed on AIM in London as well as in their home jurisdiction so that their shares can be marketed to investors in the UK.

Because the company is non-UK resident it will not pay UK capital gains tax on capital gains on UK property, but it will pay UK corporation tax on income deriving from the UK. It will pay corporation tax on income and capital gains according to the tax regime in its home jurisdiction.

The shareholder, if a UK tax payer, will pay UK income tax on dividends received (at 32.5%) and will pay UK capital gains tax on any capital gains made from selling shares in the company.

There are complex anti-avoidance provisions in the UK tax regime which could have adverse consequences for the shareholder (for example, by imputing the company's capital gains to the shareholder) and specialist advice should be taken before investing in any such company.

Examples are:

| | |
|---|---|
| Squarestone Brasil Limited - | investing in Brazilian shopping malls (incorporated in Guernsey, listed on AIM) |
| China Real Estate Limited - | investing in China (incorporated in Jersey, listed on AIM). |

(f) Off-shore investment company with variable capital (usually in Dublin). These are attractive to some funds because they allow for flexibility in investment objectives. A few UK property funds have been set up this way.

(g) PAIFs (Property Authorised Investment Funds) - a PAIF is an authorised OEIC investing mainly in property or property-related interests and that has elected to be a PAIF. Provided certain conditions are met, a PAIF is exempt from tax on the income arising from its property-related assets (like a REIT), and so is attractive to tax exempt investors such as pension funds or charities. PAIFs are a recent innovation, and none have yet been launched to the public. A couple have been promoted to pension funds and other institutional investors, by CBRE, and a couple of existing funds have announced they intend to convert themselves into PAIFs – Royal London Exempt Property Unit Trust, and a Threadneedle fund.

(h) Derivatives_– Real estate derivatives are financial instruments which give investors a return that reflects the performance of the direct property market. There are also some residential real estate derivatives. They are an emerging market in the UK aimed at institutional investors and high net worth individuals.

The plus point of derivatives is that they allow investors to buy or sell real estate exposure easily, cheaply and quickly. Stamp duty is not payable on property derivative transactions, provided the instruments are structured so as to give no rights or interest in the land. However, liquidity is an issue. Though the volume of trades is rising, an active secondary market has not yet developed.

The derivatives currently available include:

- Property income certificates. PICs are Eurobonds, so technically speaking they are bonds rather than derivatives. But they pay investors a quarterly return based on IPD's all-property total return. On maturity, investors receive the face value of the bond adjusted for movements in the index over that time. A bond with an embedded property swap, they are issued sporadically. The minimum investment varies from £1,000 to £100,000.
- IPD index swaps. These are over-the-counter trades, arranged by banks. They are mainly for professional investors, since they involve substantial amounts of capital. Most swaps have been measured by the

total return on all property but trades could be on component sectors and subsectors of the IPD index, such as offices and shopping centres, and between sectors.

(i) SIPP investment – It is possible to invest in commercial property via a Self Invested Personal Pension (SIPP). Tax-exempt property unit trusts are often structured as feeder funds into other products, like limited partnerships, in order to give SIPP investors access to them. It is even possible for a SIPP to invest in a building that is occupied by its beneficiary's business. For example, the owner of a small business can invest his SIPP in the office building which it occupies. However, these arrangements are subject to strict criteria and must be done on a commercial basis, that is, the rent paid must be a market rent.

SIPPs can invest in residential property via designated vehicles, including UK REITs and collective investment schemes. However, direct investment in residential property is taxed punitively.

SIPP investors can borrow up to 50% of the fund, unless it is categorised as a 'genuinely diverse commercial vehicle'. It is also possible to form designated SIPP syndicates to buy property via a SIPP. Specialist advice should be obtained for this.

The normal age-related rules for pension contributions apply to the level of annual contribution to the scheme that can be made benefiting from income tax relief.

The rules on drawdown of funds are complex. Broadly, 25% of the fund can be extracted on retirement tax-free. The remainder is used to buy an annuity, the income from which is subject to income tax.

The pension fund itself is exempt from tax on income and capital gains.

## REITs - why do they matter?

The UK property industry campaigned for many years for the Government to allow a tax efficient means for individuals to invest in commercial property.

Investors in commercial property have suffered double tax on rents – corporation tax for the owning company on the rents received from the tenant, and income tax for the shareholder on the dividends distributed by the owning company (see box below).

**Pre REITs**

| | | |
|---|---|---|
| Shareholders | | |
| ↑ | Dividend £64 – plus income tax | £16 |
| Company | | £80 |
| ↑ | Rent plus development profits – less corporation tax | £100 |
| Property | | |

Total tax = £36

Tax efficient vehicles have been developed in many other countries and have an important role both as significant players within the property investment market and in offering individuals a means of investing in the property investment market as an alternative to conventional pension products.

In the US, real estate investment trusts, or REITS for short, have become a major part of the property market and have by and large replaced property investment companies. In Australia special kinds of tax efficient A-REITs (previously known as listed property trusts or LPTs) own most of the commercial investment property and have expanded into the US and the UK. For example, Westfield (owner of Westfield London, Westfield Derby and Westfield Stratford City) and Lend Lease (Bluewater owners) are A-REITs.

In the years before REITs became possible in the UK, an increasing range of complex structures were developed to achieve tax efficient results, particularly for institutional investors.

Following successful lobbying by the UK property industry and the introduction of new REIT structures in France, Japan and Singapore, UK REITs came into existence from 1 January 2007 and allow a tax efficient structure, so avoiding double tax on rental income, subject to significant conditions. Since then, Germany and Italy have also legislated for similar vehicles and a number of other countries are in the course of doing so.

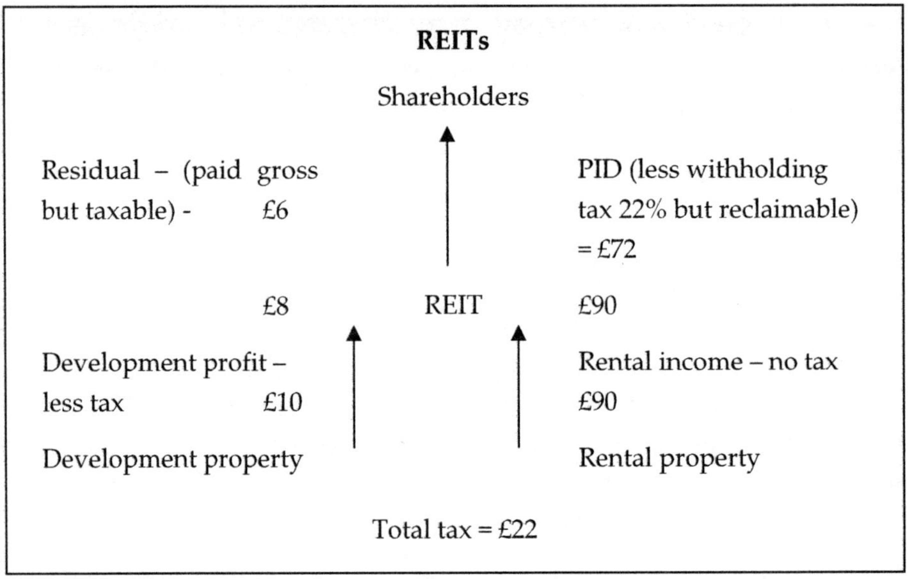


The UK government sought to achieve a balance so as to reduce the tax losses it was suffering through the complex structures developed to avoid tax, while making REITs more attractive to investors than the existing property investment companies, so that (in theory) the increased tax received by the Government at investor level would off-set the loss of tax 'given away' at company level, while maintaining an appropriate level of regulatory control to protect investors. The tax exemption applies to both income and capital gains achieved by the company from its investment properties, but not to its profits from development.

The principal conditions for qualifying as a UK REIT are that the company must:

1. Be resident in the UK for tax purposes.
2. Be listed on a recognised stock exchange. That includes, as well as the London Stock Exchange, the stock exchanges in Jersey, Guernsey, Dublin and Luxembourg but not the alternative investment market (AIM) in London.
3. Derive at least 75% of its income from rents.
4. Have at least 75% of its assets in investment properties (as opposed to development sites, or holdings in other companies or limited partnerships etc).
5. Pay out 90% of its property investment income in dividends each year.

6. Have investment income of not less than 125% over the interest payable on its debt.
7. Own three or more properties (although a shopping centre, for example, will count as multiple properties because there are multiple tenants).
8. Not own a property representing more than 40% of the value of the company's assets.
9. Not have a single shareholder holding more than 10% of the shares in the company.

In practice, all of the major UK property companies already listed in the London Stock Exchange at the beginning of 2007 have converted to REIT status and now have the benefit of the preferential tax status it confers, apart from a few whose focus is on development rather than investment (so would fail the 75% income test) - for example, Quintain and Helical Bar - or whose emphasis is on residential rather than commercial (so may struggle to achieve the 90% of gross income for distribution test) - for example, Dorrington and Grainger Trust.

Only a couple of new REITs have been created since 1 January 2007, partly because of the cost and complexity of achieving listing on the London Stock Exchange, but more immediately because of the downturn in the property investment market from mid-2007.

In order to convert to REIT status, the property companies had to pay a conversion charge of 2% of the value of their investment properties, in return for which they were released from capital gains tax on the accrued gains on those assets, many of which they had held for many years. To put some figures on this, for the biggest companies, the cost/benefit in 2007, according to their published accounts, was as follows:

**Savings/conversion charge**

| | Savings £m | Conversion charge £m |
|---|---|---|
| Land Securities | 2,317 | 300 |
| British Land | 1,651 | 338 |
| Hammerson | 410 | 96 |
| Liberty International | 930 | 146 |
| Slough Estates | 460 | 73 |
| Brixton | 166 | 38 |

This was a one-off saving on historic gains, but shows the scale of the change for those companies.

For investors, one consequence of the way REITs are now structured is that instead of simply receiving a regular dividend cheque, from which tax at basic income tax rate has been deducted as with any other company, investors will receive instead two cheques, one for the distribution of profits from the REIT's tax exempt investment activities (this is called a property income distribution, or PID, and tax at 22% will be deducted before distribution), and the other for the distribution of profits from its non-exempt activities such as development, which is paid as a dividend in the same way as any other company, that is, less tax at 10%. If the shares in the REIT company are held through an ISA or SIPP or some other tax exempt mechanism it is paid gross, not net of tax. This is obviously attractive to pension funds and other tax exempt investors.

The REIT legislation is fairly new, and it will take time to mature. Changes are likely, perhaps to simplify the 'start up' process for new REITs or to include companies already listed on AIM, or to make it easier for residential investment companies to qualify (for example by making allowances for the higher property management costs they inevitably incur), but those changes are not yet visible.

## Thumbnail sketches

Property companies - by market value (all REITS except where marked*)

| Company | 2009 Low | Share price at 1 April 2010 | Market Capitalisation at 1 June 2009 | Market Capitalisation at 1 April 2010 |
|---|---|---|---|---|
| Land Securities | 322.00 | 678p | £3,680m | £5,090m |
| British Land | 295.00 | 487p | £3,202m | £4,178m |
| Liberty International *** | 278.00 | 510.5p | £2,073m | £2,900m |
| Hammerson | 202.00 | 395p | £2,028m | £2,470m |
| Segro ** | 12.84 | 318p | £1,505m | £2,360m |
| Derwent London | 445.50 | 1,381p | £850m | £1,450m |
| Great Portland | 127.00 | 311p | £559m | £1,020m |

| | | | | |
|---|---|---|---|---|
| Estates | | | | |
| Shaftesbury | 236.50 | 390p | £532m | £896m |
| Big Yellow | 147.50 | 340p | £396m | £413m |
| Helical Bar * | 244.00 | 340p | £369m | £317m |

There are 22 REITs in all, and 29 non-REIT property companies, on the London Stock Exchange.

Note: * Helical Bar is an investor/trader and therefore not a REIT.

Note **: Segro took over Brixton Estate during 2009.

Note ***: Liberty International separated into 2 companies, Capital & Counties Properties plc and Capital Shopping Centres Group plc, in May 2010.

*What do they own?*

Land Securities - principally offices – including much of Victoria in London.

British Land – offices and retail – half of Broadgate in the City and half of Meadowhall Shopping Centre in Sheffield, and a number of Sainsbury and Tesco stores.

Liberty International - Capital & Counties Properties owns offices plus a part share in Earls Court, and a chunk of Covent Garden. Capital Shopping Centres – obviously – owns shopping centres.

Hammerson – principally offices plus Brent Cross Shopping Centre; also office and retail property in France.

Segro (formerly Slough Estates) – mostly industrial and storage property in the South East.

Derwent London - mostly offices in Central London.

Great Portland Estates - mostly offices and retail in Central London.

Shaftesbury – Carnaby Street and part of Chinatown.

Big Yellow – storage and distribution warehouses.

It is noteworthy that apart from Hammerson and to a lesser extent Segro these companies limit their investment to the UK, and generally most of the value of these properties is in London and the South East.

# CHAPTER 9 PROPERTY DEVELOPMENT

## The big picture

Property development has given the UK its suburbs and its housing estates, its office blocks, shopping centres and 'leisure parks'. From The Bull Ring in Birmingham to Canary Wharf, from Regent Street to Bluewater, from Princes Street to Regent's Park, the desire to design, build and make a profit from development has motivated speculators, investors and builders to create our cities and towns.

Some may hope to emulate Nick and Chris Candy who started their property careers by refurbishing a two-bedroomed flat in Earls Court, and now live in Monaco, in one of the most spectacular apartments in the world, with a 65 metre super-yacht in the harbour.

On a more domestic scale, many of us have built an extension, or a loft conversion, or a 'home office', or plan to do so, or have bought a property which has already been 'developed'. A few of us have built a house for ourselves, or dream of doing so.

Although little noticed in the general news media, 'self build' is more common than you may think – it is estimated that 20,000 new self-build homes are started in the UK per year, and in times when the volume house builders have had to cut back dramatically, that represents a significant proportion of the overall housing starts – 25% of the estimated 80,000 private sector housing starts in 2009, and much the same as Taylor Wimpey, the largest UK housebuilder.

Extending your existing property to make it more suitable to your changing needs may also be an attractive option in a world where 'climbing the property ladder' by moving to a larger house is difficult because of the lack of supply in the market, the challenge of selling your own house, the limited availability of mortgages, and the heavy cost of moving, particularly SDLT (stamp duty) at up to 5% of value.

So in this chapter we will identify some basic guidelines for property development; explain briefly the regulatory controls on development (that is, town planning and building regulations); spell out what you can do without needing planning permission; and address some of the 'green' issues and opportunities in carrying out property development, either by improving your existing property or by building a new one.

Before we get into detail, the risks of property development should not be overlooked. Two developers of Canary Wharf became insolvent before the skyscrapers we see today were completed; Battersea Power Station still lies derelict 25 years after plans for its redevelopment were first proposed; the saga of Chelsea Barracks illustrates the unpredictability of the planning system.

The combination of increases in costs, delays through the planning or construction process, or unexpected drops in market values have bankrupted many an amateur and professional property developer.

## Guidelines

Property development is, in principle, a very simple way of making money: you own or buy something, improve it and sell it for more than the cost of buying and improving it. Not rocket science, but it is easy to get it wrong through poor judgement, poor timing or just bad luck.

The experts say there are four basic rules:

(1) Buy well.
(2) Add maximum value.
(3) Control costs.
(4) Sell well.

### What does 'buy well' mean?

It means (assuming you are buying to 'do up' rather than improving your existing home) buying at a price at or below market value for the property without the improvements you intend to make, and where the improvements will be reflected in a higher value when you come to sell.

*How do you do this?*
This is about spotting potential, or identifying hidden value.

Look for a property with problems you can solve.

It is an advantage to be a cash buyer, so you can move quickly; it is an advantage to know an area and property values within it well so that you know what will be attractive to buyers when you sell; it is an advantage to be able to spot the difference between relatively cosmetic flaws in a property – an ugly colour scheme, an out of date bathroom, a garden wilderness – and major structural problems like damp, dry rot or subsidence, and to have enough design nous to see how removing a non-structural wall or creating a loft extension will move the property into a higher price bracket.

Except in times when values in the property market generally are moving up very fast, it is unlikely that you will make a lot of money by buying at full market value a standard product (a three-bedroomed terraced house or semi) and doing a standard extension or alteration to it (although that may make an effective buy-to-let). You need to find the properties and opportunities that others have overlooked – those in a mess, or being sold by a non-local agent, or outside the selling agent's 'comfort zone' in terms of value, or as a private sale in the small ads in the local paper, or at an auction (although at auctions you will compete with property traders who buy and sell property for a living and may be better than you at distinguishing the goldmine from the money pit).

If you are clear about the area and type of property you want, nothing is more effective than leg work. Watching the ads and prices in the local paper's property section, checking the local agents' shop windows on a regular basis and looking out for 'for sale' signs - and then checking sold prices on line - will ensure that you know the market value for property in that location, so you can spot and capture the bargain when it appears.

You should aim to buy the worst property on a good street, rather than creating the best property on a poor or average street.

Talking to the local agents will also help you to understand which parts of the area they cover are 'on the way up' and which are less so, and whether local demand is for houses or flats, bigger or smaller gardens, one- or two-bedroomed flats, for buying or renting, and the price points at which different kinds of property are likely to sell. Their advice is of course free, and you can motivate them to help you by offering the carrot of the fee they may earn when you sell. In the longer term, building a relationship with them may give you access to properties off-market.

## Adding maximum value

If you want to change a less attractive property into a more attractive one, you will want to ensure that your money is well spent, and reflected to the maximum possible in the price you get when you sell.

It is likely that the most effective ways of achieving this are:

- repairing the structure (getting rid of the damp or dry rot or fixing the roof)
- cosmetic improvements (clearing clutter, clearing and landscaping the garden, updating décor)
- enhancing the existing space (reorganising the 'flow' of the rooms, updating kitchens and bathrooms, modernising the electrics or central heating)
- adding extra space (a kitchen or loft extension, opening up the basement, putting in en-suite bathrooms, adding a garage or adding garden buildings such as a home office)
- enhancing the property's amenity (creating off-street parking or building a garage, improving privacy, connecting mains services, building a swimming pool or tennis court, buying more land to extend)
- resolving legal or planning issues (extending the lease, removing a right of way across the property, removing restrictive covenants, dealing with sitting tenants, obtaining planning permission for an extension).

You need to match your expenditure to the property you start with and the area in which it sits. The extent to which you can increase value is limited by its surroundings - putting a swimming pool in the garden of a row of terraced houses is unlikely to add to value whereas the same amount spent on a loft extension to create a fourth bedroom and en-suite bathroom is likely to increase the value by considerably more than you have spent.

## Controlling costs

- Buying and selling costs.
- Design fees.
- Labour and materials costs.
- Finance fees, interest and insurance.
- Tax.

To give you a very rough rule of thumb, a loft extension or garage may cost £850-1,050 per sq m to build, a standard rear extension £1,050-£1,650 per sq m, a contemporary design rear extension £1,450-£2,000 per sq m, a basement excavation £3,000-£4,500 per sq m. These are build costs, without decoration or furnishings, or VAT.

Generally speaking, there are no grants or tax reliefs available for property development, apart from those for 'green' improvements, but there is a limited amount of tax relief available for conversion of commercial properties to flats, designed to encourage conversion of the upper floors of shops back to their original residential use. This is known as Flat Conversion Allowance (FCA).

## Selling well – marketing, presentation and setting

Location indicators for buying – good:

- Sold boards.
- Estate agents' 'good roads'.
- Property pages week on week.
- Auctions.
- Count the skips.
- Follow new house building.
- Local authority regeneration plans.
- New employment.
- Transport improvements (Olympics, Ashford).
- Coffee shops or Waitrose.
- Good schools.
- 'Next to' areas.

Location indicators for buying - bad:

- Flood areas (use Home Check).
- Contamination (use Home Check).
- High crime (use Up My Street).

## Regulatory controls on development

The two main controls on development are the town planning system and the building control regime.

The town planning system is essentially about land use and design – making provision for appropriate uses in appropriate places, and the appropriate appearance or size of buildings. The building control regime is more technical, to ensure buildings are built properly so as to be structurally safe, with sufficient fire protection and escapes, and increasingly to maximise building efficiency; for example by improving standards of insulation, and reducing water and energy usage.

The planning system derives primarily from the Town and Country Planning Act 1947 – now replaced by the Town and Country Planning Act 1990 – which requires each local authority to set policies and allocate land for housing, industry, offices and other uses, and requires developers to build in line with those policies through the planning permission procedure. Over the last 60 years this post-war public-spirited prescription for regeneration has become a vast, complex and inefficient machine which frustrates those who operate it (mostly, the local authorities) and those who need to use it (applicants and those who wish to object to applications). There have been several attempts to improve it[98] but the fact is that the planning system cannot entirely reconcile policies with the opposing views of developers and existing owners, in either urban or rural areas.

The Coalition Government is changing the system again, with the intention of 'returning decision-making to local councils'. This is likely to cause some uncertainty and, at least so far as the property development industry is concerned, the effect will be to make it more difficult to get consent.

In 2006/2007 approximately 650,000 planning applications were made in England and Wales, of which over 80% were granted. Of the 650,000 applications, 328,000, just over half, were classified as 'householder' applications – more than double the figure of 10 years earlier. Roughly 75% were dealt with by the local authority within the required period of two months from the date of application (eight weeks in the case of minor applications), meaning that 160-170,000 were not. In the same period, there were 22,687 planning appeals (17,824 of which related to residential property) of which 34% were allowed.

The applications ranged in scale from a new shopping centre or office block to a change in the height of a garden wall, the positioning of an extension or the demolition of a garage. For our purposes, in this chapter we are intending to cover the range of possibilities from demolition of an existing house and replacement by a new building, building a new house in the garden of an existing one, a side or rear extension to create a new or larger kitchen, conversion of a house into flats or vice versa, creating a loft or basement extension, building a garage, or converting a garage to living space.

So, how do you avoid your proposal getting stuck in the planning system, or worse, refused?

---

[98] Most recently the Killian-Pretty Review published in November 2008.

## Permitted development

For many domestic proposals, particularly extensions, it may be possible to take advantage of the 'permitted development' rules which were substantially widened for England (but not Wales) in September 2008 – in response to the pressure on the planning authorities from the volume of applications, shown in the 2006/2007 figures we have quoted – so that many more minor proposals are automatically permitted and an application for planning permission is not required. The housing minister, when announcing the new rules, estimated that 80,000 applications per year could be avoided. So, you may be able to avoid an application by adjusting your needs or design to fit within the permitted development, or PD, rules.

These PD rules are not easy to follow or to apply to particular situations. If you are unsure what they mean in your particular case, we recommend that you obtain advice from the planning department of your local authority, although there may be a cost for this. If you do not agree with their advice, or want to obtain guidance on how to proceed before meeting them, it may be wise for you to consult a local architect or a specialist planning consultant who has experience in dealing with that local authority. The architect or consultant will charge you a fee based on the time they spend but the savings in wasted time they can achieve for you are usually worth it.

There is plenty of scope for misunderstanding or misinterpretation or lack of knowledge of the PD rules as they are relatively new, and materially different from those within which local authorities and designers have operated for many years and so have become familiar with. The new rules are generally less restrictive than the previous ones, but in some respects more so (for example, paving over your front garden now requires planning permission unless the surface is porous - a reaction to the 2007 floods – and the manufacturers of tree houses have found themselves unexpectedly caught by the need for planning permission under the new rules). In some situations the old rules (which in broad terms allowed extensions of up to 10% by volume) were more generous than the new ones, which are more precise.

Also, before seeking to use the PD rules, check carefully that your property or proposal is not affected by any special protected status, for example if the property is a listed building or in a World Heritage Site or in a National Park or Area of Outstanding Natural Beauty, or in a conservation area. The PD rules do not benefit listed buildings but do still generally benefit properties in a conservation area, although not the other special areas, but the local authority can exclude some or all of the PD rules by a special order known as an Article 4 Direction. Also, if the proposal involves removing a tree subject to a tree preservation order, or a tree which is within a conservation area, then you may need consent for its removal, even if the main proposal does not require planning permission because of the PD rules.

The PD rules for England[99] are set out in the Town and Country Planning (General Permitted Development) (Amendment) (No. 2) (England) Order 2008, Schedule 2 Part 1. In summary, so far as they relate to residential properties, they mean that planning permission is not required for ground floor rear extensions or loft conversion, subject to limits relating to distance from the boundary of the property, or cubic volume. The detail is complex but important, so we set it out as follows:

## Class A – extensions and improvements

Are permitted development subject to the following limits and conditions:

- No extension forward of the principal elevation or side elevation fronting a highway.
- No extension to be higher than the highest part of the existing roof.
- Maximum depth of a single storey rear extension of 3 metres for an attached house, (that is a semi or terrace) and 4 metres for a detached house.
- Maximum depth of a rear extension of more than one storey of 3 metres including the ground floor.
- On article 1(5) land no permitted development for rear extensions of more than one storey.
- Maximum eaves height of extension 3 metres within 2 metres of the boundary.
- Maximum eaves and ridge height of extension no higher than the existing house.
- Side extensions to be single storey with maximum height of 4 metres and width no more than half that of the original house.
- Two storey extensions no closer than 7 metres to rear boundary.

---

[99] These do *not* apply in Wales.

- Roof pitch of extensions higher than one storey to match the existing house.
- Materials to be similar in appearance to the existing house.
- No verandas, balconies or raised platforms.
- Side-facing windows to be obscure-glazed; any opening to be 1.7m above the floor.
- On article 1(5) land no cladding of the exterior.
- On article 1(5) land no side extensions.

## Class B – roof extensions

Are permitted development subject to the following limits and conditions:

- A volume allowance of 40 cubic metres for terraced houses.
- A volume allowance of 50 cubic metres for detached and semi-detached houses.
- No extension beyond the plane of the existing roof slope facing onto and visible from the highway.
- No extension to be higher than the highest part of the roof.
- Materials to be similar in appearance to the existing house.
- No verandas, balconies or raised platforms (this catches roof terraces).
- Side-facing windows to be obscure-glazed; any opening to be 1.7m above the floor.
- Extensions to be set back, as far as practicable, at least 20cm from the eaves.
- Roof extensions are not to be permitted development on article 1(5) land.

## Class C – roof alterations

Are permitted development subject to the following limits and conditions:

- Any alteration to project no more than 150 millimetres from the existing roof plane (intended to allow for roof replacement and Velux-type windows).
- No alteration to be higher than the highest part of the roof.
- Side facing windows to be obscure-glazed; any opening to be 1.7m above the floor.

## Class D – porches

The erection or construction of a porch outside any external door of a dwelling house.

## Class E – outbuildings, enclosures, swimming pools and oil and gas containers

Are permitted development subject to the following limits and conditions:

- No building, enclosure, pool or container forward of the principal elevation fronting a highway.
- Buildings to be single storey with maximum eaves height of 2.5 metres and maximum overall height of 4 metres with a dual pitched roof, or 3 metres for any other roof.
- Maximum height 2.5 metres within 2 metres of a boundary.
- No verandas, balconies or raised platforms (this catches tree-houses).
- Maximum 50% coverage of the garden.[100]
- In National Parks, the Broads, Areas of Outstanding Natural Beauty and World Heritage Sites the maximum area to be covered by buildings, enclosures, containers or pools more than 20 metres from the house is limited to 10 square metres.
- On article 1(5) land, buildings, enclosures, containers or pools at the side of properties will require planning permission.
- Within the curtilage of listed buildings any outbuilding will require planning permission.

## Class F – hard surfaces

Are permitted development subject to:

- Any surface installed in the front garden of more than 5 square metres to be either porous or to run-off to a porous or permeable surface.

## Class G – chimneys, flues and soil and vent pipes

Are permitted development subject to:

- The height being less than one metre above the highest part of the roof.
- On article 1(5) land,[101] no installation on the principal or a side elevation that fronts a highway.

---

[100] If the existing house was built before 1948, it is the size of the house in 1948 which must be used in this calculation.

[101] Article 1(5) land is defined to include conservation areas as well as National Parks, the Broads, Areas of Outstanding Natural Beauty and World Heritage Sites.

### Class H – microwave antenna

The installation, alteration or replacement of a microwave antenna on a dwelling house or entrance.

## Solar panels

Solar panels are permitted development on a principal or side elevation visible from a highway in conservation areas and World Heritage Sites (they are already permitted development elsewhere).

Different rules apply to public sector buildings such as schools and colleges; to agricultural buildings and forestry; to caravan parks; and to commercial properties.

## Making a planning application

You apply to your council for planning permission. Application forms are available from them, in most cases online. A fee will be payable. Planning applications are decided in line with the Council's development plan unless there are very good reasons not to do so. Points that will be looked at include the following:

- number, size, layout, sitting and external appearance of buildings;
- proposed means of access, landscaping and impact on the neighbourhood;
- availability of infrastructure, such as roads and water supply; and
- proposed use of the development.

It is not necessary to make the application yourself. If you wish, you can appoint an agent (for instance, an architect, a solicitor, or a builder) to make it for you.

Anyone can make an application, irrespective of who owns the land or buildings concerned. However, if you are not the owner, or if you have only part-ownership, you have to inform the owner or those who share ownership, including any leaseholder whose lease still has seven or more years to run, and any agricultural tenant.

The system is similar for related applications such as those for listed building consent (to alter a listed building), for conservation area consent (to make changes to a property in a conservation area which require specific approval, including demolition) or for a tree preservation order consent (to prune, lop, remove or replace a protected tree). It is important to use the right forms.

Set out below is the Government's (they think) easy to understand flow chart for a planning application, from www.planningportal.gov.uk.

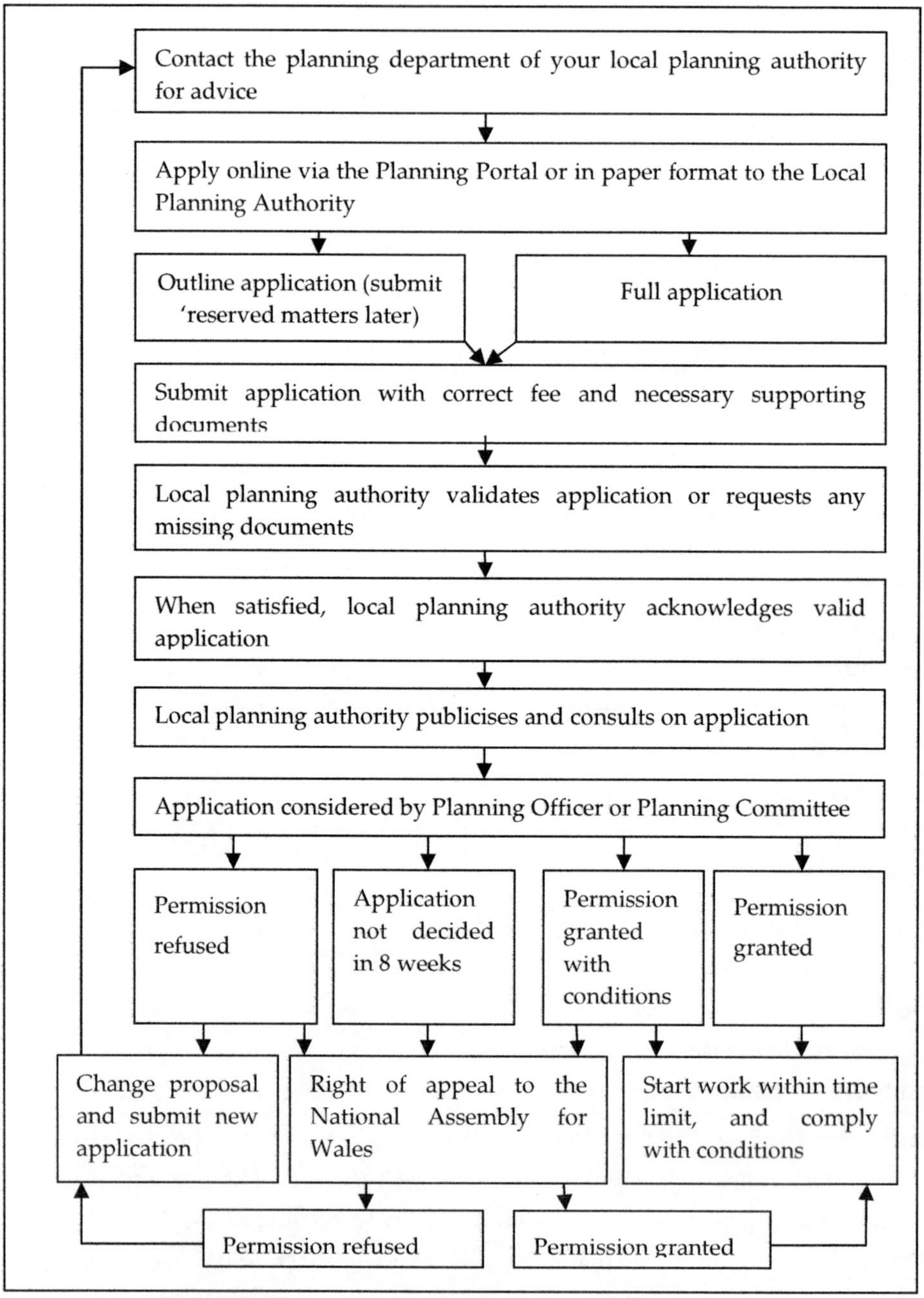

## Penalties for breaching planning controls

There are serious penalties for breaching planning controls, whether by carrying out building work without permission when it was required, building something different from what was approved, failing to comply with a condition on a permission, or changing the use of a property without permission.

Local authorities can require a breach to be rendered (by an enforcement notice - usually preceded by a planning contravention notice as a warning). If the landowner does not comply that is a criminal offence, usually punished by a fine. In more serious or urgent cases the local authority can secure a stop notice – requiring works to stop immediately – or seek an injunction from the courts. In extreme cases, the local authority can require the landowner to demolish the offending building, and even go in and demolish it itself (and charge the cost to the owner). It is also possible for the local authority to claim any profits made by the landowner – for example in renting out a building for a non-permitted use.[102] There are rights of appeal in most situations.

Most owners, of course, comply at least once they have realised they are in breach of the law (or have been found out).

However, as an illustration of the vagaries of the planning system, compare two cases reported in early 2010.

In *Welwyn Hatfield Council v Secretary of State for Communities and Local Government and Another*, the story was that the landowner, a Mr Beesley, obtained planning permission to construct a hay barn. In fact, he built a house that looked like a hay barn on the outside. He and his wife lived in the house for four years, and then applied for a 'certificate of lawfulness of existing use or development' – a way of getting effective approval – on the basis that even though he had built the house without planning permission it was now too late for the Council to do anything about it. As the breach related to use, the 'safe after' period was four years. If he had built something physically different from what the Council approved, it would have been ten years. Not surprisingly, the Council refused his application. Although it became apparent that Mr Beesley

---

[102] In an extreme case, the authorities have even used the Proceeds of Crime Act 2002 (originally aimed at gangs and terrorists) to recover the profits gained from an unlawful 'park and ride' scheme (*Basso v R*).

had deliberately deceived the Council when applying for planning permission, the Court of Appeal found in his favour, with the rather patronising comment that the lesson to be learnt by planning authorities is to look at the inside of buildings as well as the outside when checking after construction.

Contrast this with the story of Mr Fidler, a farmer in Surrey, who built a 'castle' hidden by forty foot high hay bales, and lived in it for four years. After he removed the hay bales to reveal the 'castle' the Council served an enforcement notice. Mr Fidler lost his appeal on the somewhat technical argument that the removal of the hay bales formed part of the process of construction of the 'castle' and because that took place within the four years before enforcement started, the four year rule did not apply to save the 'castle'.

It is understood that Mr Fidler intends to appeal.

It is worth noting that in both cases the arguments were about the procedures followed by the homeowners and the Councils, not the merits of the designs.

## Requirement for Building Regulations consent

Building Regulations apply in England and Wales to 'building work', which is defined to mean any of the following:

- The erection or extension of a building.
- The installation or extension of a service or fitting that is controlled under the Building Regulations.
- A project to alter a building where the work involved will temporarily or permanently affect the ongoing compliance of the building, service or fitting with the Building Regulation requirements relating to structure, fire or access to and use of the buildings.
- The insertion of insulation into a cavity wall.
- The underpinning of the foundations of a building.

The Building Regulations apply to all types of building, whether domestic, commercial or industrial.

Local authorities have a duty to ensure that the Building Regulations are complied with. This enforcement is often referred to as 'building control'.

### What the building control service is for

- A checking service to help achieve compliance with building standards.

- Support and advice for customers on how to end up with the result they want (this is not a substitute for professional design and construction advice).
- To help with aspects of quality (workmanship and materials), where these affect compliance with building standards.
- To ensure that all building standards have been complied with at completion.

## What the building control service is not

- Responsible for compliance with building standards, which is the duty of the person carrying out the work.
- Managing every stage of the construction process on-site. The customer and builder should make these arrangements.
- Addressing issues such as the finish and aesthetics of the final project.
- Dealing with contractual problems between customer and builder.

## The Building Regulations

The Building Regulations are highly technical and impose requirements which affect the design and materials for any building project in many ways - from requiring double glazing in all new houses, to establishing minimum widths for external and internal doors (to allow for wheelchair access), to requiring adequate ventilation in kitchens and bathrooms and near gas appliances such as fires or boilers. They are intended to correlate with British Standards (that is, BS labelling) for materials.

The Building Regulations requirements are set out in Parts A to P of Schedule 1 to the Building Regulations 2000 ('BR 2000').

The function of the Building Regulations is principally to ensure the health and safety of people in and around buildings. They provide a minimum standard in the following areas relating to the construction and alteration of buildings:

- Structure
- Fire safety
- Site preparation and resistance to contaminants and moisture
- Toxic substances
- Resistance to the passage of sound
- Ventilation
- Hygiene

- Drainage and waste disposal
- Combustion appliances and fuel storage systems
- Protection from falling, collision and impact
- Conservation of fuel and power
- Access to and use of buildings
- Access for disabled people
- Weather proofing
- Glazing: safety in relation to impact, opening and cleaning
- Electrical safety.

The BR 2000 is supplemented by detailed technical guidance contained in Approved Documents published by the Secretary of State. The guidance explains how the Building Regulations requirements may be satisfied and will be taken into account in any official compliance assessment of building work.

## Amendments to the BR 2000

The BR 2000 has been amended several times since coming into force. For example:

- The Building and Approved Inspectors (Amendment) Regulations 2007: most of those changes took effect on 6 April 2008.
- From 1 April 2009, 'Gas Safe Register' replaced CORGI registration under the Gas Safety Regulations 1998. This change was formalised, along with other minor modifications to the BR 2000, in the Building (Amendment) Regulations 2009.
- From 1 October 2009 under Approved Document G, which amends Part G of the BR 2000, all new build homes must meet a new minimum water efficiency standard and include inbuilt protection from hot water scalding in baths.
- On 18 June 2009 the Department for Communities and Local Government (DCLG) published a consultation document on draft amendments to Part L (conservation of fuel and power) and Part F (means of ventilation) of Schedule 1 to BR 2000. The amendments will come into force in October 2010. The draft amendments have been introduced to deal with climate change and aim to improve the energy efficiency of buildings.

## Applying for Building Regulation approval

To comply with the Building Regulations, a developer may do either of the following:

- Apply for approval from the relevant local authority building control department.
- Apply for approval from a private sector approved inspector.

## Local authority building control service

There are two different procedures for getting building regulations approval through the local authority building control service:

- Deposit of a full plans application.
- Giving a building notice

The building notice procedure does not involve the preparation of detailed plans and is intended for situations where the work is less complex and will be done quickly. The procedure is not available for certain types of building work such as that involving fire safety issues or drains.

## Full plans application procedure

A full plans application means that the application is deposited with the relevant local authority together with the plans and other information that show all the construction details.

The local authority will check the plans and consult appropriate authorities (for example, those dealing with fire and sewerage). The local authority is required to issue a decision within five weeks from the date of the deposit of the application. This period may be extended by the local authority, with the applicant's agreement, to a maximum of two months from the date when the plans are deposited.

If the plans do not comply with the Building Regulations, the local authority may do either of the following:

- ask the applicant to amend the plans or provide more details; or
- issue a conditional approval.

A conditional approval will either specify what modifications need to be made to the plans or specify what further plans need to be deposited with the local authority.

If the plans comply with the Building Regulations, the applicant will receive an approval notice. A full plans approval notice is valid for three years from the date of deposit of the plans. In that time the building work that has been approved must be started otherwise the local authority may cancel the approval notice.

Once the building work is in progress, the local authority will carry out regular inspections. When the work has been completed, the local authority will issue a completion certificate provided that the applicant requested one at the time of the original approval application, and provided the building works comply with the Building Regulations.

If there is any dispute between the applicant and the local authority about whether the building works have been carried out properly, the applicant may ask for the dispute to be determined by the Secretary of State for Communities and Local Government (in England) or the Welsh Assembly (in Wales).

It is important that the applicant deposits the full plans application with the local authority sufficiently in advance of the date when they intend to start the building works to enable the approval to be made.

## Building notice procedure

The applicant submits a building notice to the local authority. No plans or other details are submitted with the notice.

Once the building notice has been submitted, it is valid for three years. It will automatically lapse after three years if the building work is not started.

The applicant informs the local authority when it is about to start work. The local authority may request plans and further information before the work is started.

The local authority will inspect the work periodically and will advise if the building works do not comply with the Building Regulations.

There is no completion certificate and no facility to refer any dispute to the Secretary of State for Communities and Local Government or the Welsh Assembly.

## Approved inspectors

If an applicant seeks approval from a private sector approved inspector, the approved inspector and the applicant must issue a joint 'initial notice' to the local authority, giving the local authority notice of the intended building works. Building work can start as soon as the initial notice has been accepted by the local authority but cannot be started if the initial notice is rejected. A notice will be treated as having been accepted unless it has been validly rejected within five days of being given.

The approved inspector will:

- Advise the applicant on how the Building Regulations will apply to the building works.
- Check the plans and inspect the site.
- Inspect the work as it progresses.
  If the approved inspector is not satisfied with the work, the inspector will have to cancel the initial notice. This will terminate the approved inspector's responsibility for the building works and the local authority will then step in. The local authority may require works to be uncovered so that a full inspection can be carried out. Additional charges may then be made by the local authority.
- Issue a plans certificate if one is requested.
- This will confirm that the plans show compliance with the Building Regulations.
- Issue a final certificate to the local authority when the building works have been completed in compliance with the Building Regulations.

## Regularisation certificates

A property owner may apply for a regularisation certificate for 'unauthorised' building work, which means building work that was carried out on or after 11 November 1985, which should have been approved through the Building Regulations procedures.

The local authority will charge for a regularisation certificate.

The local authority may request unauthorised work to be 'opened up' and will then decide whether remedial work is required to make it comply with the Building Regulations as they were at the time the unauthorised building works were carried out.

A regularisation certificate is evidence (but not conclusive evidence) that the requirements of the Building Regulations specified in the certificate have been complied with.

Anyone acquiring property where they are concerned that Building Regulations have not been complied with may wish to take out indemnity insurance.

## Enforcement

If a person carrying out building work contravenes the Building Regulations, the local authority may do each or any of the following:

- serve an enforcement notice
- apply for an injunction
- prosecute in the magistrates' court.

Even if a local authority does not prosecute or take enforcement action, it will not issue a completion certificate to confirm compliance with the Building Regulations. This may cause the property owner problems when he/she comes to sell the property. A property owner may be able to obtain a 'regularisation certificate'.

### Enforcement notices

A local authority has power to serve an enforcement notice on a building owner to require the removal or alteration of work that does not comply with the Building Regulations.

The enforcement notice must be served within 12 months from the date of completion of the building work that is in breach. The date that building work is completed is a question of fact.

The enforcement notice will give the building owner 28 days to carry out the required work, failing which the local authority can carry out the work at the cost of the owner/occupier.

### Injunctions

Whether or not a local authority serves any enforcement notice under section 36 of the Building Act 1984 (BA 1984), the local authority can also apply for an injunction for the removal or alteration of any work on the ground that it contravenes any regulation or other provision of the BA 1984 (section 36(6), BA 1984).

The grant of an injunction is at the discretion of the court.

Traditionally, injunctions have not been widely used to enforce Building Regulations because of the cost involved, in terms of time and resources, in obtaining an injunction. Injunctions tend to be used for those situations that are urgent and where the cost can be justified by the risk of serious danger to health and safety (for example, where a nightclub or cinema is at risk of fire).

The case of *Cottingham v Attey Bower & Jones (a firm) (Times 19 April 2000)* has not caused any apparent increase in injunctions being used to deal with contraventions of Building Regulations. The decision did, however, rattle the conveyancing world and has resulted in the creation of a significant layer of work for lawyers in relation to Building Regulation consents, particularly in residential conveyancing.

In *Cottingham,* the buyer brought negligence proceedings against his lawyers because his house required expensive remedial works of which he had not been made aware before he bought the property. The court found that the buyer's solicitors were negligent because they had failed to:

- take all reasonable steps to obtain copies of the Building Regulation consents for work that they knew had been carried out. The solicitors had been incorrectly informed that the consents were in existence but had not obtained copies; and
- advise the buyer of the potential risk if the copies of the consents could not be obtained.

Since *Cottingham,* it is usual good practice, particularly in relation to residential property:

- For the buyer's solicitors to investigate all works carried out to the property since it was built.

  Some practitioners are generally happy to limit investigation to the previous 10 years, unless circumstances suggest a longer period. This is on the basis that:

  - investigating all works might be unduly onerous and unproductive; and

  - the 10 year period sits comfortably with the period for which planning permissions should be investigated for breach of conditions.
- For the buyer's solicitors to obtain copies of building regulation consents and completion certificates for works.
- If consents and certificates cannot be obtained from the seller, the buyer's solicitors should advise the buyer:
  - that the lack of consent or completion certificates **may** indicate that the works carried out are structurally unsound, or that consent **may** have been refused and that the buyer should refer the issue to a surveyor;
  - of the risk that the local authority will take enforcement action (an enforcement notice injunction or prosecution) and the implications of any such action being taken;
  - that a request can be made to the local authority for any missing consents and certificates, but that this might of itself alert the local authority to unauthorised works and precipitate enforcement action;
  - that indemnity insurance might be available to cover the risk that the building works do not comply with the Building Regulations or that no consent was obtained, but that the availability of insurance may be prejudiced by an application to the local authority for the missing consents and certificates; and
  - of the possibility of applying for a Regularisation Certificate.

## Prosecution (section 35 and 35A, Building Act 1984)

A local authority may prosecute contraventions of the Building Regulations through summary proceedings in the magistrates' court. Prosecutions are relatively infrequent and generally taken only for flagrant or wilful breaches.

Where the Building Regulations are contravened, the person responsible for the breach may be liable for a fine of up to £5,000 and an additional £50 per day for each day the contravention continues after conviction.

### Time limits

The time limit for a prosecution to be brought in a magistrates' court is determined by both:

- when the breach was committed; and
- which Building Regulation has been breached.

The time limits were extended in 2008 in two phases following complaints from local authorities that the original rules prevented effective enforcement of breaches of the Building Regulations where latent breaches were not discovered until after the time limit had passed. They argued that an extension of time to bring a prosecution would provide a more effective deterrent and fewer cases of non-compliance would escape prosecution.

In July 2007, there was a consultation on extending prosecution time limits. Responses indicated strong support for the proposal.

Therefore, the breach of any Building Regulation that has been committed on or after 22 September 2008, prosecution must be **brought within six months of discovery of the breach** of the Building Regulation, provided that action is taken within two years of the completion of the offending work (section 35A, BA 1984).

## The future of Building Regulations

The Department for Communities and Local Government (DCLG) has published the *Future of Building Control Implementation Plan*, which aims to make the building control system work better; to make it easier for builders to understand what standards are expected of them; and to ensure buildings comply with the high standards of safety and sustainability set out in the Building Regulations.

Measures in the Plan include:

- reducing the number of times a builder has to contact the building control inspector during a construction project;
- limiting changes to Building Regulations to every three years from 2010 (the building trade has not unreasonably complained that it was impractical to keep up with all the frequent changes); and
- improving the inspection and enforcement regime for buildings.

# Green issues and property development

## The big picture

As we have all heard by now, there are major environmental issues which will increase and affect the way we live. Climate change is likely to increase the risk of flooding and other extreme weather events; paradoxically it is also likely to lead to water shortages; as the world's oil reserves diminish the availability and cost of energy will increase, and new sources of energy will have to be found; we will also need to continue to contend with the pollution caused by current and historic industrial activity.

Buildings, and in particular housing, have a major part to play in improving our performance: it is estimated that 27% of the UK's $CO_2$ output is from our homes. On average, each household in the UK creates about six tonnes of $CO_2$ per year.

The construction industry has historically been one of the least efficient about reuse of materials, saving of energy and taking account of future constraints. Quite apart from our individual 'good intentions' to improve our environmental performance, there are sound and self-interested reasons to take account of these changes in the way we live, and the way we carry out property development in particular, because of the inevitable increases in the cost of energy and water - significant savings can be made - and the tightening noose of regulation which will require the use of more sustainable and energy efficient materials and construction methods.

It is estimated that 70% of the homes that will exist in 2050 have already been built, so adapting existing homes and flats, as well as reducing the environmental impact of new buildings, is really important. The University of Salford is conducting an interesting experiment using a typical period terraced house as a testbed to identify potential improvements.

The UK Government has set some ambitious targets to limit climate change:

- to cut the UK's emissions by 18% from 2008 levels by 2020;
- to ensure all new homes in the UK are carbon-neutral (known as Code 6 in the trade) from 2016, and from 2013 to achieve a lower standard known as Code 3;
- to generate 12% of heat from renewable sources by 2020; and
- to ensure all homes in the UK are carbon neutral by 2050.

Whilst there is some scepticism about all this, (the definition of 'zero carbon' is far from clear), and housebuilders' organisations claim that the additional requirements will add £30,000 to the cost of an average house, there are signs of progress:

- the first six zero carbon homes have been built at Upton, Northamptonshire;
- the first large scale zero carbon housing scheme is under way by Barratts for 195 homes at Hanham Hall in Gloucestershire for houses, and Kevin McCloud's smaller scheme in Swindon has received planning permission; and
- zero carbon new build homes are exempt from SDLT until 1 October 2012 (up to £500,000).

In the 2009 Budget, £435 million was allocated towards energy and resource efficiency for households, business and public buildings over 2009-2011, £525 million for offshore windfarms, £405 million for low carbon manufacturing industries, and several tax benefits for 'green' investment.

The Coalition Government has said that environmental issues are high up their agenda and, although details may change as they bring forward proposals, the general direction is likely to be similar to that of the previous Government.

There is a huge volume of well-meaning but often duplicated or contradictory material available on how to improve the 'green credentials' of your home. Only some of it is promoted by those making a profit out of selling you the means to make those changes. The most authoritative and disinterested source of information is in our view the Energy Saving Trust (www.energysavingtrust.org.uk) which is a Government-backed charity tasked with reducing the impact on the environment of the way we live.

They promote a series of simple but dull changes in the way we live our lives which will significantly reduce energy and water consumption:

- replacing light bulbs with low energy light bulbs (older models are being phased out anyway);
- turning off lights (one for parents…);
- ensuring that electronic equipment is off, not on standby, overnight;
- generally minimising car use;
- recycling waste;

- composting organic waste (needs a decent-sized garden and is not practical in dense urban areas);
- taking (short) showers rather than baths;
- draught-proofing doors and windows;
- turning down thermostats on central heating (boiler, cylinder and individual radiator thermostats) and reducing washing temperatures for washing machines and dishwashers;
- heating only the rooms you need, when you need them.

On the building side, some straightforward measures include:

- insulation of lofts and cavity walls: in an uninsulated house, 33% of heat loss is through the walls, 26% through the roof, 18% through (closed) windows, 12% through ventilation and 11% through doors and floors;
- carrying out energy assessments and putting in controls.

An EPC identifies (broadly) the energy standard of a home and potential improvements. Although usually prompted by a house move (as part of the HIP) you can get one from an energy assessor at any time. More specifically, you can use a plug-in energy monitor to test how much electricity different appliances use. An example is the Eurosaver power meter. Smart electricity meters will be in all UK homes by 2020, encouraging efficiency in power usage;

- water metering;

In terms of 'easy fixes' for existing buildings, the Energy Saving Trust gives estimates based on a typical three-bedroomed house of:

- insulating loft with 250-300mm of insulating material - cost £500 without a grant, £250 with a grant, saving £150 a year;
- insulating cavity walls – cost £500 without a grant, £250 with a grant, saving £115 a year or £400 a year for older properties;
- insulating the hot water tank – cost £12, saving £45 a year;
- replacing an old boiler – cost varies, saving up to £235 a year;
- double glazing – cost varies (prices start at £650 per window for sash windows), saving £135 a year;
- solar panels – cost £3,000-£5,000, saving £55 to £95 a year;
- sustainable materials;
- power generation - wind turbines, which use wind to generate electricity for house use (although they are rarely cost-effective in cities or suburbia);

- ground source heat pumps, which use pipes buried in the garden to extract heat from the ground. This is usually used to warm water for radiators or underfloor heating systems – it is particularly suitable to replace oil-fired or LPG or coal heating systems if you have enough outside space;
- air source heat pumps, which use temperature differences between inside and outside to provide heating (rather like air-conditioning in reverse);
- 'passive ventilation' – reusing the air extracted from kitchens and bathrooms to heat incoming air (although this cannot be used in a house where there is an open fire);
- mini hydroelectric systems, to generate small-scale electricity from, for example, a stream in your garden;
- solar thermal systems (solar panels which produce hot water, or photovoltaic cells which produce electricity);
- water butts[103] – rainwater can be collected and used to water the garden water or wash cars, and in the washing machine and toilets. This could save 50% of household water use;
- using grey water – this is water that is lightly soiled so must be filtered and treated before it can be used to flush toilets or water gardens;
- bore holes – by drilling down to the water table or an underground stream you can get your own water supply. Expensive (£2,500 minimum) and messy, but permanent - needs a licence from the Environment Agency and may need planning consent. Contact The Well Drillers Association (www.welldrillers.org.uk);
- local or very local combined heat and power production.

A list of useful websites and books on green homebuilding can be found on page 364.

## Incentives for Energy Production

With the laudable objective of encouraging large numbers of householders to adopt a greener approach to energy saving, the Labour Government announced two schemes to provide financial incentives. Whilst the Coalition Government has not yet confirmed these schemes, it is likely to do so.

---

[103] Called in polite company 'rainwater harvesting'.

These are part of the drive to provide 15% of the UK's energy through renewable means by 2020. The first, known as the Clean Energy Cash Back Scheme, started on 1 April 2010 and introduces 'Feed-in Tariffs' so that the Government will pay householders for electricity they generate themselves from photovoltaic solar panels or wind turbines or mini hydro electric systems – even if they use it themselves. This is additional to the saving on bills.

If you fit a photovoltaic system to your existing home to generate electricity, payment will be at a rate of 41.3p per unit of electricity generated; lower rates apply to new build properties. Payments for wind-generated energy are up to 34.5p per unit, and for water-generated up to 19.9p. See www.decc.gov.uk for details.

To be cynical, you may now be bombarded with sales literature for solar or wind or hydro systems; these need careful analysis to establish which is most effective for you. The Energy Savings Trust (www.energysavingtrust.gov.uk) will help.

A further incentive system is due to be introduced in April 2011 under the name 'The Renewable Heat Scheme' to reward house builders who install equipment such as air and ground source heat pumps, biomass boilers and solar thermal panels (which heat water).

There may be a substantial cost attached to the installation of these systems, and it is wise to assess the payback period carefully.

For both schemes, there may be teething problems – for example delays in the approval process for the eligibility of equipment – but in principle the schemes are clearly attractive, particularly to 'self-builders'.

# CHAPTER 10 BUYING ABROAD

The benefits and challenges of choosing and buying a property in the UK are magnified – rendered in Technicolor – when buying outside the UK. The fulfilment of a dream is somehow more emotionally satisfying than achieving a necessity; but if that dream turns sour it feels like a complete disaster.

So the image we have of buying a property abroad is either, on the one hand, sipping a glass of local vino and watching the sun set over the iridescent sea, or in a hot tub in the snow or, on the other hand, pitying the retired couple who have lost all their life savings in an unbuilt Bulgarian ski resort or a Spanish villa which is to be demolished.

Yet the guiding principles are the same as in the UK:

- be clear about what you want, and why
- budget carefully
- research the market carefully
- make sure you understand the buying process
- think about how sellable the property will be.

In addition, you need to take into account – and recognise in yourself:

- the need to adapt culturally
- the language barrier (even in the US)
- currency risk
- tax and inheritance consequences.

The British public has embraced both travelling and buying abroad in a way far beyond that contemplated in the days of exchange controls (for those too young to remember, the amount of currency one could take outside the UK was limited to as little as £50 as recently as 1967).

According to Grant Thornton, British-owned properties outside the UK have trebled from 102,000 in 1995 to 300,000 today. Of these, Spain and France are by some distance the most popular locations.

Of course, for many people the opportunity to buy abroad has become available because of the enormous growth in value of their UK home, and to a lesser extent the relative strength of the pound against other currencies until 2007.

This chapter includes some generic advice about how to choose where and what to buy, and more specific advice about the buying process in the most popular (or at least most advertised) countries, namely:

Spain
France
Portugal
Italy
Switzerland
Cyprus
US (specifically Florida)
Dubai
South Africa.

Properties in many other countries are of course advertised for sale or featured in the UK press - to take a random selection from the Sunday Times Home Supplement, you could buy in Austria, Barbados, Belgium, Canada, Columbia, Croatia, Kenya, Mauritius, Morocco - but we cannot cover everything. Perhaps not surprisingly, the ads for properties in Estonia, Latvia or Bulgaria have been replaced by 'how it all went wrong' stories.

Whilst much of this chapter could apply to investment and commercial property, we are focussed on residential property - either for your own use or for holiday letting. Investing in commercial property, or in residential property for a longer term letting, has further implications and complications which would require more detailed description than would fit comfortably into the scope of this book.

So where do you start?

As with any property purchase, the three phases are:

- deciding what you want
- finding it
- buying it.

The place *not* to start, beyond playing the 'what if' game, is in the sales office at your holiday resort, or at a 'special exhibition' at a hotel in the UK, where you will be given the hard sell. Just as with buying a UK home, you may be lucky and find the perfect property first time around, but the chances are that you will not. You can by all means use these as a source of some, perhaps one-sided, information about the resort or development, and asking prices, but it would be very unwise to commit yourself to anything without time to think about why and what and where to buy, and to research the market properly.

We suggest that if you are thinking of buying abroad, start by analysing your own motives and desires:

- is this primarily a permanent purchase, or temporary (in other words are you buying to keep, and maybe retire to, or to trade on for a profit)?
- is this for you to live in, or to use as a second home, or for investment? If for investment, will it be for holiday letting or long term lets? (If so, do you have experience of doing this in the UK, and do you have the time and the skills to manage it?)
- if you want a property to 'do up', either for yourself or for letting or sale, do you have the time and skills (and money) to do this at a distance, and do you have experience of doing this in the UK?
- what are your financial resources? What is your UK property worth, net of any mortgage, how much 'free' cash do you have, what do you need to keep aside for unexpected costs, such as seeing an elderly parent into nursing care? For how much longer will you be earning? What do you need to reserve for pension payments? What pension will you actually receive? Will you expect to fund children through university and into their own first homes?

It is likely that, if you are being realistic and can convince your other half that you are, and you do have the time, skills and money to embark on your 'buying abroad' mission, you will fall into one of three categories of buyer:

(1) *The owner.* That is, you are buying a property for you and your family to use and live in, now or later. You will let friends and family use it from time to time but will not let it commercially.

(2) *The financial investor.* That is, you are buying the property to make money, either by creating an income from letting or a capital profit from developing and selling on (the days of buying off-plan and selling on quickly at a profit have passed into history or myth, at least for the next few years).

(3) *The hopeful investor.* That is, you are buying the property to live in or sell eventually (you will decide later); you hope to cover the running costs by

letting out the property most of the year, keeping back a couple of weeks a year for yourself, and you hope that the property will go up in value.

Those falling into the first two categories are most likely to be motivated to choose the right property with care to satisfy their different motives, and to manage themselves and the property to achieve their aims; those in the third category, who are probably the majority, are at risk of taking short cuts to buying, and in managing the property and the letting process, and of running out of energy and becoming disenchanted over time as the effort involved in managing and letting seems to increase and the benefit of owning seems to decrease. So, if you are in that third category, we suggest you project yourself forward two, five and 10 years from today: think about the grind of advertising for lettings, managing bookings, arranging weekly changeovers such as cleaning and laundry, arranging regular decoration and replacement of kitchen equipment and linen, for perhaps little immediate financial benefit after utility and service charge costs, currency devaluation and tax.

If you do fall into this third category, a useful test of whether you are treating this as a hobby or an investment is to ask yourself which weeks you will reserve for yourself to spend there – the peak high earning summer holiday weeks (in the sun) or the New Year/half term weeks (in the snow), or the off season (November?) – *every* year?

Perhaps you really want a timeshare or fractional ownership. We have a section on this later in this chapter.

If we have not completely put you off the idea of buying abroad, please read on ….

## Deciding what you want

As with any property purchase, research is essential, and the same fundamental criteria apply as in the UK. Location is the most vital; your field of search is not constrained by commitment to job, school or location so there is a world of choice.

However, most buyers do not start with a globe and a pin. Perhaps you have a family connection to a particular country, or at least a smattering of the relevant language, and have worked or enjoyed a holiday there, or been recommended to it by someone you trust.

Some will prefer rural isolation in, say, France or Italy, others will prefer the sociable mix of, say, a golf complex in Florida, Spain or Portugal. Most properties tick one or more of the following boxes:

| | | | |
|---|---|---|---|
| In a city | | In the country | |
| Near the sea | | In the mountains | |
| Newly built | | A wreck with potential | |
| In a resort complex | | Miles from anywhere | |

For the owner, personal preference is obviously the key. For the financial investor, the availability of a market for letting and resale is the key. For the hopeful investor, a balance between the market for letting and personal preference is desirable.

If you are thinking of buying abroad, analyse your own motives and desires before you start. How long do you expect to keep the property? Is it for the foreseeable future or for re-sale after a defined period? Unlike house moves in the UK, it is relatively rare for owners to trade up to accommodate a larger family, or to downsize, except for purely financial reasons.

For an owner, the considerations for choice of location should include the following:

- language and currency;
- buying costs (and obstacles to buying and residence);
- ongoing maintenance and tax costs;
- accessibility from the UK (allowing for the possibility that Ryanair, EasyJet, BA or charter airlines may drop certain routes, or make them seasonal, but not forgetting train services);
- accessibility to local facilities, for example shopping, banks, churches, social and leisure activities, healthcare;
- weather throughout the year (some parts of Spain, France or Italy get pretty cold and wet in the winter; some parts of the Middle East are extraordinarily hot in the summer);
- seasonality (some ski resorts have real life and activities throughout the year, others close from April to December);

- cost of living (*everything* is more expensive in Dubai or Switzerland than in the UK, even if tax free); most things are cheaper in Florida or South Africa than in the UK;
- availability and reliability of internet access and, if it matters to you, UK or other English-speaking TV or radio channels;
- the size and surroundings of a particular property, including the risk that the view from your terrace may be blocked by future development;
- personal security (it may be unfair to single out South Africa, but many do express concerns);
- cultural differences (especially for single women);
- inheritance laws – a complex area, which in many countries is very different from the UK;
- regime stability;
- (if you intend to improve the property) the complexities and costs of managing building works at a distance.

For an investor, choice of location considerations should include the following:

- language and currency;
- buying costs (and obstacles to letting or sale);
- ongoing maintenance and tax costs;
- the size and permanence of the potential letting market, whether for holiday lettings (will climate change render a low ski resort unusable?) or longer job-based lettings (the Dubai bubble has burst);
- the pricing of lettings, and the competition for tenants - obviously there is both higher demand and higher competition in a city such as Paris or Brussels or Venice but little demand for long term lettings in holiday resorts;
- tenant demand for particular size units - single occupancy, couples, families - or particular requirements - air conditioning, swimming pools;
- whether the likely tenants will be British, local or international;
- accessibility from the UK and elsewhere;
- accessibility to local facilities, such as pools, golf courses or the sea;
- weather all year around;
- seasonality - the length of the summer or ski season varies significantly according to resort; conversely a villa in the Caribbean will not let during the hurricane season;

- the infrastructure for lettings – the availability of reliable letting and managing agents, cleaning and maintenance companies;
- internet access;
- personal security (gated communities are attractive for holiday lets, concierges for city flats);
- constraints and tax on resale;
- regime and legal system stability.

For our (by now battered and bruised) hopeful investor, both these long lists of location considerations need to be taken into account in order to maximise letting prospects and use in the short term, and saleability or occupiability (if there is such a word) in the longer term.

In order to assess letting potential of the property, put yourself in the shoes of the tenant and look through their eyes - what will make them choose this property rather than the hundreds or dozens of others with which yours will be competing, within the same complex, if it is in one, or on equivalent complexes elsewhere? Look at 'holiday apartment' or 'gite' websites to see what you are up against, and consider what would make you choose one property against another.

In addition, think about the adaptability of the accommodation itself: you may be able to anticipate reconfiguring it for your own use, for example, by converting an outbuilding to add a bedroom or studio or teenagers' annex, or buying an adjoining field for privacy, or (in an apartment block) buying the flat next door or above or below in order to combine them. However, if the property is in a tightly controlled environment such as a golf complex, it is unlikely that major external changes will be allowed.

Read the summaries following this generic section to compare buying and tax costs in different countries.

## Finding what you want

Once you have narrowed down your focus to a particular country, area and property type, we suggest the following research to help you select your preferred property:

Research via the internet – there are many websites with details of properties including those of the larger UK residential agents, who have international sections or links on their main websites. Some also have offices in the popular cities and resorts. The established UK property websites have international sections, as do the Times and Telegraph newspaper sites. There are also useful websites with advice on letting abroad – although remember they want you on their list! There is a list of useful web addresses on page 363 and in the individual country sections at the end of this chapter.

Others carry listings of overseas properties for sale, and in some cases offer useful 'how to' guides, but remember they are essentially advertising sites on behalf of sellers. They are good for research but not a replacement for your own knowledge, or for legal advice.

Try before you buy. Take one or more holidays in your chosen area, at different times of year, in and out of UK school holidays and, particularly if you are planning a long term move, rent in the area for a few months before committing yourself.

Read up in more detail about the country of your choice - most public libraries have a selection of books about buying in the most popular destinations which go into more detail than we can within the scope of this book. Lots of the property websites also have further resources for research - www.themovechannel.com covers the most popular countries and makes many books available online.

Talk to as many local agents as practicable in the area you have chosen. Bear in mind that in most countries estate agents do not exist, or perform the same role, as in the UK. For the most popular locations for the British, UK agents have set up their own offices in the Costas, Paris, the Cote d'Azur and Dubai, or local agents have adapted to British ways, for example in the Dordogne and Tuscany, but elsewhere you may need to adapt to local ways of finding and viewing properties. As an example, in the US it is common for a buyer to employ a property agent to find a property (and mortgage finance).

## Buying it

Assuming you have got this far, you have assessed your own needs, selected your country, area and property type, done your research and found your dream. No doubt you are raring to go.

Before you get going:

## Budget

You need to make a realistic financial assessment of your own resources and budget, allowing not just for price but buying costs, and if you plan to let or develop, the projected income to achieve the letting and projected expenditure on the building, so you have a realistic budget to work to. Broadly, this will follow a format similar to that we have set out in the chapters on buying, letting or property development in this book, but you need to bear in mind two additional factors.

First, the cost of visits to supervise the purchase, and then the letting or developing. Factor in not just flights but also hotel stays, car hire or other transport, and the need for multiple trips to decide on design and furnishing options, to meet the mortgage company or bank manager or the local mayor's office, or just to find the nearest Ikea. Secondly, bear in mind the cost and volatility of currency exchange rates and the likelihood that you will need to make several payments at different times when the exchange rate for sterling may have improved or deteriorated. If you are at your budget limit, currency changes can be really painful. At least for larger amounts, you can make worthwhile improvements on the currency conversion rate you achieve by using a specialist currency broker, and they can also advise you whether and how to buy currency in advance in order to be certain you will have the necessary funds in the right currency when you need them. They can also guide you through some countries' requirements for approval or notification of larger transfers (for example, Italy).

## Plan

Before you take the next step, make sure that you think long term. Think carefully about your family's needs if you are buying for yourself, and how they will change as your energetic 10-year-old turns into a sulky teenager or absent student, your own future pattern of working, and your commitments at home to sport or pets or ponies or mothers-in-law.

So, you have passed all those tests, you have found the property you want, you have made sure you have the funds available: what happens next?

## Process

Of necessity, this next section is full of generalisations. We have provided summaries for 10 of the most popular destinations at the end of this chapter, but we can give only the briefest of explanations. If you want to be fully informed you will need to research the specifics applicable in the country you have chosen. Bear in mind that in some countries, for example Switzerland, the US or Germany, the law, custom and practice, as well as taxes, vary from country to country or state to state or region to region.

Remember also that changes do happen, particularly on tax rules and rates, so make sure you get up-to-date information (for which the internet is not reliable). The information in this chapter is up-to-date as at 30 June 2010, but change is constant.

In most of the popular countries, the property buying system is well established and reputable, although different from the UK. We strongly recommend that you employ a local English-speaking lawyer to advise you on the purchase, and to ensure that you are aware of the local tax and inheritance laws. It may well be wise for you to take advice in the UK as to your tax and inheritance position before you launch into the purchase. Some UK firms of solicitors specialise in advising on overseas purchases. We mention a couple at the end of this chapter so you can look at their websites which may be useful in providing a little more detail than we can within the frame of this book.

A good general starting point is the free guide 'Buying Overseas Property Safely' available from the Association of International Property Professionals (AIPP) at www.aipp.org.uk.

In most European countries, the system and the role of the lawyer is significantly different because the procedural (and usually tax) aspects of the property transfer are dealt with by a government-appointed or government-approved official called a notary (see the separate section in this chapter, 'The Role of the Notary'). He is there to ensure that the transaction is properly carried out. He is acting for both parties, not only for you. He will not provide legal advice as to whether it is appropriate to buy, or carry out due diligence beyond some formal checks, so you will need a separate lawyer acting for you to ensure those things are carried out properly. The notary also will often not be able or willing to operate in English.

Although lawyers vary according to personality the world over, of course, you will tend to find that in most European countries they are more academic, perhaps more gentlemanly, than UK solicitors but rather less 'commercial'. If there is a peculiarity on the title they may give you an extended essay on the history of it, rather than a straight answer as to whether it matters to you or not. Conversely, in the US you will find that the lawyers tell you how to take the best commercial advantage of your position in ways you may find aggressive.

As with any other professional, if you can get a word of mouth recommendation then that is desirable. Do not fall into the trap of using the lawyer suggested by a developer. A notary, however, is an independent and regulated official, often the only one in a particular area, so you should be able to rely on his/her independence.

It is wise to take inheritance law advice before embarking on any formalities of purchase, because in many countries those laws differ very significantly from what we assume in the UK, which is that property and other assets will go in accordance with your intentions as set out in your will. In those countries where the inheritance law derives from the French Napoleonic Code, including Italy, Spain and Portugal and their former colonies, the Napoleonic Code imposes a mandatory sub-division of the value of the property which may include both the children and the parents and siblings of the person who has died. This set of rules overrides any will. Consequently, careful thought is needed before you enter into any contracts: for example, as to which name to buy in. In some circumstances it may be appropriate to buy through a company, normally a company based in a country that is not subject to the same rules, for example a Gibraltarian company for Spain. It may be too late to change this once you have entered into the purchase contract so you need to be clear how you will proceed before you sign anything.

Assuming you have all those ducks in single file, the process of making an offer and having it accepted is, as in England and Wales, firstly verbal, and then usually confirmed with a short memorandum and a small preliminary deposit. Beware that this can be interpreted, notably in France, as a legally binding commitment, so take advice *before* signing anything.

At this stage, in most countries, the property is not off the market and, as in the UK, you are relying on the goodwill of the vendor to stick with you.

However, the second stage of a formal legally-drawn agreement, and a larger deposit (at least 10% but in many countries more than that, sometimes up to 50% in Italy or Portugal) follows as soon as is practicable. This needs to be coordinated with the offer and availability of mortgage funds if you are borrowing, and with your lawyer or the notary carrying out the necessary searches and investigating the seller's title to make sure that they are able to sell. In a few countries (notably Switzerland and Cyprus) you also need to apply for and obtain a governmental permit before you can buy.

Unlike England and Wales, in some countries, notably France, the purchase contract may be signed subject to mortgage funds being made available - this enables the contract to be signed earlier than it otherwise would be.

During this 'due diligence period', if you have in mind any works to the property, particularly in major renovation or rebuilding, it is wise to get at least preliminary drawings prepared and to establish what the local authority approval procedure will be, and to obtain local advice, and maybe meet the relevant officials at the local authority. Your lawyer will advise you on how best to proceed with this.

For the perils of not carrying out this due diligence carefully (and sometimes the consequences even if you do) read the separate section in this chapter: 'The Pain in Spain'.

By the time you sign the contract you should be sure that you have all the funds available including enough to cover the costs of buying, that you know what you are getting and the constraints on it, and that the lawyers have checked that the title is good and have carried out all the necessary searches (or, in the US, arranged title insurance). This is when the main deposit is payable. The deposit is often held by the notary where there is one.

In most countries, the system of carrying out surveys and valuations that we are familiar with in the UK does not really exist, so you will need to assess the structural state of the building and any risks yourself. It may well be worth employing a local builder to assess the property as to what works are required to put it into habitable condition, or to comply with local building codes or to establish whether your 'grand design' is viable, and what the likely cost and timescale may be. If there is any risk of doubt about the boundaries (particularly with rural property, particularly in Italy) it is worth employing a site surveyor (called a geometer in Italy) to check exactly that the boundaries comply with what you think you are getting. In any event, you should check any plans carefully on site, to ensure the 'paper' boundaries match the 'physical' boundaries.

## Buying from a developer v buying second hand

Unlike in the UK, a high proportion of holiday home purchases abroad are from developers, often in purpose-built complexes. In Dubai or parts of Spain, Portugal, Cyprus, Switzerland or Florida that is all you can buy. It is important to allow for the differences which follow from buying from a developer.

As we mention on page 76 in relation to UK property, there can be significant advantages; the property should be in good condition and need less maintenance at least initially, and be built to modern standards of, for example, thermal insulation; you may have the opportunity to improve design details (at a cost), and some white goods or even furniture may be included in the price. You also have the potential advantage that if there is a later problem, for which you have to chase down the seller, you may have more success with an established developer who has an interest in you being positive about their after-care service, than an individual seller of a second-hand property who may be difficult to trace, or to persuade to take action, once they have your money.

On the other hand, as we spell out in 'The Pain in Spain' section below, some developers (and their agents) cut corners, or fail to get the paperwork right, or run out of money part-way through a development with consequences which can be disastrous.

In some countries – including Spain – protection for buyers do exist, limiting or protecting deposits, requiring guarantees to be provided and imposing building standards or insurance cover. These vary from country to country, and you (as always) will need local legal advice to ensure that you understand the significance and implications of what you are signing before you do so. Before you commit, it is worth doing some research, including asking around and asking your lawyer, about the reputation of the developer for quality, and its financial strength. Don't fall for the old trick – which you wouldn't accept in England – of using the lawyer recommended by the seller.

In some countries, there are also tax differences between new-build and second hand properties – VAT may apply to new-build but not second-hand, or different rates of registration fees, or capital gains tax on sale.

So, the moral is, do not assume that the rules of the game are the same elsewhere as they are at home. Even if the underlying principles for buyer protection are similar – and they generally are – the procedures can be very different.

*Valuations?*

In most countries you buy the property in its condition at the time of signing the contract so it is important to inspect the property before signing to ensure that it has not deteriorated since you first saw it, or that any works the seller agreed to do have either been done, or are provided for in the contract.

Depending on the country and procedures, completion is usually 3-4 weeks after exchange of contracts, and again is formally carried out in front of the notary unless a power of attorney is used, the underlying intention being that the notary is satisfied that both seller and buyer are fully aware of the transaction and the documents they are entering into. You will have to transfer the funds to the notary for completion, including all taxes payable, in advance, so that they hold the necessary monies at completion (in the US, you may use an escrow account set up through the lawyers).

You also should have in place buildings insurance as the risk is now yours if the building burns down or is damaged (at least in Switzerland, buildings insurance is compulsory – rather like third party car insurance, for the benefit of other people rather than oneself).

Either the notary or the lawyers will then deal with registration at the Land Registry, and the payment of relevant transfer and local taxes to ensure that the transaction is properly recorded. If there is a mortgage over the property involved then further registration fees are likely to be needed.

Then, it is all yours!

One important follow-up point is for you to check that the registration of your ownership is completed and to get a copy of the registered transfer document for your own records, preferably with a translation into English, as you are likely to need this for both the local and UK tax authorities in the future. It also ensures that the notary or lawyer finishes the job they were paid to do.

## The role of the notary

In many continental European countries, notably France, Spain, Portugal, Italy, Germany and Switzerland, the principal actor in transferring ownership of properties - what in the UK we call 'conveyancing' – is not a solicitor (or equivalent) acting for each party but a notary acting neutrally.

The role of a notary derives from the legal system known as the Napoleonic Code, and ultimately from Roman law. The notary's responsibility is to ensure that the property is accurately described and that title is properly transferred and registered with the appropriate Land Registry. In most countries the notary is also required to ensure that the appropriate transfer taxes (and VAT if applicable) and registration fees are paid. He or she is acting in an administrative capacity and is independent of either seller or buyer. In most of the relevant countries, the notary is a government-appointed official, although in some countries he or she is a government-approved but self-employed professional.

In some countries, the notary also acts as an estate agent, holding details of properties for sale within his or her local area.

The notary takes care of the mundane but vital procedures required to identify the property in words accurately, to draft the sale and purchase agreement and the deed effecting the transfer of land, and any mortgage binding on the property itself, and to deal with registration of the transfer and mortgage at the Land Registry and pay any applicable registration fees and taxes.

Usually, the formalities require both seller and buyer to attend in person in front of the notary to identify themselves (bring your passport!), to hear the document to be signed read out aloud, and to sign the document with the notary acting as witness.

Attending in person can be avoided by using powers of attorney to appoint a local lawyer to act on your behalf, but there is something to be said for the formality of the notary procedure. Although we sophisticated Brits may find it all rather quaint, it does emphasise the seriousness of the event itself, and the commitment you are entering into, in a rather more satisfying way than the faceless process of English solicitors, and of course it is also a good excuse for a celebration.

There are differences in the scope of the notary's role between different countries. In France part of his or her duties include carrying out searches to check title, and ensuring that the seller provides a pack of required searches, for example for lead, asbestos, termites, gas, electricity and energy and for outstanding municipal charges (the cost of water or drainage connections or road improvements, for example) and outstanding mortgages, so the need to employ a separate French lawyer is reduced (although we do advise it anyway). In Switzerland, the notary also makes the necessary application to the cantonal authority for a permit to buy, on the buyer's behalf. In Spain, the notary's role is limited to transfer of title matters, including drafting the contract and transfer and registering the transfer, and you will need a separate lawyer (*abogado)* to check the seller's entitlement to sell, carry out searches (which are particularly vital for the reasons described in 'The Pain in Spain' section) and to check for outstanding municipal or mortgage liabilities. In Portugal, the notary will merely witness the signing, and the buyer's lawyer will deal with checking title, searches, drafting the documents, paying the taxes and registering the transfer.

The notary is regulated by state authorities and the rules of the notary profession, which also set scales of charges which are rarely negotiable. As well as dealing with transfers and mortgages, in most countries notaries will also prepare wills. They are not tax or inheritance law experts, and do not have an international perspective, so you should take advice on these matters from a specialist (before signing anything, even the initial contract). Following the death of the owner, the notary will process the transfer of the property to the heirs in accordance with the inheritance laws of that country, and any will, including dealing with any taxes and registration fees then due. If the notary also drafts a will for you, the fee for that will be for you to agree. VAT will be payable on the notary's fees. Most notaries operate in their local language, not English. You may need to arrange (and pay separately for) translations of key documents such as the sale and purchase contract, the transfer deed, any mortgage documents and any constitutional documents for any co-ownership arrangement, or a company you have used to buy through.

The notary in Continental Europe is not the same as the 'notary public' known in the UK, whose function is to witness and validate important legal documents (usually related to international trade or shipping) or produce certified copies for use in various other countries, but not to draft or process them. You may need to use a UK notary public to witness and validate a power of attorney you give to a lawyer or other representative abroad to enable them to perform a property transaction on your behalf, particularly for Spain and Portugal.

## The pain in Spain

Spain has been the most popular holiday home country for the British, and other Europeans, for many years.

Its property development industry has been red hot to meet demand, and consequently the factors which have affected property markets everywhere have affected Spain more powerfully than elsewhere. There are also problems which are particular to Spain but have affected holiday home buyers disproportionately. The British media have therefore reported more 'shock horror' disaster stories about holiday homes in Spain than anywhere else.

The reasons why Spain, or at least some coastal regions of it, has been popular are still in place – the climate, a critical mass of developments and social facilities, a ready supply of villas and apartments to suit UK buyers, and ex-pat communities – and provided that you use some common sense and take appropriate precautions, particularly by getting legal advice from an experienced Spanish lawyer, the 'shock horror' stories should not put you off.

First the macro factors:

As with elsewhere in the Eurozone, the change in the relative strength of sterling against the Euro since 2007 means that Spanish prices are relatively more expensive than they were for the British (the converse of the logic of Cristiano Ronaldo moving to Real Madrid ...). This is bad news for British buyers, particularly when compared to say, German, Dutch or Irish buyers who are not affected by the exchange rate change. It is, of course, good news for those Brits who bought when the pound was stronger. Also, as with most other property markets, the boom period up to 2007 has been followed by a crash in 2008 and 2009. Because the boom in Spain was exceptionally powerful – prices in the holiday areas rose on average by 270% between 1996 and 2006 – the crash has been exceptionally severe and prices are quoted as falling by 19% between

2007 and 2009[104] and in practice sales have virtually stalled. Inevitably, for some owners and some developers, and their banks, the crash has turned to bust. The number of housing starts collapsed by 60% in 2008. One of the largest Spanish property development companies, Martinsa-Fadesa, went into insolvency in July 2008 and others such as Polaris World have teetered on the edge of insolvency. Spanish banks have generally survived but have huge risky debts (€165.5 billion of 'potential troubled' loans according to the Banco de Espana in March 2010). The banks most affected are the savings banks (*caja de ahorro*) who lent heavily to property developers, and some of these are now having to be rescued by others.

Funds for new developments, and in some cases completing existing developments, are therefore not available. That may also mean that any deposit you may have put down is difficult to recover. All of this may be good news for selective new buyers, but not for sellers. Thirdly, the strength of demand from (mostly) unsophisticated buyers inevitably drew in some dishonest sellers or developers or speculators. An example highlighted by the Sunday Times was a land investment company called Fortuna Estates – read *Times Online* for the sorry tale.

As we have said, these problems are not unique to Spain: there are reports of unfinished developments and bust developers all over the world, including the UK, and many reminders that property values can go dramatically down as well as endlessly up – but there are six legal issues which have impacted in Spain, particularly on holiday home buyers, more severely than elsewhere. An aggravating factor is that because of the distinction made in Spanish law between rural and urban land, if compensation is available at all it is usually based on the rural price even for developed property.

First, where the property was built within 100 metres of the coastline: by the Coast Law of 1988 (and a previous law of 1969), intended to protect the Spanish coastline from damage from development, the buyer of a property must obtain a certificate from the National Coastal Authority stating that the property is not within 100 metres of the coastline. The coastline is defined by that Authority and there is scope for argument about where it should be – it could be defined

---

[104] Source – Tinsa.

by a coastal flood five years ago – and the Coastal Authority can and will redefine it from time to time, if a new port or marina is built. The fact that zoning approval or planning permission exists for a development is not sufficient to satisfy or override this Coastal Law requirement. If the property is within 100 metres of the coastline it is illegal and the Coastline Authority can require it to be demolished. There are rights of appeal, and if the illegality is caused by the Coastline Authority redrawing the boundary, then there may be a 30 year retention period, but clearly you will not want to be exposed to this risk. If it is even remotely possible that the property you are looking at could be subject to this risk, you must get your lawyer to check this point.

Secondly, where the property was built without planning permission. By way of background, developing property in Spain requires three levels of permission:

- Zoning: prepared and adopted by the local authority (for example to designate zones for development or preservation or conservation) but the regional authority can review and alter the plan.
- Planning Permission (*'plan partial'*): prepared by the developer and approved by the local authority (for example to authorise building and road design for a particular project).
- Building Licence: prepared by the developer and approved by the local authority (for example construction details, services etc).

In addition, before a property can be connected to public utilities, or a valid mortgage given, the local authority must issue a *'licencia de primera ocupacion'*. Some unscrupulous developers connected temporary unofficial electricity and water supplies without obtaining this licence so that buyers completed on and paid for their properties, leaving the unsuspecting buyer with a fight with the local authority to get the licence later.

Some planning permissions issued by local authorities have been illegal because they contravene the zoning plans, for example by permitting building construction on zones reserved for local services such as schools, parks or playing fields. Notoriously, in Marbella, this happened on a large scale (leading ultimately to the arrest and conviction of the mayor and several other officials in 2002 and again in 2006) after the regional authority reviewed the zoning plans and invalidated some of the permissions. In these circumstances there may be a claim for compensation against the local authority, although it will be based on the rural value and not the developed value or the price paid.

In other cases, the house or apartment block may have been built without planning permission, because (before the changes in the law made as a consequence of the Marbella scandal) it was common for the developer to start construction and selling off-plan at the same time as applying for the planning permission and building licence. If the developer did not achieve those permissions, the off-plan buyer is entitled to recover its deposit but the developer may not have funds to pay. The developer should, by law, provide a bank guarantee to the buyer to cover this risk but frequently did not.

Thirdly, the Spanish government and other authorities have compulsory purchase powers enabling them to expropriate property in order to construct roads, railways, etc. There are rights of challenge both against the principle of expropriation and the valuation figure. This, in broad outline, is no different from the system applicable in the UK or most other European countries, but because Spain is (or has been, at any rate) more active in developing its infrastructure, partly to accommodate the expansion of its tourist economy, the likelihood of compulsory purchase impacting on existing, even recently developed, areas is higher than elsewhere.

Fourthly, in relation to new build properties, part of the construction permit process involves the developer carrying out works and paying fees to connect into the central services – estate roads, water, sewage, electricity, gas and telephone. If a developer is dishonest or struggling for cash, it may claim that the building is complete at completion, and therefore payment of the balance of the price is due. Even if the services are connected, these may be temporary or unofficial. If the price is paid and completion takes place, the cost of permanent connection may in practice fall to the buyer, with the developer having disappeared.

Fifthly, unlike in the UK, mortgages attach to the land and are not necessarily repaid and released on a sale. Consequently, on buying a property, including buying a plot from a developer, you can also buy responsibility for the mortgage. This can easily be checked out at the local land register where any mortgages must be registered; again, your lawyer should confirm that they have done so and that any mortgages have been released.

A high profile victim of this was Sir Geoff Hurst (and friends) who bought apartments at Aloha Royal near Marbella off-plan, paid the whole price before they were built, and then found that the developer could not transfer good title to the apartments.

Sixthly, declared transfer prices have often been significantly lower than the real price paid – which saves the buyer transfer taxes and maybe ongoing property-related taxes, and saves the seller capital gains taxes. This is illegal. The Spanish authorities have not always been very effective in enforcing this in the past but they are increasingly taking enforcement action against those who abuse the system. This is not unique to Spain and the habit of under-pricing and the threat of enforcement happens elsewhere too, notably in Portugal and Italy.

All of these problems can and should be familiar to an experienced Spanish lawyer. Any of the first three should be a sufficient warning not to proceed with this particular property, and any of the last three should be covered in the purchase contract so that you do not complete and/or pay anything beyond the deposit unless they are satisfactorily dealt with.

A further aggravating factor is that (unlike the UK) there is no time limit on enforcement by the local authority of (for example) building in breach of planning, so problems can arise many years after the property has been built or bought.

## Raising the money

For many, but certainly not all, the desire and opportunity to buy abroad, whether as owners or investors, arises around the time the children leave home and the mortgage on that home is finally paid off, so that both time and money are more easily available.

Therefore, a relatively higher proportion of overseas purchases are for cash. However, if you do need or want to borrow to fund your purchase, three main options to consider and price are:

- raising money against your UK home by re-mortgaging, or increasing your existing mortgage
- borrowing in the UK for the purchase abroad – several UK banks offer packages specifically for this, notably HSBC and Barclays

- borrowing in the relevant country - either through a local branch of a UK bank, or through the local bank.

The benefits and drawbacks of these alternatives vary from country to country and according to your individual circumstances. In many countries, mortgaging a property there will incur additional notary and registration fees and sometimes stamp duty; in France interest payable to a French bank may be tax deductible against rental income but interest payable to a UK bank may not; in Switzerland interest rates are usually lower than the UK; in Florida it is normal to arrange for banks to put in competitive bids for your money before you make your offer to buy, so that you know you have the funds available. There are risks and possible benefits in borrowing in the same currency as applies to the property, depending on future currency movements. Some banks offer hedging facilities, although the amounts and periods available may make them too expensive for most people.

Initial bank fees and interest rates vary significantly from country to country and from time to time, as they do in the UK, so we suggest you investigate this as part of your budgeting exercise before making your final offer.

## Tax

This is only a very brief summary and we recommend you take specific advice applicable to your circumstances.

If you are a UK resident, you must declare income from a non-UK property and, subject to your overall tax status, that income will be taxable. The same reliefs apply as for UK property: that is, costs of letting, mortgage interest and the cost of certain repairs may be deductible. Bear in mind that mortgage interest is deductible but mortgage capital repayments are not.

In many countries, income tax will be payable on income from property in that country, even if you are not resident there. Tax reliefs may be different – costs of letting, mortgage interests and running costs may not be deductible.

The UK has double tax treaties with all of the countries covered in this book (and many more), so that credit is given in the UK for tax paid in the country where the income arises from the property. In order to achieve this you will need to prove that you have registered for tax in that country, filed a tax return and paid the tax.

In the past, if you owned foreign property through a company and occupied the property yourself for part or all of the year (but remain a UK tax resident), you were potentially chargeable to UK tax on the benefit in kind that use represented. Most people were not aware of this and therefore did not declare it on their UK income tax return and were potentially liable for tax for past years, including interest and penalties. In the Finance Act 2008 legislation was introduced to provide an exemption from this tax charge for a director or other officer of the company or a member of such director's family or household if, basically, the company is wholly owned by such director or such director and other individuals, the property is the only asset of the company and the only activities of the company are matters incidental to that ownership. There are some detailed conditions which should be checked, but normally it should prevent the charge arising. This exemption was introduced with retrospective effect.

UK residents will also pay UK capital gains tax on gains made on selling overseas properties, subject again to UK reliefs and exemptions and double tax treaties. Again, capital gains on selling may be taxed in the country where the property is situated as well, for which double tax treaty relief may be claimed. Deductions against capital gains or the percentage of capital gains taxable may differ from the UK.

This book is not aimed at UK non-residents. In view of the increase in the top UK income tax rate to 50% from 5 April 2010, a number of readers may think spending time abroad or moving abroad 'permanently' is a way of avoiding UK tax.

The question of whether a person is or is not resident in the UK is a complicated one and depends upon all the facts. However, even where a UK resident leaves the UK permanently and would otherwise be treated as resident in another jurisdiction, they are nevertheless treated as continuing to be UK resident if visits to the UK average 91 days or more per tax year.

There have been two significant recent tightenings of these rules. Previously HMRC's practice was to ignore both the day a person arrived in the UK and the day a person departed the UK in calculating the 91 days but now an individual is usually treated as spending a day in the UK if he is in the UK at the end of that day, that is the day of arrival is treated as a day in the UK. Secondly,

HMRC revised their general guidance on residence in April 2009 and now state that the act of leaving the country is not likely to be sufficient evidence by itself that you have left the UK permanently and have become non-resident and not ordinarily resident, and so even if the number of days spent in the UK is less than 91, connections with the UK such as retaining a property in the UK, visiting the UK regularly for work purposes, or retaining formal or informal social ties in the UK through clubs or memberships, sending your child to a UK boarding school or university, visiting clubs, societies or friends may all undermine a claim to be non-resident. The guidance notes give these indications as examples rather than a definitive test, and it remains to be seen how literally and how effectively HMRC interprets these guidelines for individuals. Greater clarity may only come through test cases in the courts.

An example is the Gaines-Cooper decision in February 2010. Mr Gaines-Cooper, an international businessman, moved from the UK to the Seychelles in 1976 but retained links with the UK including an estate in Oxfordshire where his wife and son lived, and he kept his collections of paintings, guns and classic cars. Mr Gaines-Cooper lost his appeal to the Court of Appeal, and so will be taxed as a UK resident.

Finally, bear in mind that UK and local tax rules change frequently, that the UK tax authorities are increasingly under pressure to recover tax 'avoiders' wherever they may be, and that the tax authorities worldwide are increasingly effective in penetrating so-called tax havens in pursuit of criminal or terrorist funding, so they are suspicious of complex arrangements. So our advice is: don't try to be too clever!

## France - sale and leaseback

The French government has a 'Residence du Tourisme' scheme, usually called 'leaseback' in English, which is a way to buy a property in France at a discounted price and cover some of your mortgage costs by allowing it to be rented for some or all of the year.

This scheme is now being advertised in the UK for British buyers. It applies only for properties having 'Residence du Tourisme' status, which can be villas, apartments or, for example, ski chalets. They must be sold furnished. If it is a new build, there is a discount equivalent to a waiver of the VAT which would otherwise be payable (19.6% of the headline price). If it is a second-hand property, the discount may only be 5.5%. In both cases, the VAT must be paid at the time of purchase and then claimed back.

Most properties are available on the basis that the buyer can use it for up to 16 weeks per year (the dates for which must be fixed in advance), and it will be rented out through a managing agent at other times. In some cases it is a condition of the particular scheme that the buyer is not permitted to use it at all and renting is full-time.

This letting arrangement lasts for a pre-agreed period of between nine and 20 years, and then the property is yours.

## Timeshare and fractional ownership

'Timeshare' is simple in principle: it is a contract with the owner of a resort complex to use a unit within it for a fixed period of time - usually one or two weeks in each year - for a fixed number of years.

It has (for Daily Mail readers at least) unsavoury connotations of high pressure sales techniques on Spanish Costas, and certainly there are some schemes to be avoided, but there are a number of reputable and well-organised timeshare operations, mainly US in origin.

'Fractional Ownership' is newer and also American in origin and a little more complicated: you will buy a portion of the ownership of the unit within the complex, or membership of a club owning several schemes, which gives you the right to stay at that unit say, for four or six weeks in each year. The added attraction is that you own something (rather than it being just a contractual arrangement), so if the developer/operator of the resort fails, you have an asset which will not disappear. This is somewhat illusory - if the operator fails it is likely that the facilities you want to use such as the swimming pool, spa or golf course, will fail to appear, or will not be maintained, or will disappear so that your fractional ownership may not be sellable. However, the fractional ownership is usually permanent rather than for a fixed number of years.

Neither timeshare nor fractional ownership should be seen as an investment. Neither is likely to increase significantly in value or be easy to sell or borrow against; both will have hefty management and service charge costs, and fees for 'extras' such as spa treatments or for the use of tennis courts or golf courses. It is unlikely that you will have much control over those costs or the rate at which they increase or the quality of the services provided once all the units have been sold.

It may be better to consider the price you pay for your timeshare or fractional ownership as advance payment for a series of holidays in the same place which will have the benefit of familiarity, and perhaps higher quality facilities than you would pay for annually.

It may be possible to let surplus weeks either through the resort managers (who will charge a sizeable commission) or privately.

The US-style model - promoted for example by Hilton[105] and Marriott[106] is for the timeshare or fractional ownership unit to be built as part of a larger complex containing one or more hotels, resort facilities (usually including golf) and some (often many) villas or apartments for outright sale. This type of scheme is common in the US and Caribbean and is becoming more common elsewhere. The nearest equivalent resorts in Europe are the La Manga Resort in Spain and Quinta de Lago and Vale do Lobo in the Algarve, although these include a high proportion of owned units, as well as some 'vacation clubs'.

One valuable add-on may be the club membership through which weeks can be traded for weeks elsewhere. Good examples of this are RCI (Resorts Condominiums International) which operates a points-based system - (www.rci.com) and Interval International (www.intervalworld.com). Interval has links with Marriott, Four Seasons and other US hotel or resort operators. Most are in US-style resort complexes, although a few urban schemes are also being developed, principally in New York City or Las Vegas.

So, for example, once your children have passed school age it may be possible to trade a popular week in Spain during August for four weeks somewhere hot during the English winter or for two weeks in South Africa in October.

Key points to check before you buy are:

- what week(s) do you really want (and look ahead)?
- what facilities will be available at that time of year?

---

[105] www.hiltongrandvacations.com

[106] www.marriottvacationclub.com

- what management and service charges will apply (and what constraints are there on increases)?
- what are the 'extras' and the prices of those?
- what fees will the management apply for letting surplus weeks?
- what club benefits apply or are transferable to other resorts or locations?

The nearest UK equivalent club is the Holiday Property Bond which offers 'weeks' in a variety of properties in the UK and Europe which it owns, using a points-based system. As the name suggests, it is structured as a life insurance bond. Its target audience can be detected from its 'face', Sue Barker, and its advertising in National Trust, RHS and RSPB magazines.

## Co-ownership and running costs

In each of the countries we have focussed on, running costs are payable in addition to the purchase price and fall into two categories: namely local and other taxes, and maintenance costs and service charges.

We have briefly summarised the on-going taxes in the relevant country sections. Bear in mind these will vary from time to time and place to place and you should check these carefully at the time of considering a purchase. Local taxes are in most cases the equivalent of council tax so are paid for services that the local council or commune provides, such as road repairs, water supply, drainage, rubbish disposal and so on. In some cases these are divided between different levels of local authority, at town, regional and national level.

In most cases they are assessed according to the notional value of the property which is set at the time you buy and not likely to change unless you carry out significant works to the property – rather like the rateable value which used to apply on a property by property basis in the UK before the introduction of the poll tax and then the council tax, which achieves a similar result by banding rather than individual property by property values.

In some jurisdictions, notably France, wealth taxes apply, again usually based on the 'notional value' of the property. Many of these apply to non-residents rather than locals so if you achieve residency in that country you may get the benefit of not paying these taxes.

In addition, there will be maintenance or service charges if your property forms part of a complex or an apartment block. These will be payments towards shared facilities such as water supply, drainage, communal landscaping and roads. These charges will be governed by the terms on which you purchase, and in some cases the community scheme that you are required to sign up to at the time of purchase. It is unlikely you will have much control of the amounts or opportunity to check whether the sums demanded are actually spent as described.

Finally, in the case of apartment blocks or complexes there will inevitably be shared costs such as maintenance of the common areas, including gardens, which may include rubbish disposal facilities, laundry, saunas and health club type facilities and swimming pools. Whilst the legal mechanism for running these facilities and sharing the costs varies from country to country, it is fair to say that most are rather more effective, and allow a greater degree of input into the way things are run, than the UK system allows. In many countries the purchase of a flat includes ownership of a share of the freehold or equivalent of the block as a whole so that once all the flats are sold, the block is run by a residents' committee or a board of directors consisting of residents, who would normally appoint a managing agent. There can be tensions where there is competition for use of facilities, or variation between the extent to which different owners use the facilities (particularly the British who are not in the habit of acting co-operatively in this way). There is usually a constitution or set of rules which deals with the proceedings of the guiding committee and the method by which decisions should be made. It is wise to obtain a copy of this (translated if necessary) for reference if need be.

In France, this arrangement is called co-propriétée; in Switzerland, PPE; in the US, condominium, or sometimes co-operative (which is limited to certain cities, and usually to upmarket developments within them).

It is, of course, to achieve this fluency in managing blocks that the commonhold system has been introduced in the UK although to date it has not achieved much popularity.

## Spain

| | |
|---|---|
| Area: | 195,364 sq miles. |
| Population: | 46.6 million. |
| Language: | Spanish. |
| Currency: | Euro. |
| Buying constraints: | None. |
| Buying costs: | Legal fees – 1-2%. |
| Notary's fees: | 0.2%-0.3%. |
| Transfer tax on resale (ITP): | 6-7%; on new properties - VAT of 7% plus stamp duty of 0.75-1%. |
| Registration fees: | approximately 0.2%. |
| | Note: The land value tax on sale known as 'plus valia' is the seller's responsibility but is sometimes paid in part or fully by the buyer. The rate varies by local authority. |
| | Note: The 'declared value' is often less than the price actually paid, to minimise taxes but this practice is illegal – see 'The Pain in Spain'. |
| Taxes on ownership/wealth: | Community taxes (IBI) are payable based on the value of the property. These vary and should be checked locally. Non-residents pay an annual wealth tax of a small percentage of the declared value of the property. |
| Taxes on rental income: | For non-residents, income tax (IRPF) is due at 24% on actual rental income; a notional charge is made if the property is not actually let, based on 2% of the declared value. |
| Taxes on sale: | Capital gains tax (bien immueble) is payable on sale, although there are exemptions where another property in Spain is being purchased, or where the owners are over 65. |

Note: A deposit of 5% of the purchase value is required from a non-resident at the time of purchase, to ensure that capital gains tax is paid. This is held by the tax authorities and is returnable if the tax is paid.

Inheritance constraints / pitfalls:

Property in Spain is subject to the Civil Code which regulates who inherits what, in a similar way to France – take legal advice on this before deciding in whose name the property is bought (that is, before signing the contract) and consider making a Spanish will. Inheritance tax laws vary by region.

Pitfalls:

See 'The Pain in Spain'.

Useful jargon:

abogado – lawyer

agencia inmoliara – estate agent

arras or senal – deposit

comprador – buyer

contrato private de compraventa - sale and purchase contract

escritura (de compraventa) – notarised property transfer deed

escritura (publica) - transfer

finca – literally, a farmhouse, often a plot of land or a detached house with land. It can include a villa as well as a traditional building if outside an urban area.

hacienda – tax office (formally called Agencia Estatal de Administration Tributaria)

IVA –VAT

notario – notary

Registro de la propriedad – Land Registry

urbanizacion – housing estate or development

valor cadastral – declared rental value

| | | |
|---|---|---|
| Useful websites: | www.spanishpropertyinsight.co.uk | (agent) |
| | www.hiddenspain.co.uk | (agent) |
| | www.kuhn-partner.com | (agent) |
| | www.johntaylorspain.com | (agent) |
| | www.timesonline.co.uk/spanishproperty | |
| | www.spanishproperty.co.uk | (agent) |
| | www.thepropertyfinders.com | (agent) |
| | www.tuspain.com | (agent) |
| | www.50connect.co.uk | (agent) |
| | www.britishexpat.co.uk | (agent) |
| | www.belegal.com | (lawyers) |
| | (formerly www.marbella-lawyers.com) | |

## France

| | |
|---|---|
| Area: | 260,558 sq miles. |
| Population: | 65 million. |
| Language: | French. |
| Currency: | Euro. |
| Buying constraints: | None. |
| Buying costs: | Agents' fees of up to 10% if not included in the sale price (look for the letters FAI on property details, which means the agents' costs are included in the price).<br>Registration tax: 0.715% for newer properties where TVA applies; 8.09% otherwise. |
| Taxes on ownership/wealth: | An annual tax of up to 1.8% of value if the value exceeds €790,000 (but the value of a French bank mortgage may be offset).<br>Taxe d'habitation – a local tax payable by the occupier.<br>Taxe Foncière – a national tax payable by the owner.<br>Taxe assimilée – an additional tax in holiday resorts for maintenance of public facilities.<br>These are based on 'rentable value'. |
| Taxes on rental income: | 'Impot sur le revenue' – 25% if the income is not more than €76,000 per annum (for furnished lettings). A standard deduction is made for unfurnished lettings. |
| Taxes on sale: | Non-residents must pay 16% of the property's value (not the gain in value) in tax if they sell within five years; the rate reduces by steps to zero after 15 years. For property held for less than two years, the rate is 40%. |

| | |
|---|---|
| Inheritance constraints/pitfalls: | French inheritance laws impose sharing of French assets between the descendants of the person dying (or his/her parents, if there are no children) and any surviving spouse. An English will cannot override this. French law advice and a French will are advisable. Inheritance tax is payable at up to 40% (except on the share going to a spouse – this change is recent) but can be offset against tax due in England. For an unmarried couple, the inheritance tax rate is up to 60%. The intended inheritance position should be considered and written into the purchase contract, that is before any legal commitment. |
| Pitfalls: | Beware of early commitment - a simple exchange of letters, even a reservation form, can be a binding contract. You can (and often should) include conditions in the 'compromis de vente', the formal purchase agreement: for example, obtaining mortgage finance, obtaining planning permission, or the seller carrying out repairs. The 'offre de vente' or 'offre d'achat' are one-way contracts, to be avoided.<br><br>Note also that planning permission is needed for letting. This law is usually ignored, but the authorities in Paris have started to enforce it. |
| Useful jargon: | acte authentique (or acte de vente) – the property transfer<br><br>avocat – lawyer<br><br>clauses suspensive – conditions in the contract<br><br>compromis de vente – purchase contract<br><br>dossier de diagnostic techniques (DDT) – the pack of search reports<br><br>notaire – notary |

plan communale – register of planning applications

TVA - VAT

Useful websites:

www.propertyvision.com (agent - owned by HSBC Private Bank)
www.winkworth.fr (agent)
www.frenchestateagents.com (agent)
www.frenchpropertyinvestor.com (agent - linked to the above)
www.ernalowproperty.co.uk (agent)
www.investorsinproperty.com (agent - for Alpine property)
www.pierre-vacances.co.uk (developers - leaseback specialists)
www.frenchentree.com (advice and agent)

## Portugal

| | |
|---|---|
| Area: | 35,645 sq miles. |
| Population: | 10.7 million. |
| Language: | Portuguese. |
| Currency: | Euro. |
| Buying constraints: | None – although before signing a purchase contract the buyer must obtain a Fiscal Number (NIF) from the tax office local to the property. |
| Buying costs: | Notary fees including document tax – previously 1% of value approximately, now fixed fees of around £153 per transaction.<br>Transfer tax (IMT) - up to 6% of value.<br>Legal fees – 1-1.5% of value (plus VAT).<br>Registration fees - £125 plus fees for registration of a mortgage.<br>Note: VAT is also payable on new construction so if buying new or off-plan check whether VAT is included. |
| Taxes on ownership/wealth: | Local property tax (IMI) at 0.8% of rateable value (in rural areas) or 1.1% - 1.3% of rateable value (in urban areas) payable every six or 12 months depending on value. |
| Taxes on rental income: | For non-residents, income tax is due at 25% on letting income. Mortgage interest is not deductible. |
| Taxes on sale: | For non-residents – capital gains tax at 25% on the gain. For residents – capital gains are aggregated with income and income tax applies – up to 40%. |
| Inheritance constraints: | No inheritance tax applies if property in Portugal passes to close relatives. In some circumstances, Portuguese law imposes 'enforced heirship', which over-rides a will. |
| Pitfalls: | As in Spain, the declared value of the property has often been under-stated to reduce taxes. The Portuguese authorities are increasingly enforcing the law to require |

full value to be declared. This can be difficult to agree with the seller.

The penalty for not paying the IMI is that the state can sell the property.

The usual deposit on re-sale is 10-12% of the purchase price. If the buyer defaults without good reason, there is a penalty of double the amount of the deposit. On new-builds the deposit is usually 30%, with the balance in stage payments.

Useful jargon:

| | |
|---|---|
| advogado | lawyer |
| contrato de promessa de compra e venda | purchase agreement |
| Conservatoria de Registro Predial | Land Registry |
| escritura de compra e venda | the transfer deed |
| mediador autorizado | licensed estate agent |
| valor metrical | rateable value |

Useful websites:

www.winkworth.pt (agent)
www.algarveprop.com (agent)
www.algarveteamproperties.com (agent)
www.pureportugal.co.uk (central and northern Portugal) (agent)
www.apropertyinportugal.com (agent)

## Italy

| | |
|---|---|
| Area: | 116,346 sq miles. |
| Population: | 60.2 million. |
| Language: | Italian. |
| Currency: | Euro. |
| Buying constraints: | None – although the buyer must obtain a tax identification number (codice fiscale) from the Italian authorities before making an offer to buy a property or signing a contract. |
| Buying costs: | Notary fees – approximately 1% of the purchase price.<br>Transfer tax – up to 10% (in three parts). New properties are subject to VAT rather than stamp duty.<br>Registration fees – 4% for an Italian, 11% for a non-Italian.<br>Estate agent's fee – often shared between seller and buyer, often 3% each.<br>Note: if buying from an individual the registration fee is based on the 'cadastral' value which is usually substantially lower than market value. If buying from a company the fee is based on market value. |
| Taxes on ownership/wealth: | There is no wealth tax. The local commune will raise a property tax (ICI) based at 0.4%-0.7% of rateable value, plus 'tassa comunales' to cover refuse disposals etc. |
| Taxes on rental income: | Rental income must be declared and is taxable at between 19% and 46% depending on the amount. |
| Taxes on sale: | Capital gains tax is not payable on the gain unless the property has been owned for less than 5 years. |
| Inheritance constraints: | Difficult: take advice! |

| | |
|---|---|
| Pitfalls: | Italian bureaucracy and the tax system are especially baffling and local advice is essential. If buying from a family, disputes as to ownership are common.<br>The import and export of currency is controlled, and transfers of over €10,000 must be declared.<br>Deposits tend to be higher than elsewhere – deposits of 30%-50% are not uncommon. If the buyer defaults without good reason before completing, there may be a penalty of double the amount of the deposit.<br>In rural areas neighbouring farmers may have the right to match any offer (known as 'prelazione').<br>For rural and older properties the legal description may not match reality and a specialist surveyor (geometra) may be required (before buying!). |

Useful jargon:

| | |
|---|---|
| avvocato | lawyer |
| caparo penitenziale | deposit |
| compremesso di vendita | preliminary sale contract |
| notario | notary |
| proposto d'acquisto | offer to purchase |
| Registro Immobiliare | Land Registry |
| rendita cadastreal | rateable value |
| rogito | the property transfer deed |

Useful websites:

www.italianskiproperty.com (agent)
www.gkitalianproperty.com (agent)
www.italianproperty.eu.com (agent)
www.casatravella.com (agent)
www.propertiesinitaly.net (agent)
www.thepropertyfinders.com (property finder)

## Switzerland

| | |
|---|---|
| Area: | 15,940 sq miles. |
| Population: | 7.7 million. |
| Language: | French, Swiss-German, Italian, Romansch. |
| Currency: | Swiss Francs. |
| Buying constraints: | Under the Lex Koller, non-Swiss citizens require a permit from the relevant canton to buy property in Switzerland. Permits are limited in number (currently 1,500 per year) and are restricted to certain areas and types of property. Application for the permit is made by the notary. This process may take three months or more, particularly towards the end of the calendar year. |
| Buying costs: | These vary from canton to canton. The main variable is transfer tax. In Valais this is around 1.5% of the purchase price or in Vaud around 3.3% of the purchase price. |
| | Notary and land registration fees are around 1.7% in total, in addition. |
| | Fees for registration of a mortgage are extra, and based on the value lent. |
| Taxes on ownership/wealth: | Property tax is 1.3% of rateable value. Tourism tax is 1.75% of rateable value. Local land taxes are also payable. |
| Taxes on rental income: | Tax is not payable on rental income in Switzerland. |
| Taxes on sale: | Capital gains tax is payable. The amount depends on the size of the gain and the length of time the property has been owned. |
| Inheritance constraints: | Swiss inheritance laws will apply, and may override any UK will. It is advisable to take specific advice, and usually to make a specific will and lodge a copy with the notary. |
| | Inheritance and wealth tax vary by canton and (unless you are resident in Switzerland) are only |

| | |
|---|---|
| | payable on Swiss assets. |
| Pitfalls: | Property and funding costs are expensive.<br>Buying requires a permit; sale within a fixed period (for example, five or 10 years) may be restricted.<br>Not in the EU, so residence rights are limited. Non-Swiss can only occupy for thee months at a time, or six months per year in total unless they obtain a residency permit B (annual) or C (permanent). A non-Swiss family can only own one property in Switzerland between them.<br>A company cannot be used.<br>Letting is up to a maximum of 11 months plus one week per year. The owner or family or friends are required to use the property for three weeks of the year. |
| Useful jargon: | Notar/notariat — notary<br>Promesse de vente et d'achat — purchase contract<br>PPE ('propriété par étage') — a form of common ownership, where the owners of apartments also own the building and common parts communally. |
| Useful websites: | www.alpinehomesintl.com (linked to Savills) (agent)<br>www.investorsinproperty.com (agent for Alpine property)<br>www.myswitzerland.com (tourist information)<br>www.pureintl.com (agent)<br>www.swissproperty.co.uk (agent)<br>www.swisspropertyguide.com (agent)<br>www.swissworld.com (general information) |

## (Southern) Cyprus

| | |
|---|---|
| Area: | 3,572 sq miles. |
| Population: | 793,963. |
| Language: | Greek, Turkish. |
| Currency: | Euro (from 2008). |
| Buying constraints: | Approval needed for non-Cypriots to buy – only one property allowed and there is a maximum size limit. EU citizens are not subject to these restrictions.<br><br>Exchange control approval may be required from the Central Bank of Cyprus for fund transfer (without this, getting the funds out again following sale will be prevented). |
| Buying costs: | Deposits are usually 10% for a resale, 20%-30% for a new build.<br><br>Legal fees – 1.5%.<br><br>Stamp duty – 0.15% up to €170,860; over that figure 0.2%.<br><br>Transfer tax – 3%-8% depending on value plus VAT at 15% on new build properties. (This is not always included in the advertised price.)<br><br>Registration fee for mortgages – 1% of amount secured. |
| Taxes on ownership/wealth: | A small annual ownership tax based on property value (up to 0.4%, over €850,000), plus annual municipal and sewage taxes, of between €80 and €170. |
| Taxes on rental income: | Yes, up to 30%. Approval is required from the Cyprus Tourism Organisation (CTO) although this is often ignored. |
| Taxes on sale: | Yes, capital gains tax at 20% *less* certain allowances. |
| Inheritance constraints: | No inheritance tax or equivalent if you are tax |

| | |
|---|---|
| | resident in Cyprus and have a Cypriot will. |
| Pitfalls: | The Title Deed requisition system is seriously inefficient – registration may take over 10 years, making re-sale, mortgages and even alterations very difficult. |
| | Note: land ownership in Northern (Turkish) Cyprus is likely to be disputed and confiscation is even possible – (see *Apostolides v Oram,* a case in the European Court of Justice). |
| Useful jargon: | donum — a measure of area – 3 donums = approx 1 acre |
| Useful websites: | www.buysellcyprus.com (agent) |
| | www.aphroditehills.com (developer) (a large 5-star luxury resort with golf near Paphos) |
| | www.minthishills.com (developer) (likewise) |
| | www.cypruspropertyassociates.co.uk (agent) |
| | www.skek-creea.com (Cyprus Real Estate Agents Association) |

## Florida

| | |
|---|---|
| Area: | 65,795 sq miles. |
| Population: | 18.3 million (plus 85 million visitors per year!) |
| Language: | US English. |
| Currency: | US Dollar. |
| Buying constraints: | None. |
| Buying costs: | Legal fees – 0.5% - 1% of value.<br>Transfer tax – 2% plus 1-3% if a mortgage is taken out.<br>Title and search insurance – 0.5%-0.2%.<br>Note: There are additional taxes if a mortgage is obtained; together 0.0055% of the mortgage amount. |
| Taxes on ownership/wealth: | Annual property taxes are around 1% of the value of the property per year. |
| Taxes on rental income: | Will be payable, and withholding tax at 30% will apply. Mortgage interest and other deductions can be claimed. |
| Taxes on sale: | Capital gains tax – take local advice as it varies according to personal circumstances. |
| Inheritance constraints: | No 'forced heirship' |
| Pitfalls: | Many buyers employ an agent (realtor) to find a property and finance and to negotiate for them.<br>Bear in mind that law, procedures, costs and taxes vary within the US from state to state and even from county to county within Florida.<br>For example, there are restrictions in some popular areas on short-term rentals.<br>Beware of ARMS – mortgages with low initial rates, higher later.<br>UK visa requirements are fairly simple for holiday visits but living in the US requires a 'green card' |

which is much more difficult to obtain.

Useful jargon:

| | |
|---|---|
| ARM | adjustable-rate mortgage |
| condominium (or 'condo') | a building complex jointly owned by the individual building owners, or a unit within such a complex |
| contingency | a condition in a purchase contract, such as 'subject to survey' |
| closing | the completion date/process |
| 'earnest money' | initial holding deposit |
| Escrow account | a means of holding the purchase deposit |
| Title insurance | the way title is guaranteed |
| 'turnkey' | ready to move in, including furnishings |

Useful websites:

www.escape2usa.co.uk (agent)

www.britishhomesgroup.co.uk (agent and mortgage broker)

www.realtor.org (National Association of Realtors)

www.more.com (price comparisons and useful links)

## Dubai

| | |
|---|---|
| Area: | 1,588 sq miles. |
| Population: | 1.4 million (2006). |
| Language: | Arabic. |
| Currency: | UAE Dirham. |
| Buying constraints: | No prior approval is required. |
| Buying costs: | No notary fees.<br>Registration fee – 1.5% (plus 0.25% for a loan). |
| Taxes on ownership/wealth: | None. |
| Taxes on rental income: | None in Dubai. |
| Taxes on sale: | None in Dubai. |
| Inheritance constraints: | Inheritance tax is governed by sharia'a (Islamic) law. Advice should be taken. A local will may be required. |
| Pitfalls: | Until 2006 freehold purchase was not possible for non-UAE citizens. It is now, but only in certain areas and through certain developers.<br>Market collapse in 2009; many new build projects may never be finished; there is no resale market yet.<br>Rents for letting have been capped by the Government.<br>Residency visas for ex-pats have been reduced to six months.<br>Some western (bad) habits remain culturally inappropriate.<br>UK-style mortgages are not available; all loans are through 'sharia'a-compliant' structures such as 'ijara' or 'murabaha'. |

BUYING ABROAD

Useful websites:

www.dubaipropertygroup.com (agent)

www.dubaipropertysale.com (agent)

www.selectproperty.com (agent)

www.bhomes.com (agent)

## South Africa

| | |
|---|---|
| Area: | 471,443 sq miles. |
| Population: | 49.3 million. |
| Language: | Afrikaans, English, Southern Ndebele, Northern Sotho, Southern Sotho, Swazi, Tsonga, Tswana, Venda, Xhosa, Zulu. |
| Currency: | Rand (ZAR). |
| Buying constraints: | No but exchange controls restrictions may apply - declaration is required, rather than approval.<br>A temporary or permanent residence permit may be required. |
| Buying costs: | Legal fees – up to 2% (usually seller and buyer share a lawyer and maybe the cost).<br>Transfer tax – 5% - 8% depending on value and purchaser's legal status. |
| Taxes on ownership/wealth: | Under review. |
| Taxes on rental income: | Yes. Income tax applies, according to personal circumstances. |
| Taxes on sale: | Capital gains tax is payable at 25%, above ZAR 1 million.<br>Note: There are rules as to retention and accounting for part of the sale price at the time of sale. |
| Inheritance constraints: | No, but estate duty is payable on assets in South Africa (currently 20%). |
| Pitfalls: | Offer to purchase can be immediately binding – so take legal advice before offering! Also take care that the offer does not also appoint the selling agent as your mortgage broker.<br>Maximum mortgage available from local banks is 50% of value, except for those proposing to become permanent residents (but mortgage interest rates |

| | | |
|---|---|---|
| | are high). | |
| Useful jargon: | bond | mortgage |
| | sectional title | a form of communal ownership within a resort or gated community, subject to regulations (like UK commonhold) |
| | share block | an older form of communal ownership where 'owners' hold a share in a company which owns the land and buildings |
| | suspensive conditions | conditions in the purchase contract to which it is subject |
| | 'voetstoots' or 'as is' | properties are usually sold as seen so the buyer takes the risk of defects |
| Useful websites: | www.ieasa.org.za (Institute of Estate Agents) | |
| | www.myproperty.co.za (agent) | |
| | www.sahomebuyers.co.za (advice and agency) | |
| | www.privateproperty.co.za (agent) | |
| | www.propertygenie.co.za (agent) | |

# AFTERWORD

This book was conceived in mid-2007 and written between mid 2009 and early 2010. During that time, the most severe banking crash since the 1930s hit property markets across the world. Average UK house prices fell by 20-25%; UK commercial property dropped by roughly 50% in value: in both markets, buyers stopped buying. The number of house sale transactions fell by half from 1.48 million in 2007 to 727,000 in 2008 (according to the Daily Star).

Major banks and mortgage lenders teetered on the brink of insolvency, although only a few fell over the precipice, and those that did fell into safer hands (apart from Lehman Brothers). Share prices for the major house builders and property companies fell by up to 90%. Meanwhile headline interest rates dropped to their lowest level since the Bank of England came into existence in 1694, although mortgage interest rates for new loans did not follow.

Without wishing to oversimplify, a great deal of the pain of these value falls has been felt by shareholders and those living off interest, and developers and their banks. Many individuals and families have managed their finances by simply delaying moving, or by upgrading their existing property instead.

Writing in early 2010, there are signs that the worst is over and that both the wider UK economy and the property market are starting to recover – latest research indicates that in prime central London prices for flats have risen by over 10% and for houses by over 15%, since around Easter 2009, and that the 'ripple effect' in house prices is visible beyond central London. The Government has announced new initiatives to provide funding to complete stalled developments for social housing and to extend the discounted 'HomeBuy' schemes to first-time buyers. The private sector is looking more seriously at 'build to let'. Green initiatives have multiplied, the 'permitted development' rules have been re-written, and the letting market has been 'hygienised' by the introduction of tenant's deposit protection and landlord licensing systems.

We cannot make predictions, but because of the fundamentals of the UK property market – a growing population (latest ONS statistics predict a rise from 61 million to 70 million by 2029 – that is, an increase of 425,000 people per year), an increasing number of households, growing pressure from those who have delayed moving house, a lack of supply of new property either to buy or to rent and the continuing British fixation on owning one's own home - it is hard to see how the property you desire now will not be desired more by someone else in the future. That does not mean your home can or should be a means to 'get rich quick'.

At a personal level, in those two years, David, one of the dedicatees of this book, who originated the 'where do I start?' conversation mentioned in the introduction, has bought a flat with his partner; his parents have bought an apartment in Austria; Ruth is working on plans for a kitchen extension to her house. One of the co-authors has bought a second house for use as a holiday rental property, and the other has bought a house to let for now and then extend, to make his own future family dream home. So, even in the worst market for UK housing since at least the early 1990s, things do happen.

We hope you have found, and will continue to find, this book useful. We do not pretend to have all the answers, or even to know all the questions, but if you are now more confident in knowing where to start in buying your dream home, and how to make that dream come true, we have achieved our objective.

# APPENDIX 1: PROPERTY IN SCOTLAND AND NORTHERN IRELAND

## Property in Scotland

### Buying and selling

The property system in Scotland is substantially different from that in England and Wales.

For example, many solicitors also act as estate agents and advertise properties for sale, and it is usual to lodge offers through solicitors.

Most importantly, under Scottish law when you make an offer to buy a property, and the seller accepts your offer, a binding and enforceable contract is made. 'Subject to Contract' does not apply. You can make an unconditional offer – that is, just price – or a conditional offer – that is price plus conditions such as 'subject to survey' or 'subject to mortgage'. The acceptance can also be subject to conditions – for example that the buyer's survey condition is cleared within say two weeks.

It is common, if more than one buyer has 'noted an interest' in buying, for the seller to set a 'closing date' for offers. Often, the marketing material will ask for 'offers over', say, £150,000.

The terminology used is also different: the offer/acceptance procedure is known as 'missives'; the conditions are 'purified' as they are cleared; the point when they are all cleared is called 'concluding missives' and a deposit of (usually) 10% then becomes due; the property transfer document is known as a 'disposition'; the completion date is known as the 'settlement date' or 'date of entry'.

Land ownership in Scotland was originally based on the feudal system. The basic principle, going back some 900 years, was that apart from the Crown, nobody owned land absolutely but each proprietor held a subsidiary title to land, subject to certain conditions (known as feuhold). The important element about any system of land tenure is evidence to support the claim of the person entitled to the land. In the early days of the feudal system this evidence was provided by the ceremony of 'giving sasine'. The word sasine is derived from the old French word 'seiser' meaning 'to seize'. This ceremony was performed every time a feudal grant of land was made.

In the ancient ceremony of 'giving sasine' dating back to the 15th century, the parties would meet with a number of witnesses on the site of the land being granted. The feudal superior would make a verbal grant of the land and hand over earth and stone as symbols of the land being transferred. This signified that the feudal superior was delivering possession. This was known as symbolic delivery, and was essential to the ceremony of giving sasine. If the right was not of land, the tokens would be different, for example symbols given in a grant of salmon fishing rights were a net and cobble.

The Abolition of Feudal Tenure, etc. (Scotland) Act 2000 was designed to modernise the system of land ownership. Feudal superiorities and most attendant rights, such as the right to collect feu duty, were abolished with effect from 28 November 2004. Some rights relating to the use and management of property were preserved.

The 'Registers of Scotland' (www.ros.gov.uk) maintain various historic registers – notably the Register of Sasines dating back to 1617 – which are gradually being overtaken by a state-guaranteed map-based register similar to the Land Registry in England and Wales.

Administering the registers was originally the responsibility of an officer of state known as the Lord Clerk Register. In 1928 the duties transferred to the Keeper of the Registers and Records of Scotland. In 1948, the office was split into the Keeper of the Records of Scotland (preserving the records and registers) and the Keeper of the Registers of Scotland (compiling and maintaining the registers).

## Renting

The system for renting residential property is also substantially different from that in England and Wales.

All private landlords are required to register with the local authority (or authorities) where they are, or will be, renting out property. Non-registration is a criminal offence. The local authority will consider whether the landlord is a 'fit and proper person' before allowing registration (so complaints from tenants about bad practice will be taken into account).

The 'Houses in Multiple Occupation' licensing system also applies.

Most private rented sector tenancies are subject to a repairing standard under the Housing (Scotland) Act 2006 which imposes obligations on landlords to put and keep properties, appliances and furniture in reasonable repair and safe.

Most new tenancies will be a 'short assured tenancy' which is roughly equivalent to an assured shorthold tenancy in England and Wales. 'Assured' or 'regulated' tenancies are more secure. The Tenancy Deposit Protection Scheme does not yet apply in Scotland.

## Property in Northern Ireland

The structure of the house buying market in Northern Ireland is similar to that of England and Wales, although Northern Ireland has a separate legal and Land Registry system.

As in England and Wales, properties are advertised on websites and in local newspaper(s) and sold though estate agents. The conveyancing process is carried out by solicitors for the seller and buyer, who are regulated by the Law Society of Northern Ireland and have a monopoly on conveyancing (so there are no equivalents of licensed conveyancers). Fee comparisons can be made by getting quotations.

Generally, the process is similar to England and Wales with some differences in terminology (for example replies to enquiries and searches are called 'certificates'). The Land Registry set-up (called Land and Property Services) is a little different. The long-standing 'Registry of Deeds' system (which maintains a record of summaries of purchase and mortgage documents provided to it by solicitors when purchases happen, collated by name rather than property address) is being gradually replaced by a map-based Land Registry similar to the England and Wales version. That transition is about 50% complete. Meanwhile the two registration systems exist side by side (see www.psni.gov.uk).

The private rented sector in Northern Ireland has increased in scale dramatically since 2001 – it has almost trebled in number of properties, while the public rented sector has reduced by a third.

Major legal changes aimed at improving the quality of tenanted property were introduced in 2006. The protection for landlords given by the 'Assured Shorthold Tenancy' and the protection for tenants given by other forms of tenancy in England and Wales do not apply in the same way, but tenants do have some legal protection against poor quality accommodation and harassment and eviction. A registration system for landlords is not yet in place but is likely to be introduced, according to 'Building Sound Foundations', a review published in March 2010 by the Department for Social Development (www.dsdni.gov.uk). The 'Houses in Multiple Occupation' licensing system does apply. There is no tenancy deposit protection scheme yet but the DSD is proposing to introduce one.

# APPENDIX 2: USEFUL WEBSITES

## Finding a tenancy

www.easyroommate.com

www.gumtree.com

www.roombuddies.com

www.spareroom.co.uk

## Property search websites

www.findaproperty.com

www.homes24.co.uk

www.primelocation.com

www.propertyfinder.com

www.rightmove.co.uk

www.globrix.com

www.zoopla.co.uk.

## First time buyer websites

www.firsttimebuyermag.co.uk (monthly magazine)

www.firstrungnow.com

www.directgov.uk

www.moneysupermarket.com (for mortgage comparisons)

www.lcplc.co.uk (for mortgage repayment calculator)

www.nationwide.co.uk (for mortgage repayment calculator)

www.halifax.co.uk (for mortgage repayment calculator)

www.alliance-leicester.co.uk (for mortgage repayment calculator)

## Nationwide firms of agents

www.savills.com

www.knightfrank.com

www.yourmove.co.uk

www.reedsrains.co.uk

www.countrywide.co.uk

www.cluttons.com

www.jackson-stops.co.uk

www.johndwood.co.uk

## National and London newspapers websites

www.timesonline.co.uk

www.telegraph.co.uk

www.homesandproperty.co.uk (Evening Standard).

## Auction sale sites

www.auctionpropertyforsale.co.uk

www.ukauctionlist.com

www.propertyauctionnews.co.uk

These all require you to sign up to a subscription fee.

## 'Nosy neighbour' websites

www.mouseprice.com

www.nethouseprices.com

www.upmystreet.com

www.houseprices.co.uk

## Affordable Housing

www.shared-ownership.org.uk

www.shared-equity.net

www.homebuy.co.uk

*Housing Associations*

L&Q/Metropolitan Home Ownership (www.housingoptions.co.uk) who manage access to all affordable housing in London as agents for HomeBuy.

Family Mosaic (www.familymosaicsales.co.uk)

Genesis Homes (www.genesishomes.org.uk)

Hyde Housing (www.hyde-housing.co.uk)

Home Group (www.homegroup.org.uk)

New London (www.newlonhomeownership.co.uk)

Notting Hill Housing Association (www.nottinghillhousing.org.uk)

Thames Valley Housing Association (www.tvha.co.uk).

*Private developers*

Barratt Homes (www.barratthomes.co.uk/offers)

Taylor Wimpey (www.taylorwimpey.co.uk)

Asset Trust Housing (www.assettrusthousing.com)

Crest Nicholson (www.crestnicholson.com)

Gallion Homes (www.gallionsha.co.uk)

Miller Homes (www.millerhomes.co.uk)
Countryside (www.countrysideproperties.com)
Pocket Living (www.pocketliving.com) for small flats in London.

## UK Holiday letting

English Country Cottages (www.english-country-cottages.co.uk)
West Country Cottages (www.westcountrycottages.co.uk)
Welcome Cottages (www.welcomecottages.com)
www.holidaylettings.co.uk

## Letting property abroad

www.holidaylettings.co.uk

## Overseas property search

Association of International Property Professionals – www.aipp.org.uk
www.findaproperty.com
www.property-abroad.com
www.homesoverseas.co.uk
www.properties-in-europe.com
and the usual suspects – rightmove, primelocation, findaproperty, and the larger UK agents.

## UK solicitors specialising in overseas purchases

International Property Law Centre[107] – www.internationalpropertylaw.com
Croft Baker Solicitors – especially for France and Switzerland www.croftbaker.com
Pannone – www.pannone.com
Phillips International Lawyers – www.phillipsinternationallawyers.com
Prettys (Ipswich) – especially for France - www.prettys.co.uk
Withers – especially for Italy – www.withersworldwide. com

The Law Society also has listings of UK law firms with offices outside the UK[108] although that does not mean the relevant firm is qualified to carry out residential property purchases or sales in that country. It also has a listing of local firms of lawyers in various countries[109].

[107] The International Law Partnership LLP run by John Howell has ceased to trade
[108] www.lawsociety.org.uk/choosingandusing/findasolicitor.law
[109] www.lawsociety.org.uk/documents/downloads/international

## Guidance on green issues

### *Websites*

www.energysavingtrust.co.uk

www.diy.com/oneplanethome (part of B&Q's website)

www.biggreenhome.org.uk (an initiative from the National Home Improvement Council in conjunction with British Gas), www.nasba.org.uk, www.selfbuildalliance.co.uk

www.plotsearch.co.uk (subscription based)

www.plotfinder.net

www.nasba.org.uk

### *Books*

*Renovating for Profit* by Michael Holmes

*The Housebuilders' Bible* by Mark Brinkley

*The Book of Green Homes* (case studies from Homebuilding and Renovating magazine).

# INDEX